Stunting in the cinema

Also by Arthur Wise

Non-fiction

Reading and talking in English (1964)
Communication in speech (1965)
Spoken English for CSE (1966)
Your speech (1966)
Weapons in the theatre (1968)
Talking together (1968)
Talking for management (with Nan Wise) (1971)
Us Northerners (with Sid Chaplin) (1970)
The history and art of personal combat (1971)

Fiction

Days in the hay (1960)
The little fishes (1961)
How now brown cow (1962)
The death's head (1962)
The day the queen flew to Scotland for the grouse shooting (1968)
Leatherjacket (1970)
Who killed Enoch Powell? (1970)
The naughty girls (1972)

STUNTING

in the

CINEMA

ARTHUR WISE
DEREK WARE

St. Martin's Press
New York

Affiliated publishers
Macmillan & Company, Limited, London
also at Bombay, Calcutta, Madras and Melbourne

To Paddy Ryan

Contents

Illustrations

Illustrations

The Last Grenade, 1970. Eddie Powell using a fire harness.
Also effects devised by Pat Moore
Those Magnificent Men in their Flying Machines, 1964. Ken
Buckle doubling for Gert Froebe, see page 99
No Blade of Grass, 1970. Stunt girl Cyd Child in action
(*Daily Telegraph*)
The Damned, 1961. Jack Cooper at the wheel
Monte Carlo or Bust, 1967. Marc Boyle at 55 mph shooting on to
a moving ferry
The Flight of the Phoenix, 1965. The death of Paul Mantz
(Johnny Hagner)
Frank Tallman, veteran flier doubling for Cliff Robertson
(Associated Press)
The Great Race, 1965. Davy Sharpe doubling for Tony Curtis
(Johnny Hagner)
How the West was Won, 1963. Bob Morgan doubling for George
Peppard (Johnny Hagner)
The Desperados, 1966. Roma Gorrara pitching through 'toffee
glass'
The Daredevil Man, 1971. Terry Walsh. A 35-ft fall (ICI)
Moll Flanders, 1964. Max Faulkner on his way to a watery
landing (Associated Press)
A real mirror being broken by Karate expert Alan Chuntz
Doctor Who, BBC television, 1970. Roy Scammell falls 45 ft
The Boss, 1946. Harvey Parry, Paul Stader and Saul Gross
handcuffed together in a difficult fall
A Cadbury commercial, 1970. Alf Joint's dive of 157 ft,
see page 114

Acknowledgements

We are indebted to a very large number of people for help with the book at every stage of its preparation, but we should particularly like to record our gratitude to the following: Mick Arnup; Felix Barker of the London *Evening News*; Bowie Films; British Film Institute; Kevin Brownlow; Ken Buckle; John Burns of BBC *Look North*; Miss Judith Chisholm; Jack Cooper; Gerry Crampton; Dave Cresswell; Mrs Angela Cretney; K.W. De Witt of Fox's Glacier Mints Ltd; Fire-Proof Textiles A.G. of Zug, Switzerland; John G. Hagner of the Stuntmen's Museum, Palmdale, California; Eric Hope of York Castle Museum; Librarian, University of York; Librarian, York City Libraries; Henry Marshall of the Society of British Fight Directors; Pat Moore, Special Effects Director, of P. Moore & Co.; R. W. Parry of John Mackintosh and Sons Ltd; Roy Scammell; Bob Symes-Schutzmann of BBC *Tomorrow's World*; Peter Turpin and Mrs Nan Wise.

In addition we would like to thank the following publishers for permission to quote from their books: Chapman & Hall, for *Menageries, Circuses and Theatres* by E. H. Bostock; Secker & Warburg, for *The Parade's Gone By* by Kevin Brownlow; G. Bell & Sons, for *Schools and Masters of Fence* by Egerton Castle; The Bodley Head, for *My Autobiography* by Charles Chaplin; Collins, for *Fairs, Circuses and Music Halls* by M. Willson Disher; Heinemann, for *My Wicked, Wicked Ways* by Errol Flynn; Weidenfeld & Nicolson, for *Gladiators* by Michael Grant; Gollancz, for *Houdini: The Man Who Walked Through Walls* by William Lindsay Gresham; Ian Allan, for *Railways in the Cinema* by John Huntley; Allen & Unwin, for *My Wonderful World of Slapstick* by Buster Keaton, with Charles Samuels; and for *Comedy Films, 1894–1954*

Acknowledgements

by John Montgomery; David Higham Associates, for *The English Circus* by Ruth Manning-Sanders; John Farquharson, for *The Film Till Now* by Paul Rotha; Arthur Barker, for *The Big Man* by Mike Tomkies; Argus Press, for *Photoplay*, July 1965; The Times Newspapers Ltd; Naseen Khan and M. McNay for articles in *The Guardian*.

Introduction

This book is about stunting, but since that word has a number of different meanings it might be as well if we outline the area with which we are concerned. It is that aspect of entertainment which is spectacular and almost entirely visual in its appeal, and which involves a certain danger to the performer which he can only overcome by skill.

Such a definition excludes a good many dangerous human activities, but not all. It excludes attempts to climb Everest and to break the land speed record, since the motivation behind these activities is not the desire to entertain. And stunting is a form of entertainment. But it does not exclude such a feat as Karl Wallenda's high-wire walk over Georgia's Tallulah Gorge in July 1970. The walk, a thousand feet long across a seven hundred foot drop, was spectacular, entirely visual and highly dangerous. It called on all Wallenda's skill and its intention was to entertain. Wallenda, in fact, remarked at the time that the applause of an audience was 'music to my ears'.

Nevertheless, Wallenda's walk was not what we would regard as stunting. The walk was an end in itself whereas the stunt is only a means to an end. The stunt exists within a dramatic framework. Its purpose is to further the dramatic process of which it is a part. It must always remain subservient to that process. If a stunt is not consistent with plot and character then it has failed, however spectacular it might be.

There is a further point that separates stunt work from all other forms of spectacular physical action. It has to do with the nature of reality. Wallenda crossed Tallulah Gorge as himself. His

13

particular form of entertainment did not require him to shed his own character and assume that of someone else. This is not true of the stuntman. When Fairbanks leapt a thirty-foot moat with the help of a trampoline in the 1922 production of *Robin Hood*, he did so in the character of the Earl of Huntingdon, not as Fairbanks. This labile ability, the ability to shed one character and assume another, is the mainspring of acting. Quite simply, then, the stuntman is an actor with a highly specialised skill. But however specialised that skill is, he remains first and foremost an actor.

There are many misconceptions about stunts and the men who perform them. Perhaps the most widely held is the view that all stunts are faked, that what one sees on the cinema screen did not take place in reality. It is perfectly true that the sophisticated techniques of the cinema can be used to give the illusion of reality. By using back-projection or double exposure, an actor can be made to appear hanging by his finger-tips twenty storeys up over a city centre street, when in fact his feet are no more than a couple of inches above the studio floor. Such an illusion is not a stunt and therefore does not concern us here. Conversely, if the actor is filmed when he is *in fact* hanging twenty storeys above the street, then that actor is performing a stunt. This is the element of entertainment with which we are concerned. It is an element that is very old and yet has seen its most impressive developments only recently, during the comparatively brief life of the cinema. In consequence, it is with the cinema that we are principally, though not exclusively, concerned.

We should perhaps stress that the book is not about stuntmen as such, although without them the phenomenon of stunting as we now know it would not exist. We have mentioned the names of many stuntmen, but we are well aware that there are many others whom we have not mentioned. In a book about stuntmen rather than stunting, they would of course all appear, but in this particular book we have had to be savagely selective. To those who might very naturally feel that examples of their work would have made a particular point more effectively than the examples we have chosen, we can only apologise.

Introduction

There is another problem that should be mentioned since it has certainly left its mark on the book. It is the problem of sheer lack of information. We have, of course, talked to many professional stuntmen about their work and we have seen their performances in the flesh and on film. But very few of them have ever put down records of their work on paper. In consequence, a good deal of information on the early stuntmen is simply not available. Other information, appearing in brief articles in a wide range of publications, is conflicting. Even in the spelling of names there is little agreement. Perkins' christian name appears as both Jean and Gene. Charles Hutchison frequently appears as Hutchinson. Perhaps Locklear has suffered most: his surname varies from Look Lear to Lock Lear, his wartime flying rank has appeared as both sergeant and lieutenant and in various publications his christian name is spelt Amer, Omer, Ormer and Omar.

In deciding which of these variations to pick we have leaned heavily on such writers as Brownlow and Goodman who, by interviewing some of the early creators of film action who have since died, have produced almost the only source material available. In this respect we are perhaps most indebted to Dick Grace whose autobiographical writings appear to be the only works written entirely by a major stuntman. Where there has been conflict over the spelling of the name of a person known to Grace we have accepted his spelling of it. There is only one exception to this and that is in the case of Leo Noomis. Grace spells the name 'Nomis' and 'Nomes', but there is such a weight of evidence against these spellings that we have ignored them.

The date of a film appears in the text when the title of the film is first mentioned, and subsequently only when there might be confusion about which version of a particular film is being referred to. All films mentioned in the text have an index entry which gives their dates.

Arthur Wise, York

Derek Ware, London

1 The early star performers

Elements of the stunt

The stunt as we now think of it was born with the cinema, but many of its elements have existed since the first group of performers sought to excite the first audience.

A fresco from Knossos in Crete, almost 4,000 years old, shows young people engaged in 'bull-leaping', the practice of somersaulting over the back of a charging bull which was originally associated with religious celebrations. Illustrations of a similar age show Egyptian acrobats and tumblers performing. Etruscan and Roman gladiatorial combats, horrific though they must have been,

Illustration: The Whirlwind (1920). 'Lightning' Charles Hutchison dives 18 feet.

B

contain many of the elements of stunting. Professional gladiators were skilled through long and arduous training. Their combats involved a degree of personal risk that no modern stuntman would have considered justified for a moment. The contests in which they were involved took place before vast audiences—the arena at Pompeii, for example, had a seating capacity of 20,000—which expected to be entertained by the performance and enjoyed a high degree of participation in it. But the actual slaughter of animals and human beings in the arena was an essential part of the entertainment, and in this of course it differs fundamentally from modern stunting. Severe injury and death were essential ingredients of the gladiatorial combat. By contrast, all the modern stuntman's skill and ingenuity are directed to the avoidance of personal injury.

The chariot race, which is such a dramatic high-spot of both film versions of *Ben Hur* (1926 and 1959), was perfected in Rome. Skilled horsemanship was certainly seen in the Roman arena. Willson Disher mentions the stunt of a rider leaping from the back of one horse to another at full-gallop as being associated with the Roman 'games', and points out that 'trick-riding, generally supposed to have been first practised towards the end of the C18th, is reported both in Homer and Montaigne'.[1]

The fair, dating from pre-medieval times, had a considerable array of side-shows which required as much physical skill and judgement as does the modern stuntman. Sword-swallowing, fire-eating, rope-walking, tumbling and dangerous performances with animals were all associated with the itinerant fairground before they became more closely linked with the circus and the music hall. Pepys refers to Jacob Hall—'a mighty strong man'—as being skilled in 'dancing on the rope', and also to the professional 'gladiators' of the seventeenth and eighteenth centuries who gave public displays with sharp weapons. Castle[2] quotes the following passage from Josevin de Rocheford's *An Account of a Journey to the British Isles* (1672):

We went to see such a combat, which was performed on a stage in the middle of an amphitheatre, when, on the flourish of trumpets and the beats of drums, the combatants entered, stripped to their shirts. On a signal from the drum, they drew their swords and immediately began to fight, skirmishing a long time without wounds. They were both very skilful and courageous. The tallest had the advantage over the smallest, for, according to the English fashion of fencing, they endeavoured rather to cut than to thrust in the French manner, so that by his height he had the advantage of being able to strike his antagonist on the head, against which the little one was on his guard. He had in his turn one advantage over the tall man in being able to give him the Jarnac stroke, by cutting him on the right ham, which he left in a manner quite unguarded. So that, all things considered, they were equally matched. Nevertheless, the tall one struck the little one on the wrist, which he almost cut off, but this did not prevent him from continuing the fight, after he had been dressed, and taken a glass or two of wine to give him courage, when he took ample vengeance for his wound; for a little afterwards, making a feint at the ham, the tall man stooping in order to parry it, laid his whole head open, when the little one gave him a stroke which took off a slice of his head and almost all his ear. For my part, I think there is a barbarity and inhumanity in permitting men to kill each other for diversion. The surgeons immediately dressed them and bound up their wounds; which, being done, they renewed the combat, and both being sensible of their respective disadvantages, they therefore were a long time without receiving or giving a wound, which was the cause that the little one, failing to parry so exactly, being tired with his long battle, received another stroke on his wounded wrist, which, dividing the sinews, he remained vanquished . . .

In most respects this might be a description of a fight in the theatre of the period, except that the wounds that are inflicted are real wounds and the blood real blood.

Stunting in the cinema

Stunt tradition in the theatre

Only in the theatre is there any tradition of true stunting. The Romans mounted re-enactments of battles which were ostensibly theatrical, although the theatrical element no doubt took second place to the spectacle of actual blood-letting. 'Another very ambitious project,' says Michael Grant,[3] 'was organized by Claudius, whose Triumph of AD 44 staged in the Campus Martius enacted the realistic capture and sack of a town, followed by the surrender of the enemy's leaders.'

In the medieval mystery play, actors had certainly to endure considerable physical hardship on occasion, though it is questionable whether this involved any particular skill. Nicoll[4] mentions the crucifixion scene from one of these plays performed in France in 1437, in which the actor playing Christ 'would have died on the rood-tree, for he fainted and was like to have died had he not been rescued'. He refers too to Jehan de Missey, a priest who 'took the part of Judas, but hung too long and fainted and was like dead; for his heart failed him, wherefore he was hastily taken down and carried to a place near by and sprinkled with vinegar and other things to bring him round'.

But only in the Elizabethan theatre do we first find that sustained kind of action, requiring skill, involving an element of personal risk and contained within a theatrical framework, that we would regard essentially as 'stunting'. The fights in *Hamlet*, *Romeo and Juliet* and *Macbeth* must in their original productions have been of a very high standard indeed. We should remember that at this period the theatres on the periphery of the City of London were used for other purposes than dramatic performances. They were used for bear-baiting and cock-fighting.

More important from our point of view, they were used by the London Masters of Defence for the 'playing of prizes', a system of examination in which applicants for admission to the Gild of Masters fought publicly with the weapons then in vogue in order to demonstrate their skill. Many of the audience that saw the first performances of the plays of Shakespeare and his contemporaries

20

must also have seen the displays given in the same theatre by the Masters of Defence. Bearing in mind the rough and ebullient nature of the Elizabethan audience, it is inconceivable that it would not have barracked the fight scenes in the plays out of existence if the quality of action in them had compared too unfavourably with the public displays of arms given by the Masters of Defence. This view of the quality of such scenes of dramatic action is supported by the fact that at least one of the great actors of the Elizabethan stage—Richard Tarlton—was himself a Master of Defence and therefore one of the outstanding fencers of London. Indeed, we might almost regard Tarlton as the first stuntman to whom we can put a name.

A wider concept of stunting was introduced by Philip Astley, a retired sergeant-major and riding-master who opened his Amphitheatre of Arts in Westminster Bridge Road, London, towards the end of the eighteenth century. He mounted 'battles and sieges' which required a high degree of horsemanship and many spectacular effects. His son John carried these performances a good deal further. He put horses through special training schedules and we can regard him as being the innovator of the modern 'equestrian drama'. But it was Andrew Ducrow, who took over the management of Astley's in 1824, who really carried these dramas to their most spectacular peak. 'His masterpiece,' says Disher,[5] 'a sawdust classic to this day, was *The Courier of St Petersburg*, and *Mazeppa, And The Wild Horse; or The Child of the Desert* began, at Astley's on April 4th 1831, a career as the most frequently acted drama in the world apart from *Punch and Judy*.' Arising out of this circus tradition of equestrian drama, came the stage version of *Ben-Hur*, first produced in November 1899 at a cost of $71,000. 'The scale,' says Brownlow,[6] 'was immense.' An army of performers and stage hands was involved, and the chariot race was staged by having a team of horses galloping on a treadmill against a revolving scene that gave the impression of tremendous action. In the end the production was so lavish that only eight cities had theatres big enough to mount it.

Spectacle in the cinema

Spectacular effects in the circus and in the theatre could go no further. The fact that the horses in the *Ben-Hur* stage production 'pounded a treadmill' instead of actually galloping freely was itself an admission of a basic limitation of the theatre. There is a point beyond which spectacle cannot go in the theatre because of the physical limitations of the medium which are a part of its essential character.

But the cinema knows no such physical restrictions. 'The greatest thing to me about picturemaking,' says Keaton,[7] 'was the way it automatically did away with the physical limitations of the theatre. . . . In the theatre you had to create an illusion of being on a ship, a railroad train, or an airplane. The camera allowed you to show your audience the real thing. . . . Nothing you could stand on, feel or see was beyond the range of the camera.'

The cinema was more naturally the home of spectacle than the theatre could ever be, and the stunt is essentially spectacular. It was inevitable that it should develop in the cinema in a way that was not possible for it in either the theatre or the circus ring. But there were other factors that encouraged that development. The early cinema arose from a circus and vaudeville tradition, not from the legitimate theatre. Even as late as 1917, Marshall Neilan was able to say, 'The sooner the stage people who have come into pictures get out, the better for the pictures.' The circus and vaudeville tradition was a visual, not a verbal one. Partly that visual tradition was in the nature of circus and vaudeville, but in part it had been imposed legally—at least in England, the home of 'classical' theatre—by patents granted to two theatre companies in the seventeenth century, giving them a monopoly on performances of stage plays.

This monopoly was not finally broken until 1843. Disher points out that 'Astley's, The Wells and The Circus were permitted almost any form of entertainment as long as it did not have dialogue'. Whether they liked it or not, all 'non-legitimate' forms of entertainment were forced to communicate very largely in visual, non-verbal terms, and spectacular effects were the inevitable consequence. Nicoll[8] points out that when verbal communication is denied in the theatre, spectacle is the inevitable consequence. He attributes the growth of the 'spectacular' play of the early nineteenth century to the increased size of the theatres in Covent Garden and Drury Lane to the point where subtle verbal communication became impossible.

Finally, we should not forget that the early cinema was silent. Although sub-titles did exist where some brief explanation of a situation in verbal terms was crucial, the principal means of communication with an audience was visual. It seems as if the whole scene was almost deliberately prepared for the advent of that specialist actor, the stuntman, an actor whose work is entirely dependent on non-verbal spectacle.

Early stunt performers

These factors determined the nature of much early cinema. Shooting was usually unscripted and improvised. The effects aimed at were achieved entirely in visual terms. Understandably, the new freedom from physical limitations that the cinema brought, found actors and directors anxious to explore it, and it was this spectacular side that initially developed most rapidly in the cinema. The very titles of many of the early serials suggests continuous, visual action—*The Adventures of Kathlyn* (1913), *The Perils of Pauline* (1914), *The Hazards of Helen* (1914), *Lucille Love, Girl of Mystery* (1914)—and there were actresses available and prepared to act in them.

The use of the word 'actress' here is perhaps misleading, since it suggests a direct contact with the 'legitimate' theatre and few of the early cinema workers had such a contact. Indeed, if actresses like Pearl White and Helen Gibson had been trained in the classic tradition of the theatre it is unlikely that either of them would have undertaken the kind of activities that were required of them on the screen. Granted, the actress in the modern 'legit.' theatre is now occasionally required to strip naked in the course of her work—a

Horse spectacle by Mr Sampson in the late 18th century

demand that no one ever made on Bernhardt or Duse—but she is never required to play scenes like those that the early cinema actresses took in their stride. This is not to suggest for a moment that the Pearl Whites, Helen Gibsons, Mary Fullers and Grace Cunards were not splendid performers, but simply that they arose from a different tradition, a tradition of circus and vaudeville that accepted violent and frequently dangerous physical activity as being an essential part of a performer's work.

Certainly, there seems to have been no hesitation on the part of the early cinema performers to accept any situation that a director dreamed up, however dangerous it might be. Mary Fuller, for example, always did her own stunt work and, according to Lahue[9] 'never refused to perform a stunt'. The same is frequently said of Pearl White who earned the journalistic nick-name of 'The Lady Daredevil of the Fillums'.

Perhaps Helen Gibson (the second 'Helen' in *The Hazards of Helen*) is a typical example of the 'action' performers of the early cinema. She moved into films after being a rider with the Miller Brothers' 101 Ranch Wild West Show, and worked originally for Thomas Ince for $8 a day. During extra work at the Selig studios she appeared with Tom Mix, and finally moved to the Kalem studios to star in *The Hazards of Helen*. The series had a railroad background, with endless opportunities for dangerous action sequences. The first 'Helen', Helen Holmes, for example, had been tied to the moving piston of a locomotive and was 'knocked from the side of a boxcar by a mail crane'. Miss Gibson's best stunt, according to Lahue,[10] was the motorcycle sequence from one of the episodes of *The Hazards*:

Travelling at full speed on a motorcycle as she pursued a runaway freight train, she rode through a wooden gate, shattering it completely, up a station platform, and through the open doors of a boxcar on a siding, with her machine travelling through the air until it landed on a flatcar in a passing train.

In 1916, she was badly hurt when she fell between a team of

galloping horses. Yet never does it seem to have been suggested that as the star performer in a series, some less hazardous method of securing the necessary action sequences in which she was supposed to be involved would have been desirable. This horse injury, says Lahue, 'was only one of a number of injuries which Helen received during her career, however, for they were a routine part of the life of stars who did most or all of their own stunts'.

After a comparatively short career in films, Helen Gibson returned to the circus as a trick rider with Ringling Brothers, Barnum and Bailey. During the 'talkie' era, she did frequent extra work, and finally retired in 1961. Her career is not unlike that of some of the other early cinema performers. It suggests a very wide view of entertainment, a view that can embrace a variety of different media, all of which are acceptable to the professional performer. It is not the view—nor the career!—of the average actress of the 'legitimate' theatre.

The star / stuntman

What in fact was developing in the early days of the cinema was not the specialist stuntman but the star performer who was capable of doing stunts. Pathé, for example, always made a strong publicity point of the fact that Pearl White never used a 'double' in the performance of the stunts in which the audience saw her on the screen. The fact that this was not entirely true—an actor called Stevenson was killed in 1922 doubling for Miss White—is neither here nor there. It is sufficiently true to indicate what the early cinema actress was capable of and what was expected of her. Indeed, the fact that Pearl White ever reached the stage of needing a double arose only because of injuries she had sustained—particularly to her back—during the days when she had done all her own stunting in *The Perils of Pauline*.

James Morrison, at one time an actor with the Vitagraph Company of Flatbush, Brooklyn, said in an interview with Brownlow[11] that he considered a recent hip operation that had put him on crutches was the result of his doing all his own stunts in his early pictures. He recalled a skating scene in *The Nth Commandment* (1923) in which he took thirty-eight falls, and an episode during the making of *The Redemption of Dave Darcey* (1914) in which he had to climb up the side of a house. Paul Scardon, who was directing him, told him to make for a length of spouting and use it to pull himself on to the roof. He set off and half-way up the cameraman decided to change the angle. When he finally grabbed the spouting it was rotten with rust. He made the climb without even a mattress on the concrete path below and when he saw the scene later at the Vitagraph Theatre, someone behind him commented: 'You know what they do? That's all laid out on the floor, and all they have to do is crawl along it.'

There is a quality of breathtaking casualness about this kind of highly dangerous stunt which is found in much of the work of the early actors in the cinema. Joe Hamman, the French actor-director, performed a succession of stunts—particularly with horses and trains—that would now only be carried out by the most experienced stuntmen after meticulous preparation. Unfortunately all his films seem to have disappeared many years ago and we have only the accounts of them left by those who saw them. But he certainly engaged in highly dangerous fights with animals—a lion on at least one occasion and a female bear on another—and an account given by Cabat and Levy[12] of a horse and train stunt performed by Hamman suggests a sequence nowadays we would associate only with the greatest of horse stuntmen. Hamman, playing the hero, is a prisoner on a moving train. His wrists are bound, but with him in the wagon is his horse. He offers hay to the horse and in the process of eating it the animal bites through Hamman's bonds. He mounts the horse and gets it to kick a hole in the end of the wagon. Through this, horse and rider pass on to a flat wagon behind just as the train is crossing a bridge over the Canal du Midi. From the flat wagon Hamman leaps the horse over the bridge parapet and into the canal—a height of some ten metres.

Hamman also had that casual and haphazard relationship with train drivers that Sennett had. If he wanted a shot of himself leaping from a bridge on to a moving train he did not go to the expense of hiring a train and a length of track. He had 'an arrangement' with the driver of a scheduled train whereby on a prearranged signal the train would be slowed down sufficiently for the stunt to be performed. Time has added a touch of mythology to the story for it is reported that on one occasion a stunt nearly ended in disaster because the presence on the train of an inspector made it impossible for the driver to slow down. A story that is rather suspiciously similar is told in connection with Sennett's use of trains.

Hamman forms an interesting link between the early stunt actors on the one hand and such men as Harold Lloyd and Buster Keaton on the other. Whereas Pearl White was under the direction of Louis Gasnier and Donald MacKenzie in *The Perils*, and Helen Gibson, when she performed her motorcycle stunt in *The Hazards*, was under the direction of James Davis, Lloyd and Keaton were principally under their own direction. (This is not, of course, entirely true of Keaton but it is true of his earlier and most important films.) Hamman has a foot in both camps. He was his own director, yet he seems to have demanded of himself as an actor no less than any other director of the time would have demanded. The stunts he performed have an element of abandon about them that is foreign to the work of Keaton and Lloyd. Keaton, no doubt because of his family background and his experience of tumbling from his very earliest years, established the principle that in stunting there is no virtue in risk and danger for their own sakes. Lloyd subscribed to the same principle. Both of them—and many of their contemporaries—turned out films that contained elements of very real danger, but they were elements that had been calculated and prepared for. The danger had been minimised by elaborate preparation. Keaton, for example, talks of the preparation necessary for a fall from the second floor of a building that he made in the course of the filming of *One Week* (1920). To lessen the impact 'we dug a deep, very wide hole in the garden, filled this with straw, and replaced the squares of sod on top of the straw. The lawn looked solid but collapsed like paper when I fell on it. I only felt a jar at the time.'[13] Nevertheless, despite such elaborate preparation, the element of danger was still there, for he found later that he had damaged both elbows and his back.

The custard-pie slinging that many early cinema comedians went in for is not in itself a stunt. It lacks the element of real personal risk that characterises the true stunt. Nevertheless, Keaton's description of how he prepared for custard-pie work is an example of that meticulous quality that he and some of his contemporaries brought to the stunt, a quality that is now accepted as being essential if a stunt is to be successful and injury kept to the minimum. For his small part in *Hollywood Cavalcade* (1939), in which he had to throw a custard pie at Alice Faye, he built a practice pie of wood and drove nails into it until the weight was right. He practised throwing this against a target chalked on a wall until he was satisfied that he could put a real pie square in the face of Miss Faye from a distance of six feet—what he called the 'shot putt'.

Lloyd, in his conversations with Brownlow,[14] makes a clear distinction between an act of sheer physical virtuosity and a cinema stunt. He recalls the incredible feat of Bill Strothers, a professional steeplejack, in climbing up the outside of the Brockman Building in Los Angeles, riding a bicycle round the parapet and finally doing a head-stand on top of the flagpole. In his climb Strothers relied entirely on his own physical skill. When Strothers attempted the climb of a much smaller building in a film, he fell from the first floor and broke a leg.

When Lloyd himself attempted a similar climb he took infinite precautions to increase the safety margin to the maximum. Physical skill alone—as Strothers had proved—was not nearly enough. Lloyd's climb in *Safety Last* (1923), for example, took six weeks to shoot. When we see him climbing the skyscraper, he really was climbing it. The only precaution he took was to have mattress-covered platforms built some ten or fifteen feet below the windows. To test what would have happened if he had fallen, he dropped a dummy on to one of the platforms when the picture was finished. It bounced off the platform and dropped to the street below.

Stunting in the cinema

The testing of such safety devices as Lloyd's platforms, had to be left in the hands of a specialist in such matters. In the work of the early stunt actors like Lloyd and Keaton, the position of the property man was extremely important. Lloyd praises the work of Fred Guiol, and even Houdini, not particularly noted for giving gratuitous credit to those about him, mentions the debt he owed to Jim Collins, who joined him in 1908 as a technical assistant and who helped in the preparation of stunts and stunt properties.[15] Keaton blames his broken neck, sustained during the making of *Sherlock Jr* (1924) and only discovered many years later, on the inadequate research conducted into the way a particular property was likely to function. He had to leap from the top of a train to the dangling rope of a water tower. The rope released a jet of water and this was to soak Keaton and so provide the comic element in the stunt. The force of the water, however, was so great that Keaton's grip on the rope was broken and he fell with the back of his neck across one of the metal rails.[16]

To the history and technique of stunting the early actors contributed two things of major importance. They stressed the need for a high degree of physical skill and the need for meticulous preparation. Keaton taught himself back somersaults, 'butterflies' and flip-flaps in order to perfect that body control which was essential to his work. And mentioning the near-disaster of a performance in which Houdini was strapped hand and foot on a runaway horse, Gresham says: 'Harry neglected the first principle of the escapist's art; *try out the stunt ahead of time and in private*'.[17] Even Chaplin, whose technique did not really include the stunt, says: 'Violence was carefully rehearsed and treated like choreography. A slap in the face was always tricked. No matter how much of a skirmish, everyone knew what he was doing, everything was timed.'[18]

2 The rise of the professional stuntman

Doug Fairbanks

'No member of my cast was injured in any of our pictures,' says Chaplin.[19] 'It was inexcusable to get hurt, because in films all effects—violence, earthquakes, shipwrecks, and catastrophes—can be faked.' Yet despite that, Keaton had broken his neck, Kamuela C. Searle had been killed in the *Son of Tarzan* (1920) serial and Pearl White had had to employ a double because of back injuries caused by earlier film exploits. It was clear that if the spectacular element of film was to develop—or even continue at all—some change on the performers' side was inevitable. Neverthe-

Illustration: Loafers and Lovers (1926). Joe Rock and Earle Montgomery leaping on to railway wagons.

less, some principal actors did continue to perform most of their own stunts. Douglas Fairbanks and Errol Flynn are two outstanding examples.

'In my opinion,' says Keaton,[20] 'even Doug Fairbanks was merely a superior YMCA acrobat. His leaps and other acrobatics made him look better than he was, because Fairbanks thoroughly understood camera angles and used them most effectively.' This we might think supports Chaplin's contention that all film effects 'can be faked'. In fact this is not the case. It indicates no more than the growing sophistication of the medium and an increased understanding of what it could do. Fairbanks *did* leap from balconies and he *did* expose himself to real physical danger, but he did so with a clear understanding of the way in which the medium itself could help him. If he was 'for all his early acrobatics in feature films, in fact a comedian first, part cowboy second, and a costume player third',[21] then it is very much to his credit that the action sequences of *The Thief of Bagdad* (1924), *Robin Hood* (1922) and *The Three Musketeers* (1920) are so highly competent. It is also to the credit of the team with whom he worked. Alan Dwan, who directed Fairbanks, talked in his interview with Brownlow[22] of the way in which the stunts that the actor performed were corporate efforts. 'Doug's stunts,' says Dwan, 'were not actually great athletic feats, but they were stunts done with great grace.' Dwan created furniture and props that were tailored to Fairbanks' physical ability. A table was cut to the exact height at which the actor could most gracefully leap on to it. A wall up which he had to climb was fitted with concealed hand holds spaced exactly to suit the length of Fairbanks' arms. A leap was planned according to his particular skill in leaping.

This collaboration marks a considerable step forward in the development of cinema stunting. The days had gone when Griffiths could say of Mary Pickford, 'She will do anything for the camera. I could tell her to get up on a burning building and jump and she would.'

Fairbanks marks the transition, which was still to continue over many years, from the star actor who performed the majority of his own stunts to the specialist stuntman who performed such stunts on the star's behalf. Dwan confirms that Fairbanks did in fact use doubles on occasions, but in many cases they were not used to replace the star in front of the camera. Richard Talmadge, for example, did not take the place of Fairbanks when a stunt was being shot. What he did was run through the stunt a number of times in rehearsal to give Fairbanks an opportunity to assess its difficulty and the way in which its spectacular element could best be exploited. On the actual 'takes' Fairbanks was the performer.

Yet there were occasions when Dwan considered a stunt too potentially dangerous even for Fairbanks, however much it might have been 'modelled' in advance by Talmadge. On one of the films in which Dwan did not direct him, Fairbanks insisted on dropping from a balcony on to the back of a waiting horse. The horse, sensing something dropping towards it, moved and Fairbanks was injured. In Dwan's view, to risk a star in such a stunt was foolish. It called for the services of a stuntman.

Errol Flynn

Some star actors in the cinema still perform many of their own stunts but they are in a minority. Certainly one of the last of the great star actor/stuntmen was Errol Flynn. His personal background more than matched the plots of any of his films for swashbuckling action, and no doubt this is one reason for his ability to handle spectacular scenes with such ease and exuberance. 'My accomplishments,' he says, 'were strictly physical.'[23] If he had not become a star actor he might have become a professional stuntman of the highest calibre.

In *Captain Blood* (1935) Flynn was given his first lead and his performance in the film established his image permanently. 'I became,' he says, 'labelled a swashbuckler.' In it he was seen for the first time doing rope swings through the rigging and engaging in spectacular sword play. *The Adventures of Robin Hood* in colour in 1938, *Dodge City* (1939), *The Charge of the Light Brigade* (1936) and *They Died With Their Boots On* (1941) confirmed the image beyond the point where it could be changed. He complained bitterly that he had been stereotyped as a swashbuckler when he wanted to prove he was an actor as well. And yet in retrospect he recalled the spectacular aspects of his performances with a grudging pride—a pride that was in fact entirely justifiable: 'Most of the stunts that people saw in my action pictures I can truthfully say were done by me. I have fought sword fights on parapets, ridden horses over high barriers and deep gullies, and fought with Indians who were real tough stuntmen; great boys, always. In *The Adventures of Robin Hood* I did all my own stunts. Dammit, I said to myself, I am not going to be a phony.' Yet in his own introspective assessment, the motivation was more personal than artistic: 'The reason behind it was that I had fear and I had to go out and meet my own fear. If I am afraid to do something I move in on it and try to tangle with it and lick it.'

This personal motivation, which had little to do with a desire for histrionic perfection, is perhaps what made Flynn unique as a star actor/stuntman. He was an anachronism. He continued a tradition which had been established in the very early days of the silent cinema long after the conditions that had brought it into being had disappeared. He continued it in the face of considerable opposition from directors, from the studio and from the insurance companies.

In the end the changed conditions of the cinema, his own psychological and physical make-up, and time itself caught up with him. In 1953, during the making of *Crossed Swords* in Italy, he found that a leap, that at one time he would hardly have thought about, was suddenly impossible for him. 'Sure as hell,' he says, 'I couldn't do it.'

For Flynn, whose whole screen image had been of a man who will attempt without hesitation any physical hazard, this must have been a terrible admission to make to himself. It is an acknowledgement that the end of a brilliant professional career has at last been reached. It is ironic—perhaps even tragic—to reflect that the very temperament that had made him the spectacular star of *Captain Blood* and *Robin Hood*, was what in the end failed him. It also throws considerable light on an aspect of professional stunting that is overlooked. The popular image of the stuntman is of a person equipped with a fine and healthy body and the knowledge and skill necessary to use it for spectacular purposes. It is not an image that pays the least attention to those psychological processes that ultimately direct that skill. Yet Flynn's comments give us a penetrating insight into the overriding importance of such processes. At the moment of professional disintegration, Flynn can still manage a cry of optimistic defiance:

> Looking back on a career where I have had guns firing at me, explosions behind my head, horses falling from under me, big leaps to make, it is amazing to me that I am all in one piece. I still have two ears, my nose, all my limbs, and my eyes. Slightly astonishing.

Totally astonishing!

The demise of the star/stuntman

What died with Flynn was the concept of the star actor/stuntman, the performer in whom both star acting ability and specialised stunting ability co-existed. Long before his professional demise, the development of the cinema had been moving in the direction of increased specialisation in all its aspects. In the early days—the days of Mack Sennett and Keaton and the early Chaplin—film men were expected to have an all-round ability. They were expected to participate in the invention of 'gags', they were expected to perform in any scene that was put before them, they could turn their hands to setting up a scene and handling properties, they were conversant with the technicalities of lighting and camera-work in a general sense and when necessary they could direct.

Keaton is an example of this kind of all-roundness. It would be more accurate to describe him as a man of the cinema than simply as a great comic performer, just as it would be more accurate to describe Sir Laurence Olivier as a man of the theatre than simply as a great actor. But in a medium as dependent on technical innovation as the cinema has been, specialisation was inevitable. Increasing technical complexity produced specialists in make-up, lighting specialists, camera specialists and specialists in film administration. No aspect of the industry withstood the movement and the star performer was as susceptible to it as anyone else. Under the pressure of specialisation he had a choice. Star *or* stuntman. Not both.

This is not, of course, to say that since the nineteen-forties no star has ever performed his own stunts. Many of the biggest names have taken part in wild action sequences. Burt Lancaster, John Wayne, Kirk Douglas, Roger Moore are only a few of very many who have done so. But they have done so *within the limitations of their star status*. They have done so only after due regard has been taken of the dangers involved, after the risks have been calculated and minimised. They have done so perhaps because they particularly wished to. But they have not done so because participation in dangerous action sequences was regarded as an intrinsic part of their jobs. When, in *True Grit* (1969), John Wayne 'did the dangerous back fall from the horse himself', it was a sufficiently remarkable act for a star to perform for Mike Tomkies[24] to draw special attention to it.

The growth of complex spectacle

What really forced specialisation on the action aspect of cinema was the demand for increasingly complex spectacle. What was satisfactory for an early Pearl White episode of *The Perils* was no longer satisfactory in the days of the feature epic. What had been done already, palled when it was repeated. What was required was bigger spectacle and, in terms of the actors, this meant falls from greater heights, leaps from faster trains, aerial stunts of infinite complexity, stunts with horses that would have alarmed even the performers at Astley's. And inevitably, the demand became greater than the ability of most cinema actors could meet.

There is no doubt at all that many of the performers in the early cinema were fearless to the point of being foolhardy. Keaton, in Brownlow's view, 'had a degree of personal courage which, had it been displayed under conditions of war, would have won him national honors'. But courage was no longer enough. Courage is not enough to bring down a 'falling' horse on exactly the spot that the director requires it. Nor is it sufficient to guarantee freedom from injury in a 70-foot fall. And however lion-hearted an actor may be, unless he at least knows how to fly an aeroplane he can never begin to emulate the spectacular effects of an Omar Locklear or Dick Grace.

What was needed more than courage was specialist skill in action sequences, and very few actors had it. Those who did have such skill, acquired in other activities, were imported into the cinema and taught to combine it with the business of acting. Omar Locklear and Cliff Bergere entered stunting from aviation. Leo Noomis had a background of circus work. Buster Wiles, Jimmy Dolgun and Don Turner, all of whom worked with Flynn, had been cowboys. Art Acord, 'born in Stillwater, Oklahoma Territory, in 1890 . . . performed his first professional stunting in 1910 with the Dick Stanley Wild West Show. His all-round versatility in stunting and riding soon led him into motion pictures.'[25] These, and others like them, trained initially in their special skills outside the cinema, were the men who began to create and later to establish and develop, the special position of the stuntman in the cinema.

The star as a valuable property

Allied to this pressure, created by the development of the medium itself, to provide increasingly spectacular effects on the screen, was the growing need to protect the principal actors from injury. The need increased with the growth of the film budget. As budgets grew, it became increasingly necessary to preserve the maximum of continuity in shooting. In the early days of the silent cinema, the indisposition of a principal performer was an inconvenience. But with the introduction of the 'star system', with minimum rates of pay being laid down by growing technical and artistic organisations—even during the shooting of *Intolerance* in 1916, the Industrial Workers of the World (the 'I Won't Works' or 'Wobblies') had tried putting organised pressure on directors for more pay for extras—the illness of a leading player could bring to a halt the work of hundreds of people and add enormously to the budget.

Illness, of course, was unavoidable, but injury caused by the performance of a stunt was not. It could be avoided quite simply by the employment of a stuntman to double for the star, and such, with few exceptions, became the established practice. Flynn sums up the whole problem for the production companies, the problem that helped to establish the stuntman as a significant force in the cinema: 'Insurance companies wouldn't insure a picture if I did the rough stuff.' However capable a star might be in handling his action sequences himself, it was no longer financially justifiable for him to do so. The whole financial viability of a production grew increasingly dependent on the fitness and availability of the star; to protect him the system of 'doubling' in action scenes was an inevitable development. This innovation itself led to a further development of stunting: with the introduction of a specialist in the action scenes, writers, producers and directors saw still greater possibilities for the exploitation of spectacle. They were no longer restricted to stunts that the average actor could perform. They could push spectacle almost to the extremes of human endurance.

Availability of cheap labour

There is a third factor that helped to establish the stuntman in the cinema. It is an economic one and it reveals a certain human cynicism on the part of early producers and directors. The rapid growth of the film industry in America and the sudden mushroom growth of Hollywood in the 1920s, led to an influx of labour into the Los Angeles area. This labour was by no means restricted to hopeful actors and actresses looking for work in the new medium. It included circus people, stunt fliers and cowboys skilled in rodeo work. The industry could not absorb them all. 'They hung around the studios hoping to pick up an odd couple of bucks.' They formed a body of labour that was readily available to any director in need of extras who were prepared to do anything that was asked of them. 'All they had to do to get extras was go on the roof and whistle,' said Geraldine Farrar.²⁶ In the 1926 production of *Ben-Hur*, many extras were feared drowned in the sea battle. When Francis X. Bushman, playing the part of Messala in the film, drew the attention of the director to this, Niblo's reply was, 'I can't help it. Those ships cost me forty thousand dollars apiece!'²⁷

The dangers of early action

However sceptical one might have been about the degree of danger involved in action sequences, all the accounts of the *Ben-Hur* production dispel it. Whatever precautions are taken to minimise the danger, a strong element of risk remains. Launches were standing by in the *Ben-Hur* galley sequence to pick up extras who had been instructed to leap over the side of the burning trireme into the water. Yet according to many eyewitnesses of the disaster some extras were still lost. Danger can be minimised but it cannot be altogether eliminated from the action sequence.

The death of John Stevenson on the morning of August 11th, 1922, is a case in point. Stevenson was a 38-year-old actor from New York who agreed to double for Pearl White during the making of a stunt sequence for *Plunder* (1923). Stevenson, dressed in female costume and blonde wig, had to jump from a moving bus on to the steelwork of a bridge as the bus passed beneath it. He leapt from the top of the bus, failed to get a secure hold on the girder and fell. He died a few hours later from head injuries. Weltman and Lee in their book, *Pearl White, the Peerless Fearless Girl*, add details to the story which, though not affecting its salient facts, show the way in which a mythology has grown up around some of the early stuntmen. According to the writers, Stevenson was neither actor nor stuntman. He was chauffeur to the director, George B. Seitz. He pleaded to do the stunt because he needed the money, arguing that his wife and child were already employed on the picture as extras. He was killed, in Seitz's opinion, because the bus was going too quickly and because he 'fouled up on his timing'.

The attitude of the production company to the accident is interesting, since it shows the prevailing preoccupation with the image of the star, in whom, after all, its money was invested: 'Pathé, which had Miss White under exclusive contract, stoutly maintained the fiction that no doubles were ever used for her and referred all questions to the Seitz studio. Seitz refused to discuss the matter and Pearl could not be found for comment.'[28]

Early financial rewards

According to Brownlow, 'The injuries suffered by motion-picture personnel—stunt men included—were no more numerous, nor more serious, than the general run of industrial accidents,' yet at the same time 'the average career of a motion-picture stuntman was under five years. He either got injured or he got money enough to leave this most dangerous game and take up another occupation.' How, one wonders, did he manage to amass the kind of money necessary to give him his freedom? The 2,000 extras hired for *Intolerance* 'got their carfare, their lunch, and a dollar and a quarter a day.' For this they faced the real possibility of physical injury. Henabery, commenting on the shooting of the walls of Babylon sequence, says: 'The injuries were mostly of a minor nature, but we once had as many as 67 in that first-aid tent in one day.'[29]

Even assuming seven days' continuous work a week—an assumption, as we have seen, that could never be made—the maximum that an extra could take home, according to Henabery's figures, was $8.75. Even that figure was dependent on his staying clear of the first-aid tent. Talking of the general employment situation of the period, Lahue says '$7 a week was the bare subsistence level'.[30] The Keystone Cops, according to Keaton,[31] 'remained the worst-paid performers in Hollywood. At first they got only $3 a day for risking their necks. After Sennett made a fortune with *Tillie's Punctured Romance* (1914) he raised them to $5 a day.'

For performing a special stunt involving hazards beyond what was normally expected of him, an actor might receive a bonus. Eddie Sutherland was paid $15 a week as an actor in *The Hazards of Helen*. For jumping off a train he was paid an additional $5. By contrast, James Morrison was paid an all-in cash sum of $25 a week for acting and doing all his own stunts. As an example of the kind of spectacle that $5 would buy in the early days of cinema, Keaton[32] mentions a particular member of the Sennett team, Bobby Dunn. Dunn was a professional high diver. For $5 he dived eighty feet off the roof of the Hotel Bryson in Los Angeles into a tank of water nine feet long, five feet wide and five feet deep. Grace,[33] who saw the dive, says it was performed after Dunn had already lost an eye in a similar stunt, a fact which makes it all the more remarkable.

For the star actor who performed his own stunts, financial arrangements were a good deal better. Helen Gibson, who was paid $8 a week as a specialist rider for Thomas Ince, was given $50 a week by the Kalem Company for starring in *The Hazards of Helen*, and in 1921 she was getting $450 a week from Spencer Productions. For *The Perils of Pauline*—'filmed exactly as they happened'—Pearl White was paid $250 a week and in 1916 Grace Cunard 'reached the financial peak of her career . . . with a unique salary arrangement that paid her $450 a week plus 25 cents a foot over 1,500 feet per week plus 10% of the profits.'[34] By comparison with the pittance paid to the stunt-extras on *Intolerance*, these salaries appear little less than weekly fortunes, but even they looked slim by comparison with the money paid to some non-stunting stars. Louise Brooks, for example, who was never called upon to take the risks of a Pearl White or a Helen Gibson, left Ziegfeld in the twenties to accept Jesse Lasky's offer of $4,000 a week. We can see such a salary in more clear perspective if we remember that $5 bill that Henry Lehrman paid Bobby Dunn for his eighty-foot dive, and the fact that in America at that time 'it was not unusual to find many women drawing not more than $6 weekly'.[35]

The consequences of injury

However courageous and skilled the early stuntmen were—and no one can deny them that—and however driven they might have been by economic conditions, they must from time to time have wondered about injury. 'Fearless' is a word used frequently by the stars of the early cinema to describe the men who performed the most spectacular feats in their films. Yet it is difficult to believe that even Bobby Dunn, standing eighty feet above a tank containing a mere five feet of water, did not, however fleetingly, pose the question, 'What happens if I injure myself?' The simple answer, as 'Suicide' Buddy Mason saw it, was that you went to hospital. If you recovered you took up stunting again where you had left off. If you were permanently injured you left the industry altogether, or you tried for some other job within it.

The industry itself acknowledged no responsibility for injury to a stuntman, though on occasions companies were remarkably understanding and generous. When Omar Locklear and his assistant Milton Elliot were killed in an aeroplane stunt for *The Skywayman* (1925), the Fox company made arrangements for the families of the two men to receive ten per cent of the film's profits. But there was no contractual obligation on the companies to make such gestures. James Morrison says he never had a written contract with Vitagraph while he was with them. Personal insurance for the average stunt-extra was unheard of. If such insurances had existed, it is hardly likely that a man on less than $10 a week—and that only on 'good' weeks—could have paid the premiums. When Eddie Sutherland tried to talk the director (J. P. McGowan) into letting him do a rope-diving stunt in which a stuntman had been injured, McGowan didn't ask if Sutherland was properly insured. He said, 'Oh, Eddie . . . if you get hurt, your family will kill me. I know them!'[36]

The kind of precautions that an established stuntman took in 1922 to ensure the well-being of his wife and family in the event of his death in a stunt, is shown in a story which appeared in *Photoplay* in December of that year. Doubling for Jack Mower in

Manslaughter (1922), Leo Noomis had to crash a police motorcycle travelling at forty-five miles an hour into the side of a car. Noomis, before he undertook this highly dangerous stunt, asked De Mille who was directing the picture if he would 'sort of keep an eye on the wife and kids' in the event of things going wrong. 'I'll take care of them as long as they live,' said De Mille. 'So don't worry about that.' According to Leatrice Joy, the female star of the picture, Noomis hit the car and, despite the mats that had been put on the ground to protect him, he broke six ribs and his pelvis. In her opinion, the shot could have been done just as well with a dummy.

But lives continued to be risked, because there are spectacular scenes in the cinema which no amount of technical skill in film processing can fake, and dummies do not always behave like flesh and blood. The very nature of the medium created the specialist stuntman. Nothing in the future can eliminate him, except a fundamental change in the nature of the art form in which he works. 'What these men left behind,' says Brownlow of the early stuntmen '. . . was not just the bar room anecdote. Without them, an essential realism would be missing from motion pictures.'[37]

3 Stunts with horses and other animals

Pre-cinema horse spectacle

The cinema brought many refinements to the way in which the horse might be used as a vehicle for spectacular action, but it did not 'invent' horse work. Homer refers to horse spectacles, and the horse played at least as important a part as the human participants in the Roman arenas. 'Along with chariot-racing and horse-racing,' says Manning-Sanders[38] of the spectacles in the Circus Maximus, 'there were exhibitions of trick-riding. . . . Riders leaped from one horse to another as they sped round the course; they rode kneeling; they rode lying down; at full gallop they hung from their mounts

Illustration: Man of Conquest (1937). Yakima Canutt transferring.

to pick up objects from the ground. . . .' All of which we have since seen in the cinema.

Medieval Europe saw the horse trained to perform tricks in his own right. If manuscript illustrations of the period are to be believed, then horses were persuaded to carry oxen on their backs and to keep a certain precarious balance on the tight-rope. Edward II of England roared with laughter, we are told, at the 'nameless father of our equestrian clowns' who performed an act during which he fell repeatedly off a moving horse, a stunt brought to its final perfection in the cinema by such riders as Yakima Canutt. Later, Elizabethan London thrilled to the performance given in the yard of *La Belle Sauvage* by Banks and his horse Morocco. 'If Banks had lived in older times,' Sir Walter Raleigh said, 'he would have shamed all the enchanters of the world, for whosoever was most famous of them could never master or instruct any beast as he did.' So much, in Sir Walter's opinion, for all the world's riders before Banks. He might well have amended his opinion if he had lived to see Adah Menken play Mazeppa or the Christianis perform 'the suicide trick' at Olympia in the nineteen-thirties, and whatever Banks did he could hardly have matched Ray 'Red' Thompson's sixty-foot leap with a horse from the top of a cliff into a river in the early days of the cinema.

Before Astley's creation of the circus as we now know it, eighteenth-century riding masters had given public displays of horsemanship which seem to have been motivated almost entirely by a wish to outdo all rivals in sheer spectacular virtuosity. About 1768, for example, Thomas Johnson, who claimed with little historical justification to be the first man to perform feats of horsemanship in public in England, rode the following programme:

Firstly he will ride two horses, as fast as they can go, all round the course with one foot on the top of each saddle. Secondly, he will ride 100 or 200 yards on his head, his feet being directly upright. Thirdly, he will ride, without any manner of support, 300 yards, standing on the saddle with one leg only. This being a performance never before attempted by any other person in

England, it is hoped the spectators will give him such encouragement as they may think the execution of so extraordinary an undertaking deserves. The said Thomas Johnson is to be spoken with at the sign of the *Ship*, in March Street.

A Mr Sampson, riding at Joseph Dingley's Jubilee tea gardens in Islington, outdid Johnson by leaping off a galloping horse, firing a pistol, remounting, standing on his head in the saddle, reversing his position and 'hanging upside down at a most dangerous angle, his hand brushing the turf'. Mr Coningham managed to play a flute and ride two horses at the same time, whilst the incredible Daniel Wildman 'surpassed in inventiveness the whole bunch of these early trick-riders by covering his face and neck with a swarm of bees, whilst careering round with one foot on the saddle and the other on his horse's neck'. But perhaps the most astonishing programme was that ridden by Charles Hughes—at one time an Astley employee—and his wife:

Hughes . . . will exhibit at Blackfriars-road more Extraordinary things than ever yet witnessed, such as leaping over a Horse forty times without stopping between the springs—Leaps the Bar standing on the saddle with his Back to the Horse's Tail, and, *Vice-Versa*, Rides at full speed with his right Foot on the Saddle, and his left Toe in his Mouth, two surprising Feet [*sic*]. Mrs Hughes takes a fly and fires a Pistol—rides at full speed standing on Pint Pots—mounts pot by pot, higher still, to the terror of all who see her. H. carries a lady at full speed over his head—surprising! The young gentleman will recite verses of his own making and act Mark Antony, between the leaps . . .!

The establishment of the modern circus by such men as Astley and Ducrow, brought with it increased specialisation and professionalism which replaced the virtuosity of the retired military men and riding masters like Samson—'lately discharged from Lord Ancram's Light Dragoons'—and Hughes. The specialist riding horse, the 'resin' or 'rosin back', appeared, named after the technique of sprinkling powdered resin on the back to give the bare-back rider, or the rider standing on a pad, a better foothold. More sheer skill was demanded than that displayed by Daniel Wildman and his co-operative swarm of bees, and when Levi J. North performed the first recorded back somersault on a running horse at Batty's circus in 1839, he established a further dimension for the trick-rider.

Towards the end of the nineteenth century the American, Orrin Davenport, is credited with having performed the first back somersault from one horse to another, but it is perhaps with the Christianis in the nineteen-thirties that we see trick-riding carried as far as it is likely to go. Lucio, Belmonte and Mogador Christiani made 'the suicide trick' one of their more spectacular specialities. It consisted of turning back somersaults from one moving horse to another, at the same time passing themselves through hoops. Lucio—incredibly—took the trick a stage further. He performed a back somersault from one cantering horse, passing over the back of a second, and landing on a third.[39]

The rodeo and the wild west show

In this tradition of trick-riding, the modern horse-stuntman of the cinema has his roots. But it is not the only background out of which he has arisen. We must remember that in the cinema, the spectacular element has always been pre-eminently American. This is perhaps even more true of the horse-action picture than of other forms of film spectacle. It is true that Joe Hamman was turning out such pictures in France before the First World War, and in this sense he might well be regarded as the creator of the 'Western', but the Americans have developed and perfected the form and the most memorable horse-action sequences that spring to mind—the Indian chase in *Stagecoach* (1939), the chariot race in *Ben-Hur* (1926), the cavalry charge in *The Charge of the Light Brigade*—are all American.

Although America shared with Europe many of the traditions of the circus, it also had its own unique form of horsemanship developed and expounded through the rodeo and the Wild West Show. Both arise not out of a form of entertainment but out of American history elaborated through the process of time into a mythology—the mythology of the West during the nineteenth century, its opening up, its conquest and its final settlement. Yakima Canutt,* 'one of the greatest rodeo riders of all time' and World Champion All Round Cowboy from 1917 to 1924, made the transition from rodeo work to cinema horse-stunting without obvious difficulty. 'Hoot' Gibson, according to his wife Helen Gibson, had been a top rodeo rider before he started doubling for Tom Mix.[40]

In the early film Westerns, the cowboys who rode in the posses after train robbers and bad men were exactly what they appeared to be—professional cowboys or rodeo riders making a few extra dollars aside from their regular jobs. If, for a further five dollars a day, they were called upon to mount a moving stagecoach or fall off a galloping horse they did so. If they were hurt in the process, that was simply unfortunate. The late Gary Cooper, talking of his early days as a film rider, says that in his first horse-fall he was simply told by the director to throw his rifle into the air and fall off his horse. He did exactly as he was told.[41]

The rise of the horse-stuntman

Out of this background of cow-punching and rough rodeo riding, the horse-stuntman appeared. He appeared in answer to the cinema's need at the time for spectacle involving horses. There was nowhere else to which the directors of the period could turn for riders and the riders, by sheer force of circumstance, adapted their riding to the demands of the directors.

It was a new game for them. There were no trained stuntmen because nothing that had gone before had required them. They learnt their new business—painfully and occasionally fatally—as

*According to Hagner (*Falling For Stars*, E. Jon Publications, Palmdale, California, 1964), Canutt's real name is Enos Edward Canutt. The name 'Yakima' was given him in an early newspaper report.

they went on. Some, like William S. Hart, 'Hoot' Gibson and Tom Mix, became stars in their own right. Most did not. A few rose to command vast salaries—when Gary Cooper was still only a 'fall-down boy', Tom Mix, according to Cooper, was earning $17,500 a week—but most remained on an extra's pay plus an additional daily payment for stunt work.

But, as we have seen, the star-stuntman was doomed by his very stardom. This is as true in the field of horsework as in any other cinematic field. Injury to an unnamed and faceless stunt rider meant little to a production but momentary inconvenience. He could be replaced without much difficulty and the scene in which he had been injured could be reshot. But injury to a star could bring a production to a complete standstill and place an enormous financial burden on a film company. A startling example of the cost of star injuries is the case of Audrey Hepburn's unfortunate accident in 1959: 'Audrey Hepburn's serious fall from a horse during work on *The Unforgiven* (1960), cost £300,000 because of suspended production.'[42]

Such a situation gave rise to the specialist horse-stuntmen. Cooper himself had a considerable reputation as a specialist 'fall-down boy'—a specialist in falls from horses—before stardom required the use of a double for him. John Wayne performed most of the more general horse-stunts before the insurance companies and producers intervened.

But the names of the great horse-stunt riders were never those of the stars. They are names that are hardly known to the general film-going public. Names like Cliff Lyons and Carol Henry, David Sharpe, Jack Cooper, Rod Cameron and the great Yakima Canutt. Without them, the Western at least could never have become the spectacle that we now expect to see on the screen.

In the early days, as Gary Cooper said, the stuntman simply 'did as he was told'. But it was impossible to continue day after day taking the kind of physical punishment that falling off a galloping horse entails. Cooper described himself as being 'a mass of sharp edges and points' weighing only 155 pounds. To survive, it was necessary to protect those edges and points. Elbows, knees, shoulders and hips were padded. Experience taught a man how best in his particular case to hit the ground, and how to leave his horse and turn in the air in order to get into that position. The improvement of personal technique of this kind, arising almost entirely out of the need for a stuntman to protect himself from serious injury, opened up for the director the possibility of still more spectacular stunts.

The horse-stuntman, then, was faced continually with a dual problem; how to meet the new demands of the director and how to protect himself during the execution of these demands. He could no longer simply fall off his horse, since a good deal more than that was being required of him. Planning and preparation became increasingly important elements of the stunt for him. He needed to know the disposition of cameras, how much of the 'frame' he and the horse were to fill, the whereabouts of actors and properties, the nature of the ground and the exact position where the stunt had to be performed. Increasingly, too, he had to be aware of the character he was playing, and the way in which the star for whom he was doubling was playing that character in the non-action sequences. For despite his special skill with horses he was first and foremost an actor performing in front of a camera. It was indeed that fact that most separated him from his circus and rodeo antecedents. If rehearsal was possible, he rehearsed, but many stunts—the bringing down of a horse on a 'Running W', for example—preclude rehearsal. The first complete performance is the one that will eventually appear on the screen.

And so, out of the general body of horse-riding extras who were prepared to 'take a fall' for an additional five dollars, arose the specialist horse-stuntman. He was a man conversant with the grammar of the cinema, highly skilled in the management of his own body and the handling of horses, and above all able to give a creditable 'performance' in front of the camera.

The transfer

Initially—with certain notable exceptions like William S. Hart's

'Fritz'—the horses that the stuntmen rode received no particular training. Certain horses were kept for certain stunts, simply because they seemed to have a natural aptitude for them. Many ordinary cow-ponies made satisfactory 'transfer horses'—horses used by stuntmen to ride close alongside a moving train or stage-coach and maintain a consistent speed and distance so that the rider could 'transfer' from horse to vehicle in mid-gallop—because their ranch and rodeo work had required them to do something very similar with running steers.

Canutt was a particular master of transfer work, moving at full gallop from one horse on to the lead horse of a careering stage-coach, for example. Indeed, he stamped his style indelibly on such horse work with the complex stagecoach stunt he performed when doubling for Jack Randall in *Riders of the Dawn* (*c.* 1938) and again for Roy Rogers in *Sunset in Eldorado* (1943). He transfers to a fast-moving stagecoach and beats at the villain with his fists. He is knocked forward on to the backs of the horses and falls between a pair of them on to the ground. As the coach passes over him he seizes the rear axle and is dragged for some distance over the ground. Finally he manages to reclimb on to the back of the coach, cross the roof, and ultimately vanquish the villain.

How, one wonders, could any man do such a stunt and survive? Granted a certain 'undercranking' of the camera, so that the final projected image on the screen is faster than the real-life event, granted padding in the most vital places, there are still those pounding hooves to be avoided and still that long drag over rough ground to be survived before the final pull upwards on to the back of the coach. There must, one feels, be some kind of trickery to it. Men are not made like that. Mirrors, perhaps? Or hidden wires or trick photography? Canutt seems to be challenging one's view of human limitations, and one naturally resists accepting as true anything which requires an adjustment of one's personal philosophy. Yet true it is, in the sense that what one sees on the screen is precisely what Canutt did. He did it without any kind of trickery or sleight of hand. He did it because he is one of the great masters of such stunts. He did it because he has that rare ability of the top stuntman, the ability to see imaginatively how it can be done and then to control his body through the necessary movements.

The cliff leap

No training is possible, of course, for the horse required to leap with its rider from the top of a cliff into a river. 'I have never yet seen a horse perform a trick that was not a natural movement . . . that he does not do daily in his natural life,' says Tyrwhitt-Drake[43] of his experience of circus horses. And since it is not natural for a horse to leap off a cliff, it cannot be trained to do so. Nonetheless, the stunt has been performed. Cliff Lyons perhaps holds the record for the height he has fallen with a horse in this particular stunt—some sixty to seventy feet from the edge of a cliff into water. The height involved here seems well-authenticated, which is by no means always the case in the literature on stunting. George May, writing in 1939 and referring to the Lyons' stunt says, 'The highest paid single stunt performed in recent years was a seventy-foot fall on horseback into a tank of water. Cliff Lyons had to do that stunt twice and for his work—it took him an hour to do the two jumps—he collected $1,770.'[44] Theodore Taylor is less precise: 'Cliff Lyons, years ago, jumped horses into a river from a height of a hundred feet,'[45] whilst John Van Orme, referring to what one can only imagine is some latter-day Pegasus, says, 'Mary Delains rode a horse at top speed over a three-hundred-foot precipice into a river.'[46] Out of such manifestly inaccurate statements, the mythology of stunting grows and is perpetuated!

The intention behind the mounted cliff-leap is to show us a horse leaping front legs first, mane and tail streaming in the wind and the rider still in the saddle. Only rarely do we see anything even remotely matching this intention. In *Jesse James* (1939), for example, after the decision of the James brothers to escape their pursuers by leaping their horses from a cliff-top into a river some forty feet below, we see the two horses being urged towards the cliff edge. Then we cut to a picture of two totally disorientated animals falling upside down towards the water, their riders both well clear of the saddles. Before the horses hit the water, which might well have killed both of them in fact, we cut again to two horses already in the water, swimming vigorously with their riders to the opposite bank.

The stunt can be performed in two ways—either by force or trickery. Wayne recalls one occasion on which a stuntman was to take two horses off a forty-foot cliff. When the horses refused the jump they were pushed off. In the water, the stuntman was almost drowned when one of the horses tried to climb on top of him. In the end he was rescued by a colleague. His pay for the stunt was fifteen dollars.[47]

Dick Grace[48] recalls an occasion on which the stunt was performed by a combination of cajolery and force. Ray 'Red' Thompson—'who won his fame for jumping horses from cliffs into water'—attempted a sixty-foot cliff leap into a river with what Grace describes as 'a trained jumping horse'. The river had been deepened by dynamiting and the horse's approach to the cliff-edge had been levelled. Thompson galloped the horse along the approach, but the horse stopped as soon as the cliff edge came into view. The process was repeated several times with the same ultimate refusal by the horse. Thompson had the horse blindfolded, but still it refused to make the leap. The horse by this time was in a highly nervous state. Thompson 'gentled' it by stroking it and talking to it. At last he put it at the cliff edge again. At the moment when Thompson sensed that the horse was about to refuse once more, he gave it a sudden slap on the rump. Its instinctive movement forward carried it over the edge of the cliff. Both horse and rider somersaulted. Thompson, according to Grace, stayed with the horse all the way down—an exceedingly risky and unusual thing to do, particularly with an animal as terrified and disorientated as this one must have been. It is interesting to note that Grace mentions the survival of both man and animal, as if this was by no means always to be expected.

The most usual form of trickery for the cliff-fall is complex and expensive, and when one sees the final result in the cinema it is doubtful whether the effect justifies the time involved in setting up the stunt, the risk to the stuntman and the terror induced in the uncomprehending horse. A chute of planks is built. One end of the chute rests on the approach to the cliff edge whilst the other end is inclined downwards over the river. The chute is well greased and over its landward end a hangman's trap is constructed. The horse, in a state of increasing apprehension, is led up a ramp and on to the trap, its rider already in the saddle. The camera is set in motion and on a signal the trap is sprung. The horse drops a foot or two on to the greased chute and, unable to maintain any kind of foothold on the surface, it goes over the cliff edge in a state of total terror. At the earliest possible moment, the stuntman clears the saddle and falls independently of the horse. For good reasons, this was one of the stunts that gave the American Humane Association considerable cause for concern, though it was by no means the only one.

A more effective horse-leap is that seen in such films as *The Mark of Zorro* (1940), in which a horse is seen to leap the parapet of a bridge into the river beneath. The effectiveness is due to two things: the fact that the horse leaps willingly and the fact that the fall is no more than ten or fifteen feet. In consequence, the horse maintains that upright position with the rider still on its back that all horse-leaps aim at. Again, there is usually an element of trickery in the stunt, in the sense that the horse is not aware of the height of the fall beyond the parapet. If it is fitted with half-cup blinkers that obscure the lower part of its field of vision, then it can see the top of the parapet without being able to see what lies beyond and below it. It has confidence in its rider and the low parapet that it is being asked to jump presents it with no height problem. Only when it has cleared the parapet and is launched in an orthodox jump towards the river, does it realise the extent of the fall ahead. But by that time it has struck the water. It only remains for its rider to reassure it.

Trickery has played its part in other horse stunts. In *Jesse James*, for example, we see two horses plunge through a shop window amidst showers of 'glass'. Even allowing for the fact that the 'glass' was not real glass and did no damage to the horses, it seems likely that such a stunt could only be performed by trickery. If benign drops are put in the eyes of the horse to blur its vision temporarily, and it has absolute confidence in its rider, then it will perform the stunt.

Early saddle falls

In the early days of the Western film it was usual for the rider to pull up the horse before falling off. At that time such a technique was an acceptable convention. But the demand for greater realism and the improvement in falling techniques perfected by men like Canutt and practised by stunt riders like Gary Cooper, resulted in the introduction of the fall from a fast-moving horse. We saw a member of a posse shot from the saddle by an escaping gang of bank robbers. The rider fell from the horse, whilst the horse itself galloped on riderless.

But this implied a code of chivalry on the part of the 'badmen' that allowed them to shoot at a pursuer whilst forbidding them to shoot at his horse, despite the fact that a horse is a much bigger and more obvious target than the man crouched on its back. The demand for realism found such an implied code unacceptable. A man escaping from a bank raid has no such code. He will stop at nothing to get away from his pursuers. If the horse is a more obvious target than the man, then it is the horse at which he will fire. Realism demanded, then, that ways be found of bringing the horse itself down in front of the camera.

The 'pit' and the 'running w'

Apparently it occurred to no one to train a horse to fall. That was a much later development, forced on the industry by outside organisations concerned with cruelty to animals. The two notorious techniques employed during the hey-day of the Western, and still used in some modern film-making, were the 'pit' and the 'Running W'.

The pit is simply a covered hole in the ground into which an unsuspecting horse at full gallop falls. It must be constructed with a good deal of care if horse and rider are to survive without too much injury. A hole some three or four feet deep is dug in the path over which the horse is to gallop, after camera positions have been established. On the approach side, the fall is sheer, but on the exit side a slope is constructed so that the horse, once it has recovered from the immediate shock of the fall, can get out of the hole. This easy exit is essential, particularly for the safety of the rider. Jack Cooper recalls once being trapped in a pit with a fallen horse that had difficulty in getting out. The horse, in an understandable state of panic, lashed at him with its hooves.

Once the hole is satisfactorily prepared it is filled with empty cardboard boxes to cushion the horse's fall and covered with tarpaulin and earth or sods. Although the stuntman knows where the hole is, the horse cannot distinguish it from the surrounding ground. Ideally, as the horse begins to sink beneath him the stunt-man falls clear of the pit on to ground that has been previously broken up and covered with peat to break his fall. In reality, of course, there are many occasions on which he misses the prepared ground and takes the full shock with his own body.

Forms of the 'Running W' vary considerably. In one form, two wires are attached to hobbles on the horse's forelegs. The wires run up the front legs of the horse, over its shoulders, crossing under the saddle. The free ends of the two wires are firmly anchored some distance out of shot. The anchorage points can be stakes driven into the ground, trees or a heavy vehicle. The length of the wires is sufficient for the horse to be brought to a gallop. When the horse reaches the full extent of the wires, usually moving at something over twenty-five miles an hour, the wires suddenly arrest the movement of its forelegs and it falls in the most dramatic manner, usually on its chin or neck.

By contrast with this method, Fernett[49] describes the 'Running W' as

a simple arrangement comprising a long, thin 'trip cable', a loop suspended just under the chest of the mount, and a pair of special 'anklets' about its forelegs. The length of wire—usually thirty or more feet of it—was secured to a stake driven into the ground. The other end was threaded through the loop on the chest of the horse, then fastened to both the 'anklets' on the legs of the animal. When all was prepared, the horse was led to a point as far beyond the stake as the cable would allow. Then, with the camera following the action, the rider—his feet pushed into special footholds which positioned him accurately for the stunt—spurred the mount to maximum speed. As the horse passed the stake, the long trip line began to tighten, eventually becoming so taut as to suddenly pull the forelegs of the horse up to its chest. At that moment, the startled animal lunged forward, catapulting its rider beyond the point where the horse hit the ground.

Perhaps the most authoritative description of the 'Running W' is that given by Pat Moore,[50] the special effects director, who has fixed the device for a number of modern horse-fall sequences in the cinema. Moore's arrangement, illustrated on page 58, involves the use of all four feet of the horse and not just the forefeet. The equipment he uses comprises four very sturdy hobbles, lined with sheepskin to protect the pastern and fitted with D rings; a strong surcingle to go round the body of the horse and a figure of eight ring; the requisite length of wire and a set of stakes to which it is to be attached. 'In selecting the wire to do the job,' says Moore, 'the weight of the horse should be gauged and the wire dimension determined accordingly.'

To rig the device the four hobbles are fastened to the legs of the horse:

It is important to get them as low as possible. Ideally between the hoof and pastern joint. Then fix the surcingle and figure of eight ring as firmly as possible. Now take the wire and feed it through the hobbles, always lacing back through the eight ring. The last leg should be the rear right, and here the wire is tied off. The long trailing wire is then fixed back to a set of

C*

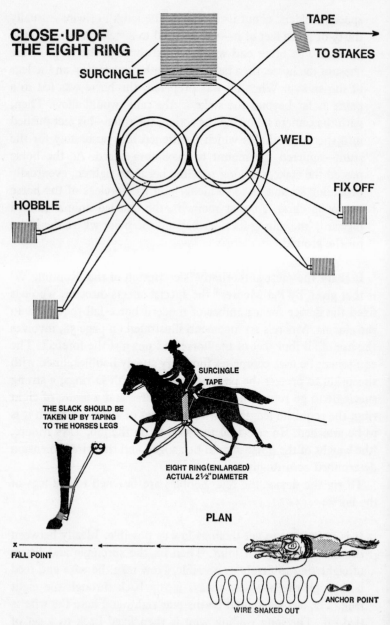

The 'Running W'. The diagram shows the 'eight-ring' in close-up and the way in which the wire is passed through it to each of the horse's legs.

stakes at the starting point. The length of wire depends on where the fall is to take place. The trailing wire is then snaked out so that it follows the horse with as little drag as possible. The last thing to do is attach the wire with tape to the saddle blanket, this stops it fouling the horse when he breaks into a gallop. Also any slack over the hobbles should be taken up by loose taping to the horse's leg. The advantage of this form of the device is that it has only one continuous wire which lessens the problem of snagging. When the horse reaches the end of its run the wire is taken up through the D rings, just as wire is run through pulleys. The central point is the eight ring and since all the feet are gathered up under the horse's stomach it must fall. The fact that there are no spare legs flying around at the time of the fall minimises the chances of one of them breaking. The eight ring is designed to help ensure that the wire is sheared, which means that when the horse lands it will not become entangled in a mass of wire. It also allows the horse to roll on from the point at which it is arrested, which lessens the impact.

The possibility of fatal injury or permanent damage to the horse is considerable. The rider is usually thrown forward in front of the horse with a certain catapult action. Although he is aware of the general position in which the horse is going to fall he cannot tell the exact moment, so that his fall must inevitably have a certain element of surprise to it. His reaction to the first moment of the horse's arrest by the wire must be sufficiently fast for him to leave the horse cleanly and give some direction to his body so that he will not land on any vital part. If, for example, his feet do not come cleanly out of the stirrups, or he has not removed them a yard or two before the fall, he cannot hope to escape with less injury than a dislocated hip. Alternatively, if he misdirects his body and lands on his head, he might well be killed.

In the case of anchoring the wire to a vehicle—a 'jeep' for example—the vehicle can follow the horse until a sufficiently good gallop has been built up. Then, when the vehicle puts on its brakes the wire tightens and the horse falls. This adds to the difficulties of both horse and stuntman. The chances of landing on ground that has been specially prepared for the fall are less than when the wire is secured to a fixed anchorage. And the stuntman cannot be quite sure when the horse is going to fall beneath him, because the moment and place of fall is controlled not by the length of the wire but by the driver of the vehicle. We can see how this variation of the device might be used cinematically if we imagine a director wishing to show a horse falling at the end of a run of two or three hundred yards. The wire necessary to control such a fall from a fixed anchorage would be so unwieldy that it would be almost certain to foul at some stage of its uncoiling.

The preparation and fixing of the 'Running W' is a highly specialised job. Pat Moore stresses the need to see that the hobbles are properly constructed and fitted so that when they are snatched by the tightening wire they do no damage to the horse's forelegs. The wire must be properly measured so that the fall takes place exactly where the cameraman expects it. In the case of the device using two wires rather than one, the wires must be secured so that the movement of both legs is arrested at the same time, otherwise a fall will take place that could add to the dangers already faced by horse and rider. The wire must be arranged so that during the build up to the gallop and during the gallop itself it is kept well clear of the horse's feet. The tensile strength of the wire must be calculated to make sure that it breaks immediately the legs of the horse have been arrested. This is particularly important where the device is fitted only to the front legs because if the wire fails to break, the horse, instead of rolling to one side or the other, will turn a complete somersault and probably break either neck or back. Such somersaults, which involve considerable danger to the rider as well as the horse, are features of many films of the nine-teen-thirties. Indeed, they seem to have been regarded as quite normal when the device described by Fernett[51] was used: 'If the stuntman failed to clear his somersaulting mount by at least 18 feet,' he says, 'he was in strong danger of being crushed to death by the animal.'

The ground where horse and rider are to fall must be properly prepared. It must be broken up with pick-axes to a depth of some six to nine inches and peat or straw laid on top or dug into it. Such care, of course, takes time and time for the film production company is always expensive. This expense, rather than sheer callousness, no doubt accounts for the lack of adequate preparation of the device during the early days of its use, and the consequent damage to horses which finally aroused the fury of the animal protection societies, particularly the American Humane Association. A properly devised 'Running W', according to Moore, can minimise the danger to both horse and rider but it cannot remove it altogether: 'No matter how well rigged, the "Running W", in my opinion, is dangerous to both man and horse.'

Moore's attitude to this particular device is interesting, since it is typical of the views of many people concerned with film spectacle involving the use of animals, and is very much at variance with the views of some critics of animal spectacle which suggest an insensitive callousness on the part of all film-makers concerned with such spectacle. Moore disapproves of the 'Running W' as a device for bringing down a running horse in front of the camera. He disapproves largely on the grounds of cruelty. It is not so much the physical cruelty of which he disapproves, since he is convinced that a properly prepared device will reduce that possibility to a minimum. But he is genuinely concerned with the nervous condition in which the 'Running W' leaves the horse after its totally unexpected and very severe fall. It is in a state of nervous panic. Its confidence has gone.

The opinion of Moore and of many specialist horse-stuntmen is that a horse can be brought down by this device once and once only. The experience is so deeply bedded in its memory that it will never again allow hobbles to be put on its legs, or if they are put on it will refuse all inducements to move. It associates hobbles permanently with some dreadful experience.

Moore's views are shared by many directors, though not all. Although animal protection organisations throughout the world have banned the 'Running W' it is still used in countries where supervision is less keen than it is in North America and in most of Europe. Why, one wonders, is it still used when it causes suffering to horses and puts their riders in jeopardy? Why do some directors still insist on it and why does Moore agree to arrange it? The answer, unfortunately, is that it produces the most spectacular and credible horse-fall the screen has yet seen. The attitude of the small number of directors who still insist on the use of the 'Running W' is understandable, even if one cannot approve of it. One can understand the dedication of a director who will spare neither himself nor anyone else in the process of capturing on film some personal inner vision. But one can understand and sympathise even more readily with Moore's position as a special effects expert. If a director insists on employing the 'Running W', despite the opposition—however tacit—that such insistence arouses, then Moore would prefer to prepare the device himself rather than leave it in the hands of a non-specialist. At least then he can guarantee that injury to the horse will be minimised.

French and Russian horse falls

Cabat and Levy[52] mention a further way of bringing down a horse, which seems to be exclusively French. This was by means of a wire attached to one of the front legs of the animal and controlled by the rider. When the horse had reached the point in its gallop at which it was required to fall, the rider pulled the wire and tripped it. Such a device must have been no less dangerous for horse and rider than the 'Running W'.

The same writers mention a Russian stunt sequence performed 'several times' by Timofeev, the Russian horse-stunt specialist. The stunt is known as the 'cut' and is performed with a *tatchenka*, a kind of war chariot dating from the First World War. The chariot is drawn by a team of horses and has some armoured protection. The vehicle is two-wheeled and carries a driver and one or two assistants operating a mounted machine-gun. The 'cut' is performed by stopping the horses in full gallop by means of wires. The vehicle runs forward over the top of the fallen animals and the driver and his assistants are catapulted forward 'some 20 metres beyond the point of impact'. It is of interest to note in connection with horse stunts that the French animal protection movement was protesting at the treatment of horses in films as early as 1920. It was almost twenty years later that such devices as the 'Running W' went out of use in America.

The cinema's attitude to the horse

The 'pit' and the 'Running W' are two devices which arose out of a particular attitude to the position of the horse in film-making. It was an attitude that hardened with the growth of the spectacular and the increasing demand for realism in the early days of the cinema, and continued until the successful intervention of the animal protection organisations in the late nineteen-thirties. It is seen most clearly in scenes of mass-action such as appeared in *Ben-Hur* (1926) and *The Charge of the Light Brigade*. The chariot race in the former and the charge in the latter are both classics of horse spectacle, and were directed by the remarkable B. Reeves Eason. Eason, who was an expert horseman and had directed low-budget Westerns, was ruthless in his approach to action. To achieve the spectacular results that he got, he needed to be. What Eason filmed really took place. For the master shot of the chariot race, Eason offered a prize of $300 to the winner, an inducement calculated to make the stunt drivers take any risks with their own lives and those of their horses. Despite the fact that Eason claimed later[53] never to have killed either a man or a horse under his direction, Bushman—playing Messala—was told by the man supplying the animals that they had lost 'about a hundred'.[54]

Errol Flynn was so upset by Eason's treatment of horses during the shooting of the charge in *The Charge of the Light Brigade* that he complained about it to the Society for the Prevention of Cruelty to Animals. In particular he complained about the use of the 'Running W', which injured the horses and caused some of them to be shot.

Flynn gives an account of what it was like to work in some of the mass horse sequences of the great Westerns when he talks of the shooting of *They Died With Their Boots On* and the death of his friend Bill Meade. He was leading a charge of four hundred cavalrymen over rough terrain in the San Fernando Valley. It was the third run-through of the day. Horses and men were tired. The camera, mounted on a car, ran beside them. Bill Meade was riding alongside Flynn when suddenly his horse stumbled. Meade got rid of his sword at once by pitching it ahead of him. By the most incredible piece of bad luck it hit pommel-first and stuck point-upwards. Meade went down with the horse and impaled himself on the weapon.[55]

Training the horse

The successful protests of such organisations as the American Humane Society brought about a revolution in horse-stunting. All devices which caused unnecessary injury and suffering to horses were banned. The notorious 'Running W' disappeared, at least as far as America was concerned. And America—certainly at that time—was the Mecca of film horse work. For some time one did not see horses falling on the screen. Riders, of course, fell off them but the horses themselves continued to gallop on. Yet the falling horse had been such a spectacular feature of horse action on the screen that it was inevitable that it would return, though in a form that would have to satisfy the A.H.A. 'All the A.H.A. asks is that animals not be forced to perform beyond their capabilities. If a horse must fall, jump or play dead, the requirement is simply that a horse be trained to do these performances.'[56]

Training took on a significance that it had not had before in film-making. The handling of horses in the cinema returned to that tradition established for so long in the circus. The attitude to horses changed. Whereas for many of the early horse stunts trickery had been an important technique in getting a horse to perform them, it now became necessary to gain the willing participation of the animal. Specialist trainers became established—men like Jack Lindell, Les Hilton, Ralph McCutcheon and Glenn

Randall—and horses were trained to perform certain special functions. At first it appeared that the need to train horses placed a severe restriction on the kind of stunts they could perform, but it soon became clear that training in fact opens up possibilities which are quite impossible by trickery. A horse, for example, cannot be tricked into falling without a rider on its back and once down to remain lying still. But it can be trained to do so. Equally a horse can be trained to stand still whilst a stuntman drops from a balcony on its back, but it cannot be tricked into doing so.

The falling horse

Of all the specialist horses that were trained for work in the cinema—the 'transfer horse', the 'self-falling horse', the 'standing horse', the 'lying horse' which will feign death, the 'crowd and band horse' which will stand unmoved by noise and bustle— the most important is the 'falling horse', the horse trained to fall at the command of its rider instead of being brought down by a 'Running W' or a pit. The training is usually long and requires considerable patience on the part of the trainer. Roy Street has trained a horse to fall properly within a month, but this does seem exceptional.

The training is conducted on the principles laid down for circus training by such men as James Fillis who insisted on the individual nature of each horse, and the Polish trainer Mroczkowski who stated his philosophy for horse training as 'time, patience, and plenty of sugar'. Gentleness is an important keynote. 'I have watched an animal trainer at work and I never cease to wonder how any man can be so gentle and unruffled,'[57] 'while the conviction grew in me that if there was any suffering involved in the matter it was borne by the teacher and not by the pupil. . . .'

The selection of the horse is important, since some horses take quite readily to being trained for this particular stunt whilst others do not. Perhaps the ideal horse would be a gelding of at least five years old. Stallions do not make satisfactory 'falling horses' and such 'falling' mares as Davie Wilding's 'Popsie' are rare.

After the usual acclimatisation period, which allows horse and trainer to become acquainted, the animal is gradually taught to fall down on command. The front foreleg is bent and tied up with rope or bandage round the knee. If possible, a saddle of the McLellan type is used. This is a large saddle capable of taking a considerable weight of equipment, with a hole just below the pommel. The lunge rope is passed through this hole and attached to the right side of the bit. The bit used varies according to the individual trainer's preference. Most are agreed that a fairly severe bit is necessary, though the degree of severity varies. The Military bit is often used, sometimes in conjunction with a curb chain under the jaw. Occasionally the severe spoon-bit has been used. When pulled it jabs the roof of the horse's mouth. One of the present writers prefers a Fulmar Improved bit with two 'T'-pieces on the cheeks of the horse. The important thing to bear in mind is that the horse ultimately will fall on a signal. It should not have to be brought down by the severity of the bit. If, when the trainer pulls on the lunge rope the horse allows himself to fall easily to the left, then he is likely to make a good 'faller'.

The first falls, of course, are best made indoors with the horse standing still and the floor covered in deep sawdust so that there is no danger of the horse hurting itself. Even minor injury to the horse at this stage is likely to make him refuse to fall for a considerable period of time. When the horse falls readily on the lunge rope, the rope is replaced by a rein. The trainer mounts and pulls the horse down with the rein. The 'bringing down on the bit' process has started. The rope is removed from the leg and the horse again brought down with the rein signal. When this has been established, the horse is brought down from a walk, then from a trot and finally from a canter.

Pulling down a falling horse

Training has made new demands on the stuntman. In the case of the 'Running W' and the pit, he has to consider only himself. The exact position of the fall was arranged by the special effects man in consultation with the director and cameraman. Now the stuntman is responsible for the fall being made in exactly the right place, he is responsible for giving the correct signal to the horse at the right time, he is responsible to some extent for the horse's safety and entirely responsible for his own.

Pulling down a horse 'on the bit' is also extremely hard work. The ground is ploughed or broken with a pick or with a special compressed air 'gun', and covered with broken peat or some other shock-absorbent material. The area which needs to be treated in this way, is not only that on which the horse is to fall but also that on which the rider himself will fall. The rider will take the horse over the course he is to run, checking on the general nature of the ground, the area on which he is to fall and the best approach run to it. He will do this not only for the benefit of the director and cameraman but also to rehearse the run for himself and the horse. The actual fall will not be rehearsed, although he may in fact have to do it several times with the camera turning until director and cameraman are satisfied with the result.

His equipment for the stunt consists of 'falling stirrups' and personal padding. The stirrups—he may have a pair or only one on the left side—are leather pouches. They are made so that the rider's feet can be removed without any risk of being caught up in them. The padding he wears will be a matter of personal choice. He may wear an American footballer's hip-pad to protect kidneys and pelvic girdle, or he may simply push pads down his pants over the vital places. His elbows and knees will also be well-padded. Collarbones are usually protected by folding the arms across them. At times a close-fitting jockey crash helmet can be worn on the head, if it does not affect the general appearance of the character being played. But most stuntmen rely on their general agility to keep the head out of danger.

Finally, the stuntman makes his run. In the course of it he goes through any moves the director has asked for. As he reaches the point of fall he takes his left foot out of the stirrup, thrusts his right leg straight and pulls hard on the right rein. As the horse begins to fall to the left, the stuntman makes sure that his left leg is clear of its body and begins his own fall towards the ground that he has prepared for himself. If the stunt has satisfied the director and the camerman, then the rider's work is finished. If not, he makes the run again.

The modern saddle fall

The 'saddle fall', is the stunt in which we see the rider fall from his horse whilst the animal itself remains on its feet. The key to the successful performance of the stunt are the stirrups. The 'step stirrups' which are used are of metal. They are 'L'-shaped so that when the rider begins his fall his feet will come clear of them without any effort on his part. The stirrups are worn quite high and when the rider reaches the point at which he must fall— perhaps in conjunction with being struck by an arrow or shot by a law-officer—he can use the stirrups as fixed points from which to push upwards with his legs and so drive himself out of the saddle and high enough to avoid the horse's rump.

The actual technique of the fall depends on the preference of the individual stuntman, but also the temperament of the horse. Some horses, for example, will automatically buck if their loins are touched so that it is essential for the stuntman to gain enough height on his push-off to clear the rear end of the horse at all costs. If he fails to do so he could, as one stuntman puts it, 'be flicked in all directions.'

The usual aim of the stuntman is to fall backwards and sideways. A fall to the left seems to be particularly favoured, though there are top stuntmen who favour falling to their right. As the stuntman leaves the saddle, clearing the rump of the horse, he turns. In the case of a fall to the right, he will turn in the air from his initial backward position to one in which he is on his right side, so that his first impact with the ground—carefully prepared beforehand— is with his right forearm and right heel. What he does from that position will be determined by two things: the need to bring the fall to a safe conclusion and the need to do so in conformity with the director's wishes. If, for example, the director wants him to finish in a face-downwards position so that the audience cannot tell that a double and not the star himself has taken the fall, then that is the position in which he must finally finish.

Falling, we must not forget, is hard work. The idea that a successful fall is handled simply by complete muscular relaxation is quite wrong. During every stage the stuntman is working to absorb shock safely, to protect the more vulnerable parts of his body, to avoid contact with the falling horse, and to place himself in that final position required by the director. The comment by Hal Needham, that the secret of a safe fall is to be 'looser than warm spaghetti',[58] can best be taken as a statement by a top stuntman anxious to preserve rather than reveal a professional secret.

Jerk harness falls

The 'jerk harness' is another piece of equipment that has appeared since the introduction of horse training. In a sense it is the stuntman's equivalent of the 'Running W'. Its purpose is to snatch the stuntman out of the saddle as if he has been struck by some irresistible force which has knocked him clear of the horse's back. In essence the equipment consists of a leather jacket, worn under the outer garments, to the back of which is attached a wire. The free end of the wire is secured to an anchor point, and when the rider has galloped to the extremity of the wire he is yanked out of his saddle.

The jacket is made to a particular stuntman's requirements since the snatch is so vicious that an ill-fitting jacket could cause body ruptures. The length of the wire is measured with great accuracy, so that the exact ground position over which the snatch will take place is known. In this way the sudden removal of the rider from the saddle can be made to coincide with a butt stroke from a rifle, a severe cut with a sword or the thrust of a lance. In the cinema, since the wire itself is invisible, the blow from the weapon appears to strike the rider out of the saddle.

The somersault fall

The Canutt brothers—sons of Yakima—are credited with the development of the 'somersault harness' which produces a particularly spectacular fall from a horse. The device was used with startling effectiveness in *The Alamo* (1960), when a cavalry officer, apparently shot, is seen to perform a complete back-somersault out of the saddle and hit the ground clear of the horse. The device consists of a jacket to which a half-hook is fitted in the middle of the back. The jacket is worn under the clothing, with the half-hook appearing through a hole in the back of the tunic. A short line is attached to the back of the saddle. On the free end of the line is a metal eye which drops over the half-hook. The rider sits sufficiently upright to stretch the line tight and throughout the somersault his bodily position is such that the line remains in tension. If the rider fails to keep this tension the eye can become detached from the half-hook and this could well lead to an unassisted back somersault from which he might land on the rump of the running horse and be severely kicked.

The rider wears 'step stirrups' taken up high so that his feet will come clear as he leaves the saddle, and at the moment of launch he thrusts himself upwards as high as the line allows him by pushing downwards on the stirrups. The line controls the rider through an arc upwards and backwards, as a piece of string will control a weight spun on the end of it. As the rider reaches a fully inverted position, almost doing a headstand on the rear of the horse, the eye on the line disengages itself from the half-hook and the rider lands on the ground behind the horse. The device must, of course, be very carefully prepared since if half-hook and eye fail to disengage the rider will be left hanging down the rear of the horse.

The drag

Perhaps the most dangerous and certainly one of the most spectacular types of horse fall is the 'drag'. On the screen we see a rider fall from his horse with one foot still caught in the stirrup and be dragged over the ground on his back. The horse, of course, must be trained not to kick out at an object being dragged behind it otherwise no stuntman would live through more than one performance. The stirrups are worn low so that the trapped foot does not have to be carried too high and so bring the back of his head into contact with the uneven ground.

The stuntman is wired from a close-fitting jacket, down a trouser leg and on to the horse by way of the stirrup. In the case of a real drag, caused by some unfortunate accident, the whole strain is taken on ankle and hip joints. But with the stunt drag the strain is carried by the wire to the jacket. The stuntman carries a disconnecting device which he can operate at any moment to separate himself from the horse. At times, he has an additional device which allows him to release the cinch band securing the saddle to the horse. With the operation of this safety device, the weight of the stuntman pulls the whole saddle from the horse's back. As with most of these dangerous horse falls, a rescue rider follows the stunt rider out of camera shot. If the stuntman is too injured by the initial fall, or too dazed to operate the release mechanism, then the rescue rider will intervene.

The horse-stuntman does not operate in isolation. He is part of a team of moviemakers. The mass horse falls in *The Alamo*, for example, are not haphazard. They are the result of meticulous planning involving not only the stuntmen but also the second-unit director, the cameraman, and the special effects and properties teams. The relationships between these various specialists are important in the planning and execution of stunts and we shall look at them in detail later.

Bears, kangaroos and other animals

The horse, although by far the most important animal in stunting, is certainly not the only one. Rome, of course, introduced a wide range of animals into its spectacles, and such creatures as the monkey and the bear have roamed Europe with their human partners for centuries. McKechnie[59] mentions twelfth-century performers who 'appeared with dogs, cocks, hares, horses, bears, camels and even lions'. Some of these creatures performed tricks, others were simply on display. But of particular interest from our point of view is his statement that 'occasionally a special thrill would be added to the entertainment by a fight between a minstrel and a bear or a lion'. Such an entertainment clearly involves that element of personal risk that we associate with stunting.

The bear seems to have been a particularly dangerous animal for this kind of activity because of its unpredictability. Manning-Sanders[60] in fact regards the bear as 'the most dangerous animal in the circus' and considers it to have been 'responsible for more accidents and fatalities among trainers than all the lions and tigers put together. For one thing, the bear has a "poker face", which reveals nothing of its mood. . . .' In support of her opinion, she records the death of William Dellah—who appeared in Bostock's circus under the name of Sargano—who was unfortunate enough to slip in a cage containing two Russian bears and two hyenas; and the death in August 1930 of Adolph Cossmy at the age of twenty-five. Cossmy was killed by a polar bear: 'Of all the species,' says Manning-Sanders, 'the polar is the most ferocious and untrustworthy.'

Bostock[61] mentions a range of animals with whom he worked in various types of entertainment. In 1891 he trained a young lion 'to leave its cage, mount the back of a skewbald pony, and ride around the menagerie', and a year later his brother, F. C. Bostock, trained a full-grown tiger so that it 'left its cage, mounted the back of an elephant, and rode round the menagerie amongst the audience'. This act was, in the opinion of the elder Bostock, 'a very risky one'.

A more successful act appears to have been the one he introduced at the Trocadero, London, in 1892, involving a boxing kangaroo. The principle behind the act was that the kangaroo should never be struck. It then considered that it was winning and put on an impressive performance. It proved a good deal more difficult than Bostock had expected, however, to find human partners for the creature who were sufficiently sober to stick to this principle.

The success with the kangaroo gave Bostock the idea of trying to promote a wrestling act between a man and a lion. For this he got hold of a 'very small, but adult, lion with a very presentable mane. A more important qualification of his for the purpose I had in view was his tameness. Sargano [the William Dellah mentioned by Manning-Sanders] used to get him to stand on his hind legs and put his forepaws on his shoulders, and in this position the lion would remain as long as Sargano chose or was able to support him. . . . In regard to the wrestling match, Sargano was simply to get the lion on his hind legs, when he [Sargano] would put his arms round the animal, make a bluff of a wrestle, and after a little, throw the lion. After a short pause the process was to be repeated.'

Sargano, in his wrestling work with the lion, clearly followed the principle established by men like Van Amburgh and Carl Hagenbeck in the nineteenth century, the principle of training through kindness. No amount of beating or cruelty would ever have produced a lion that would cooperate in the way described by Bostock, yet the training through kindness approach is comparatively recent. The position of animals in spectacular entertainment was for centuries a miserable one. During the seventeenth century lion fights took place in public in the Tower of London and as recently as July 26th, 1825, as Bostock recalls, a public fight was arranged in Warwick between a lion and dogs.

Manning-Sanders gives details of 'those brutal and humiliating exhibitions that passed for "lion acts" in the nineteenth century', in which the beasts were terrorised by the firing of guns and the beating of gongs. They were poked with red-hot irons and torches of burning pitch. When the 'tamer' left the cage of demented animals, an assistant was at hand to throw a cup of bullock's blood over him to give the illusion of severe injury. The attitude to animals that lay behind such spectacles did not entirely disappear until the intervention of the societies for the prevention of cruelty to animals. Indeed, such devices as the 'Running W', which show a disregard for the well-being of the horse, are still in use.

Cruelty and kindness were not the only approaches to animals. There was—and indeed still is—the approach based on what can only be called 'magic'. In this connection we are grateful to John Burns of the British Broadcasting Corporation for the following information:

My grandfather whose surname was Helme (christian name, I believe, Tom) was a barber in the town of Darwin in Lancashire. He died about 40 years ago (early 1930s). One day when the circus was in town he apparently said in barber's shop banter that there was nothing brave about being in a cage of lions. He boasted that any man could do this as long as he had on him something that glittered and shone to frighten off the animals. He was so sure of this that he said that with the sparkling light reflected from his cut-throat razor he'd be happy to shave a man in a den (really a cage in the event) of lions. A bet was made, the circus people co-operated, and during a performance my grandfather shaved a circus worker in that den of lions. The event was covered by the local paper and, I promise, is truly authentic.

The new approach to animal training that developed through the nineteenth century amongst the more enlightened trainers, did not, of course, remove all dangers. Bostock refers to the way in which his brother Frank was savaged at the Hippodrome in Paris by 'Wild Wallace', a particularly ferocious lion. He himself had a number of memorable encounters with animals. He was bitten by a Harlequin boa which left all its teeth in his hand. He talks of 'the stupendous crushing power of a snake' after a constrictor had nearly crushed his leg. A black bear bit off half a thumb and he was attacked and badly bitten by monkeys when he went into their cage to stop a fight. His particular dislike is for 'a wicked camel or dromedary' which he regards as 'a very dangerous creature'. 'His mode of attack,' says Bostock, 'is to seize the victim in his very powerful jaws, and, still retaining his grip, throw him up in the air; then, as he whirls the man to the ground, he brings his whole body forward and either kneels or gets the fore part of his chest on him; and he will crush the unfortunate fellow to death unless assistance is quickly afforded him. I have seen several instances of this.'

As the horse became established as an essential part of cinema spectacle through the Western, so the jungle film brought other animals into the cinema. Of course we can find examples of the introduction of animals in the very early days of the cinema. Julia Swayne Gordon, for example, played a scene with a tiger which for one terrifying moment looked as if it might make a meal of her arm, many years before the jungle vogue became established. Pearl White too, working on *The Perils of Pauline*, found herself trapped inside a mill with rising water swirling round her into which the director had put live but toothless rats.[62]

But these are isolated examples, and the use of animals in large numbers and in variety can really be said to have begun with the introduction of the 'Tarzan' theme in 1918, when Elmo Lincoln played the title part in *Tarzan of the Apes* and established a film tradition that is still with us. In an interview with Goodman[63] he gives a very modest account of what was expected of him in the Tarzan films. Most of his time, he says, was spent in the tree tops, and when he fought a lion it was an ailing specimen that had been drugged.

De Mille, directing *Male and Female* in 1919, introduced a more alarming scene in which Gloria Swanson was seen apparently being savaged by a lion. Canvas was laid on her bare back and the front paws of the lion placed on top. The canvas was gradually eased out from under the animal's paws until they were directly in contact with her flesh. Finally the lion was induced to roar by having whips cracked in its presence.[64]

The first Tarzan serial, which ran for fifteen episodes, was the National Film Corporation's *Son of Tarzan* in 1920. One incident during the making of the series is sufficient to remind us of the ultimate unpredictability of animal behaviour and the consequent dangers involved to stunt actors. Kamuela C. Searle, playing the part of a young man, was tied to a stake. An elephant was supposed to rescue him. It lifted him, carried him away, and dashed him to death. Similar behaviour by an elephant in *The Jungle Goddess*, the fifteen-episode serial that the Selig studio released in 1922, resulted in the death of a lion.

Selig is reputed to have used 470 wild animals on the series and in fact the Selig company established and maintained its own zoo. Universal, under Carl Laemmle, also established a zoo. 'Curly' Stecker was responsible for its running and for training the animals there for use in films. The need for such establishments is an indication of the popularity of animal films during the early twenties. Yet although we can presume that such films were profitable to make, they were not always easy. Work with animals posed special problems. In the 1922 serial, *A Dangerous Adventure*, for example, Grace Darmond fell off the back of an elephant and spent a week in hospital. Sam Goldwyn, writing to his brother Harry about some of the misfortunes that had been encountered during the making of the series, said that Mrs Josephine Hill, who was in charge of the animals, had been savaged by one of her own leopards. An artist on the series had almost had his hand bitten off by a lion when he had tried to shake hands with it, and a trainer suffered twenty-two wounds after being attacked by a tiger.[65]

Few of the better-known land animals have avoided at least one spectacular appearance on the screen. De Mille let a couple of Bengal tigers roam round the set of *Manslaughter*, though he took the somewhat ostentatious precaution of arming himself with a pair of pearl-handled revolvers, and when the English company, Homeland Films, made *A Spanish Love Spasm* in 1915, they used a pedigree bull for certain action scenes.

Nor has the cinema restricted itself to the use of warm-blooded creatures. In *Sparrows* (1926), Mary Pickford made three trips along a plank, carrying children over a pool full of alligators. Fairbanks, Miss Pickford's husband, was understandably furious with the director (William Beaudine) when he heard what had

happened. His remark to Beaudine, who insisted that the performance was necessary, is interesting since it refers to a technique by
which an apparently dangerous stunt can be faked: 'It's nothing
of the kind,' said Fairbanks. 'You can make a double exposure.'[66]
He was referring to the process by which two elements of a scene
can be shot separately, yet when the film is projected they appear
together. Using such a process, Miss Pickford and the alligators
would never actually have met.

No double exposure was considered necessary for Dick Grace,
of course, since he was a professional stuntman, and indeed his
contact with alligators is a good deal more hair-raising than Miss
Pickford's. In general he did not like animal stunt work, but his
approach to the alligator is characteristically professional. It should
be tackled slowly and from behind. As soon as it has been seized
by the hands, one's legs should be wrapped round its belly. From
this position it is not too difficult, in Grace's view, to push the
hands along the creature's head and hold its jaws shut.

Flynn worked with crocodiles during the shooting of *The
Cruise of the Zaca* (1954) off the Jamaican coast, but he took more
precautions than Grace. 'The reptiles' jaws were sewn up with
wire,' he says. 'We undid the wire when they ate, but then quickly
re-shut their snouts: and so I was able to work with them.'

Considering Flynn's concern for the treatment of animals on
The Charge of the Light Brigade, his technique for trying to get the
crocodiles to behave as he wished them to in front of the camera
is perhaps surprising. They became in time too tired and sluggish
to film. He tried pulling them on wires in front of the camera,
and giving them injections of adrenalin and digitalis. Finally,
remembering an earlier film in which he had seen a props man
inject ammonia into the rectum of a frog, he used the same
technique to produce movement in one of the crocodiles for an
action sequence.

Animals of every kind have made a substantial contribution to
spectacular entertainment, and particularly to such entertainment
in the cinema. On the whole, our treatment of them in order to
achieve the results we wanted has been no better and no worse

than might have been expected. The invention of such devices as the 'Running W' do not seem in retrospect particularly praiseworthy. On the other hand, it was as much as anything pressure from within the industry itself that gave the animal protection societies the necessary ammunition to restrict their use.

4 Stunts with vehicles

The train

The horse, as we have seen, has for centuries provided a means by which human stunts could be made more spectacular. Indeed, it does seem that at one time or another every conceivable means of adding to the impact of visual spectacle has been examined for its possibilities. Certainly the possibilities of vehicular traffic have not been ignored. Chariot racing is almost as old as the wheel and the Wild West shows of the nineteenth century saw the stage coach as a central piece of the dramatic spectacle. Trick cycling, either with a conventional machine or with the single-wheeled unicycle has

Illustration: Rififi in the East (1965). Patrick Bernard rides off a 78 foot cliff.

existed for many years in the circus and in vaudeville, and the eccentric cycle with collapsible frame or out-of-centre wheel hubs still forms the basis for many comedy acts.

But only with the coming of the cinema were the spectacular possibilities of vehicles fully exploited. The reason is not hard to find. The real development of vehicles which are self-propelled is quite modern. It coincides with the birth of the cinema. The modern vehicle and the cinema have, as it were, grown up together. Even the railway engine, used by George Stephenson to draw the first public passenger carrying train from Darlington to Stockton in 1825 and first seen in America on the Carbondale and Honesdale line in Pennsylvania in 1829, only precedes that very early comedy film, Fred Ott's *Sneeze* (1894), by some sixty years—a short enough time in the long history of human entertainment.

The train and the cinema seem inextricably bound up in our memories. They still are. 'Ever since those far-off days in 1905 when a wondering public in a 5-cents Pittsburgh theatre saw *The Great Train Robbery* (1903), the first film with a story, trains have been the cinema's most constantly popular actors,' says Felix Barker reviewing *Train of Events* (1949).[67] 'Quite rightly because they are big and handsome and fulfil a basic screen requirement. They move.' Keaton regarded trains and railways as 'a great prop'. 'You can do some awful wild things with railroads.' Keaton was by no means the only film man to hold this view. John Frankenheimer carried it to lengths undreamed of by Keaton in *The Train* (1964).

The first appearance of the train on film was not as part of dramatic action. It was shot for its own sake, because it seemed to contain for the very early film-makers a cinematic quality in its own right. 'The earliest experimenters were fascinated by the steam locomotive,' says Huntley.[68] In 1896, 'Thomas Edison, using a pre-cinema device known as the Kinetescope, recorded perhaps the first railway film ever, which consisted of a single scene of the *Black Diamond Express* (43ft). Later, his company was to record literally hundreds of similar railway scenes.' In July of 1895 the Lumière brothers, on holiday with their families, filmed *Arrival of a Train at La Ciotat Station*. It ran to forty-nine feet and showed no more than a puffing 2-4-2 locomotive arriving at a station. But it did show the cinematic possibilities of trains.

The Great Train Robbery saw the dramatic possibilities of the train first exploited. The year was 1903. Gun-fights take place on the train and a safe is blown open by the robbers, but the most significant scene from the point of view of cinema stunting is the fight on the tender. Two of the robbers, having climbed over the tender, hold up the fireman and the driver. The fireman seizes his shovel and makes for one of the robbers. A spectacular fist fight takes place in which the fireman is finally subdued by being struck on the head with a piece of coal used by the robber as a club. The last we see of the fireman is his body being dumped from the fast-moving train on to the track. The film established a vogue. 'Literally hundreds of one-reel railroad melodramas were made in America between 1907 and 1914,' says Huntley.[69] Many of them involved highly dangerous action scenes.

The Hazards of Helen

But it is with the serials, and in particular J. P. McGowan's *The Hazards of Helen*, that we see the firm establishment of the train stunt. As early as the first episode (1914) we see the heroine doing a dangerous transfer from a horse to a moving train, a stunt which was to be repeated in almost all Westerns involving trains during the next fifty years. Indeed, during the course of this serial, almost every train stunt that we have since seen was established at least in principle by either Helen Holmes or Helen Gibson.

Helen Gibson, for example, was at one time strapped to the piston-rod of a locomotive and travelled before the camera in that incredibly dangerous and uncomfortable position for some considerable distance. She did many drops and transfers on to trains in motion, at one time dropping from the feed arm of a water tower on to a moving train, at another leaping from one train to another. There were no devices, of course, by which she could minimise the danger of such stunts. What one sees her doing on the screen

D

she did in reality. Success was entirely dependent on her physical agility, her highly-developed sense of timing and her absolute conviction that the stunt, for her at least, was possible.

A stunt from one of her *Hazards* episodes involved driving a team of horses, standing upright on the backs of the rear two, in order to overtake a runaway train. The final transfer to the train was done by swinging from a rope that hung from a bridge. She considered her most dangerous stunt to have been a leap from a station roof on to the roof of a moving train, which she did in *A Girl's Grit* (1914), an episode in *The Hazards*, doubling for Helen Holmes. 'I landed right, but the train's motion made me roll towards the end of the car. I caught hold of an air vent and hung on, allowing my body to dangle over the edge to increase the effect on the screen. I suffered only a few bruises.'[70] Since the train was 'moving on camera for about a quarter of a mile' at an 'accelerating velocity', it would not be unreasonable to suppose that its speed by the time it reached her was approaching forty miles an hour.

The real difficulty of the stunt lay not in the leap itself, since she had practised this with the train stationary and it clearly presented no difficulties, but in the timing. What such stunts require is an inbuilt awareness of the speed of the moving object. During the course of a leap where a moving object is concerned, the spatial relationship between take-off point and landing point changes. It is quite possible to imagine a leap from a static take-off point on to the roof of a moving train in which the stuntman aims to land half-way along a carriage roof yet in fact—because of the speed of the train—lands in the gap between two carriages. It seems that in such a leap the safest place to aim at is the gap itself. At least in that way one can guarantee to miss it. Helen Gibson had this sensitivity to spatial relationships between objects in motion, but it is certainly not a gift shared by all stuntmen.

The transfer to a train from another moving object does not require this kind of judgement, since take-off and landing points are static in relation to one another, but the incredible stunt performed in *When The Daltons Rode* (1940) certainly does. In the train robbery sequence in that film, the robbers escape by leaping on horseback from a moving train on to steeply-sloping ground. The stunt, according to Everson,[71] has never been repeated. One can well understand why!

Roof running

The run along the top of a moving train, leaping the gaps between the carriages, has been a common enough stunt in the cinema's history. We saw it in *Jesse James*. Keaton performed it in *Sherlock Jr*, just before he leapt from the train roof to the rope dangling from the water tower and released such a weight of water on his head that he fell to the track and broke his neck. In the early days of the cinema, when the roof-running stunt still held its ability to thrill and amaze, it was frequently dragged in on the most unlikely of pretexts. In *The Lost Express* (1917), for example, Harelip is a villain in possession of a secret formula. To reach the compartment of the train in which he is travelling, the heroine (Helen Holmes) performs the roof-running stunt until she is immediately over Harelip's compartment. Lying on the roof she can peer through the compartment window at Harelip and the secret formula. Using a magnifying glass she focuses the sun's rays on the formula which goes up in flames before Harelip can read it. The wild plot, one feels, is simply an excuse to justify the performance of another dangerous stunt by the energetic Miss Holmes.

Harold Lloyd, the comedian, performed the roof-running stunt with a good deal more ingenuity than most. In *Professor Beware* (1938) he rode on top of a freight train on its way to New York. As the train approached a tunnel it became obvious that Lloyd must leave the train roof. We see him racing along the roof of the train, leaping the gaps between carriages, and finally escaping what seems an inevitable and very sticky end by clinging to an overhead beam. Lloyd was perfectly capable of performing such a stunt. He was at that time one of the most brilliant and courageous stunt-actors in Hollywood. Yet for some reason the effect on film did not please him. He decided instead to construct a treadmill on the side of the train opposite the camera. As the train passed between treadmill and camera, its top just masking the treadmill, Lloyd gave the impression of running along the top of the train itself, leaping in the air as his position came in line with the gaps between the carriages.

The device was not without its own risks, as he himself says: 'It really was very difficult, almost harder than running on the real train, to run on this treadmill. We had lines marked on it because I had to jump on the treadmill practically full speed. And, if I fell, there was a risk of serious injury, because the treadmill was going very fast.'[72]

Trick photography

We must certainly regard Lloyd's treadmill run as a stunt in the classic sense, since it involved considerable physical risk, although what Lloyd appears to be doing on the screen is not what in fact he was doing. But when news of such devices reached the public through the publicity media of the time and the columns of the film magazines, it added to the widely held belief that all cinema stunts were the result of trick photography.

One film which seemed to lend support to such a belief by using trick photography to mock the genuine stunt film was *He Would Act* (1915), produced by the I. B. Davidson studio in London. When the star of a film sprains his ankle while jumping off St Paul's Cathedral, a young man called Percy is given his part. 'In his first scene for the camera Percy had to be killed in a duel, in which he was run through with a sword several times, entirely without injury. "The next scene is simple," said the producer. "You have to be run over by a steamroller." Percy was then seen being flattened out by the steamroller, picked up, and pumped back to life with a bicycle pump. Finally, Percy was blown sky high by an explosion which carried him and the leading lady far into the air, blowing them both to small pieces. Unfortunately, when they picked themselves up they discovered that their limbs had got rather mixed. Arms, legs, heads, and clothes were all fixed to the wrong bodies.'[73] Yet despite popular belief the fact remains that even the most straightforward of vehicle stunts *can* be dangerous. When she was climbing on to the roof of a train in *The Wrecking Crew* (1969), for example, Gillian Aldam was caught in overhead telephone wires and broke her collarbone, shoulderblade and half a dozen ribs.[74]

Roof-top fights

Roof running naturally suggested to some enterprising director the possibility of roof-top fights. A fight on the steeply cambered roof of a train travelling at perhaps forty miles an hour is particularly dangerous. In that position the movement of the train is a good deal less steady than it appears to those riding inside it. A wind force equal at least to that of the forward movement of the train has to be contended with, and the stuntmen are subject to any sidewinds that exist.

Fortunately, close-ups of such fights—and particularly those involving stars rather than doubles—can be shot in the studio on a train-roof mock-up, so that the fight on the real train need only be shot in medium or long-shot. This means that details of the fight are not seen except in close-up and in consequence some of the dangers of the real-train fight can be minimised. Grappling can, to some extent, replace the sharp and accurate punching that close-ups require. Indeed, according to Grace, one of the prime functions of fighters on the roof of a moving train is to hold one another on rather than knock one another off. In the stunt that killed Gene Perkins, Pauly Malvern was on top of the train and Perkins had to drop from his airborne rope-ladder on to Malvern and fight him. 'Of course,' says Grace, 'Pauly was really there to help Gene land safely.'[75]

Another problem that makes the filming of a train-top fight more complex than it perhaps appears to an audience is the positioning of the camera. Cameras have, of course, been roped to the tops of moving trains so as to shoot a fight in close-up, but the result is rarely satisfactory. Movements of the train produce camera movements that do not add to the effectiveness of the scene. When Keaton was making the railway chase sequence in *The General* (1926), he shot most of it not from the engine itself but from a specially prepared road vehicle running alongside it.[76]

Economics and the 'near-miss'

The 'near-miss' between train and car, which took the breath away from the first audiences that saw it, is of course Mack Sennett's. Indeed, he must be given the credit for inventing a good deal of the stunting with vehicles that we still see in films—the wild car driving, the falling out of moving vehicles and the vehicle crash accompanied by clouds of steam and smoke. Secretly one never for a minute expects the charging locomotive to hit that Keystone Cop-loaded car. Sennett and his team seem to exercise a magical control which allows them to bring two roaring vehicles across one another's path and miss by the merest inch, yet never even touch. It looks meticulously planned and therefore entirely safe.

In fact it was, according to Goodman, entirely unplanned and entirely dangerous: 'For the train-vs-automobile encounters, Sennett would sit around with a car full of cops waiting for a real train to come along and then run the flivver right under its nose, perceptibly ageing the engineer.' At times he did make some rudimentary preparations: 'Occasionally he would make arrangements with an engineer for the train to go through Pasadena at ten miles per hour and scoot the car past the locomotive while the low-speed camera pepped up the result.'[77]

The reason of course was economic. To set up such a stunt as it would be set up today is expensive. When on another occasion he heard that a tall chimney was to be demolished he incorporated the demolition in a film. 'We couldn't have afforded to blow up a 125-foot chimney,' he said. Keaton was equally conscious of the economics of the stunt. 'None of our railroad things ever cost us anything,' he said. 'The Santa Fe people were tickled to death to see SANTA FE on the screen.'

Stunts with vehicles

The financial side of film-making is, of course, of crucial importance and stunts can certainly be expensive. When George Roy Hill, directing *Butch Cassidy and the Sundance Kid* (1970), employed horses to jump out of a railway boxcar, each jump cost him $1,000 for the horses and their stunt riders. And of the need for a detailed plan of action to be prepared by the director in advance he says, 'having a whole crew standing around at the rate of close to $5,000 an hour while you're doing your homework on the set is a kind of a luxury which pictures just can't afford any more.'[78] Nevertheless one cannot help feeling that even if Sennett had not felt the economic squeeze quite so severely as his comments suggest, he and his team would still have elected to do their stunts in the way they did. Always with Sennett and the Keystone Cops one feels that there was a certain revelling in real danger that they would not have forgone however economically unnecessary it might have been.

Since the world of film-makers is no longer full of Mack Sennetts and Keystone Cops it is perhaps fortunate that the train-car near-miss can be staged with a good deal less danger than accompanied their efforts. The rear of the car can be attached to the front of the train by wire. The wire is taken round a series of pulleys and finally across the track of the train. As the train is put into reverse it pulls the car backwards across the track. If the wire length has been adjusted correctly, the car will pass in front of the train with only inches to spare. If the scene is shot with the camera 'undercranking', the speed of the action will appear to be increased when the film is projected at the usual speed of twenty-four frames a second. If the direction of movement is also reversed, then the car and train will appear to be moving forwards instead of in reverse and the effect will be of a hair-raising near-miss.

The train crash

The idea of crashing a train in front of a camera seems to have occurred very early in the cinema's history. In 1897 R. W. Paul had filmed a crash which was set up with model trains. Between

1898 and 1906 Georges Méliès produced a number of films in his Montreeil-sous-Bois studio with spectacular train crashes in them. Perhaps the best known of these is *An Impossible Voyage* (1904). The crashes were staged with models and given credibility by the use of 'trick' photography.

The first staged crash of real trains appears to have been mounted for the Vitagraph Company's *The Wreck* (1914). An advertisement placed by the Company in *The Kinematograph and Lantern Weekly*[79] and addressed to film exhibitors, talked of the 'unparalleled degree of interest' aroused by the filming of an actual train wreck and put the cost of staging it at £10,000. The scene did in fact cause a sensation and established the train crash, complete with its complement of stuntmen, as a feature that was to be employed on many future occasions. A write-up in *The Kinematograph*[80] said, 'there will be few, in our opinion, among those who see the subject in the theatres who will not confess to having been affected in a quite unusual degree.' The writer describes the build-up to the crash and the crash itself, in great detail. He does more than describe a spectacular scene in a particular film; he reflects that special kind of involvement that all audiences feel when witnessing really effective action sequences, the kind of exhilarating awe that action directors and their team of stuntmen, cameramen and special effects men are striving to produce: a kind of inner gasp.

Keaton staged a spectacular locomotive crash through a burning bridge in *The General* but perhaps the most memorable of staged railway crashes were those in John Frankenheimer's *The Train*. When a runaway engine was taken at some sixty miles an hour into a second engine that had already been derailed, families in the area were evacuated and Lloyds, the London insurers, had already agreed a price with the owner of a café which it was thought might be damaged in the crash. Gas and electric supplies were turned off and pits dug to arrest the movement of the runaway engine once it had left the track. A reviewer of the film talked of Frankenheimer's 'obvious delight in the mechanical devices at his disposal'.[81]

The motorcar

The locomotive is a cinema character in itself, almost a star-stuntman in the old tradition. It is even given a name—*The General* or *The Texas* or *The Titfield Thunderbolt*. At times we become attached to it as we might to a human hero. We fear for its safety and marvel at its power. The motorcar, by contrast, rarely excites this involvement. We are concerned more with its occupants than with the vehicle itself. It is rarely concerned with anything more than getting people from one place to another. It provides a confined space in which gangsters can be gunned down by a well-placed burst of Thompson submachine-gun fire. It forms the inanimate neutral background against which Bonnie and Clyde are shot to death.

Yet some very spectacular things have been done with the car in the cinema. Snub Pollard, one of Hal Roach's comedians, once claimed that during his career he had 'been hit by over six hundred automobiles'. Monty Banks, during the making of one of his comedies, finished up in hospital after being roped to the back of a car and dragged down the face of a cliff. During the making of *The Submarine Pirate* (1916), Syd Chaplin slid down a rope on to a passing car from an iron girder suspended between two twelve-storey buildings, a stunt which took only two minutes to shoot and for which Sennett insured Chaplin and the Keystone Cops involved with him at a premium of $90.

The car chase

The chase is perhaps the earliest recurrent car theme, and we associate it most closely with Sennett and the Keystone Cops. Since those early silent days it is a theme that has reappeared in film after film, culminating perhaps in the spectacular car chase in *Bullitt* (1968) in which cars and drivers are pitted not only against one another but against the terrifyingly steep streets of San Francisco. Sennett, where possible, shot on location in what we

D*

should regard today as a most haphazard and unplanned way, incorporating into his film real life incidents which just happened to coincide with his filming. But he did invent a remarkable device for shooting the chase in a studio, a device to which he gave the name 'Cyclopanorama'. The device was 'a giant merry-go-round contraption with a treadmill effect on which two automobiles or a dozen cops could proceed abreast. The Cyclopanorama could be speeded up to twenty-five or thirty miles per hour, could rotate clockwise or counter-clockwise, and the scenery behind it could be altered at the drop of a scenario.'[82]

Grace[83] classifies stunts as 'major' and 'minor'. Stunts with cars fall into both categories. Grace regards the car chase as 'minor'. Also classified by Grace as minor are spectacular car skids, minor crashes and some car 'transfers'. The transfer from one car to another at less than twenty-five miles an hour, for example, he regards as a minor stunt.

The car crash

Grace does, however, regard the staged car crash at speed as a major stunt, and he mentions Leo Noomis as being one of the greatest car wrecking stuntmen of his time. Grace's comments on what he himself did when a car he was wrecking accidentally went over a cliff throw light on the lack of preparatory work on a stunt car in the early days of the cinema vehicle stunt. He did, he says, 'have sense enough to get down on the floorboards and hold on to the steering post.'

Reg Kavanagh,[84] who operated under the well-deserved nickname of 'Crash' Kavanagh, corroborates this lack of special preparation. The car in which he performed the crash in Walter Ford's *Bulldog Jack* (1935) apparently had no roll-bar to prevent the roof being crushed in on him in the event of the vehicle rolling on to its back. He mentions hitting his head on the roof at the moment of impact, suggesting that the car had no special belt to hold him in the seat, and the 'stench of burnt rubber and petrol' which he could smell after the crash leads one to believe that he used the ordinary production petrol tank instead of a miniature tank holding just sufficient fuel for the stunt.

Certainly for the lorry crash in *Forbidden Territory* (1934) no safety belt was possible. Kavanagh stresses the need to get out of the way of the steering column as it was thrust backwards on impact, and a safety belt would have held him securely in the path of this thrust. The precautions he took seem almost ludicrously minimal. He stuffed the space under the dashboard with cushions and laid cushions on the seat beside him. A second before the moment of impact he threw himself sideways on to the cushioned seat to get clear of the steering column and hoped that the cushions under the dashboard would absorb the shock of his inevitable movement forward.

Even the prepared stunt car that Kavanagh describes, and the technique for using it in a crash, seems still to be a highly dangerous vehicle. All glass was removed from it and the gear and brake handles were cut short. The knobs on the dashboard were removed. The dashboard itself was well padded and cushions were stuffed under it. But there is no suggestion that a helmet was worn and the driver is not strapped in.

Kavanagh mentions two techniques he used on impact, depending on how the car behaved. If the engine stayed in its mountings and didn't come backwards into the driving compartment, he threw himself on to the cushions under the dashboard. If, however, the impact was severe and the engine was forced backwards into the cab, he seized two leather loops fixed to the car's door pillars and lifted his body and legs clear of the engine. It is difficult to understand how he could have decided which of these two quite different courses of action to take in the time available to him.

Experience no doubt taught him the kind of behaviour to expect from a particular car in a given set of circumstances, but there is still an element of unpredictability in any crash and the speed at which he was travelling at the moment of impact must have added to that unpredictability. He talks of one crash into a building at which his speed was between forty and fifty miles per hour, and there is nothing to suggest that this was an unusually high speed.

Stunting in the cinema

The outcome of this particular stunt, in which the car and the building had been prepared so as to burst into flames on impact, stresses the danger of car crashes even when prepared vehicles are used. Kavanagh broke his ribs on this particular stunt, suggesting that he did not get clear of the thrust-back of the steering column in time.

The modern prepared car

Fortunately for the stunt driver, what a film audience is concerned with seeing in a car crash is the vehicle itself. If it goes over a cliff or—as in *The Roaring Twenties* (1939)—smacks straight into a tree with headlights blazing, it is the vehicle that concerns us rather than its occupant. Only after the crash do we ask, 'Has he survived?' Since the focus of attention is on the vehicle rather than the stuntman driving it, the modern stuntman can take precautions that would not be possible if the attention of the audience was primarily on him. He can, for example, wear both safety helmet and safety harness, and he can do preparatory work on the car itself.

In the modern prepared car all sharp objects are removed, objects against which the driver might be thrown in the crash. Where possible the windscreen is removed, though in some shots the filmic effect required makes this impossible. If, for example, the effect is of a car driving through blinding rain and striking a telegraph pole, then the rain must show on the windscreen and the wipers must be seen to be working. Roll-bars are fitted inside the car to stiffen the roof and prevent it buckling and crushing the driver if the car rolls over. In the event of a severe crash it might be thought necessary to construct a reinforced 'cocoon' of metal around the driver so as to isolate him as much as possible from the rest of the vehicle, rather like the frame of metal mesh used in some modern stock car work. The disadvantage of such a 'cocoon' is that in the event of something unforeseen happening in the crash, it is more difficult for the driver to get clear or for him to be freed easily if he is trapped in the cab.

Stunts with vehicles

The inside of the car is padded where necessary, and the driver himself frequently wears padding. The danger of fire, which can be a major hazard in any vehicle stunt, is minimised by reducing the amount of petrol carried to no more than is necessary to perform the stunt. Perhaps the most efficient way to do this is to connect the petrol feed-line to a miniature tank and make sure that the main tanks are completely empty.

All these safety measures, of course, are dependent on the director's requirements. Clearly, for example, if the car has to burst into flames on impact this will affect the kind of safety precautions that the stuntman can take. Of course he must survive the crash itself, but he must also make sure that his safety apparatus does not impede his escape from the blazing car.

The car roll-over

The car roll-over, in which we see a car driven at speed roll over on to its roof, requires the use of a ramp. Some co-operation between stuntman and the property department is necessary here, since the length and height of the ramp will affect the kind of roll-over that is finally seen on the screen. A long ramp rather than a high one usually produces the most effective roll-over. The strength of the ramp is important too, and this will be governed by the weight of the vehicle that is to run up it and the speed at which it is going to travel. A speed of about twenty-five miles an hour is generally regarded as the minimum at which a car can be successfully rolled over with the ramp.

The car is driven so that the wheels on one side only hit the ramp, and as the ramp increases in height it pushes the car over in the opposite direction. What happens to the car after it leaves the ramp depends upon its speed and the disposition of objects in its path. At speeds only a little above the minimum the car might land on the roof and skid forward in that position. At higher speeds it will roll completely over and finish again on its wheels. If a bumper catches a tree in the course of the roll, the car might cartwheel. What we need to remember is that all the precautions stunt and props men might take can only minimise the risk. They cannot remove it altogether. Car stunting remains dangerous and the car crash is justifiably classified by Grace as a 'major' stunt. According to Ken Gooding[85] Bob Simmons regards his car work in *Thunderball* (1965) as 'probably the most dangerous stunt he has performed for a Bond film'.

Car leaps

Gil Delamare, the great French stunt-driver, performed a spectacular leap during the filming in Istanbul of *FX* 18 *Secret Agent* (*c.* 1964). We see him arrive at the docks in his car, just as the boat ferry is pulling out. He turns his car directly at the ferry and leaps some fifty feet from the quayside to the deck of the ferry. To perform the stunt, according to Cabat and Levy,[86] the car had a roll-bar fitted in case it turned on its back, and Delamare took with him a hammer, a bottle of oxygen and a breathing mask in case he landed in the water. Divers were standing by and the ferry itself was attached by cables to the quay so that the gap did not become too wide for Delamare to leap. The take-off, at something approaching fifty miles an hour, was by way of a ramp that gave a rise of nine feet at an angle of about 30 degrees. To counterbalance the weight of the engine when the car was in mid-air some 1,500 lbs of lead was put in the boot, and Delamare himself, moved by some last-minute intuition, added a further 180lbs a few moments before performing the stunt.

Dangers and reality

Car stunting has certainly taken its toll of victims—among them Gil Delamare himself—though not necessarily in connection with film. As recently as 1970 John Bell was killed performing a spectacular car stunt for entertainment purposes.[87] Bell was a member of the 'Destruction Squad',

a group of stuntmen and girls who guarantee to wreck 16 cars, a bus, and a furniture van during a two-hour show. In one race two cars pulled Mr. Bell and a girl behind them on wooden sledges. As part of the act Mr. Bell, who was wearing a protection pad and crash helmet, was meant to fall off and be dragged along the track on his back for half a circuit. To excite the crowd it was prearranged that after the fall an appeal would be put over the public address system for the car towing Mr. Bell to be waved down and stopped. But the stunt miscarried. People in the crowd thought the accident was genuine and ran out to wave down the towing car . . . the driver was forced to swerve to avoid the crowd, sending Mr. Bell into a snaking action which ended with his crashing into a barrier post. He died soon after admission to hospital.

A particularly interesting statement in the report of the coroner's inquest concerns the relationship between danger and reality which has dogged the stuntman over the years. Bell died, says the writer, 'when a crowd intervened in a mock accident that they thought was real'. They would not have intervened, we can presume, if they had been convinced that the accident was 'mock'. A real accident requires human intervention because the danger involved is 'real'. Reciprocally, the danger in a 'mock' accident is also 'mock'. This widely held attitude is not as reprehensible as it may appear to those of us concerned with stunting. Entertainment has always challenged reality by showing us spectacle which we do not believe could be performed 'in real life'.

It is perhaps a very flattering, if quite erroneous, comment on the stuntman's skill that when we see a window-cleaner fall from a fifty-foot ladder we know he is going to be killed, whereas when we see a stuntman do an identical fall in front of a camera or a live audience we are equally convinced that he will survive. He will survive because in some way he is outside natural law. The window-cleaner is falling 'for real', the stuntman only falls 'for fiction'.

The analogy is not entirely accurate, of course, because the window-cleaner falls without any preparation whereas the stuntman falls only after he has calculated the height of the ladder and checked the security of the rig on which he expects to land. The stuntman has done what he can to minimise the danger, but he has not eliminated it. His calculations may be wrong. He may miss his rig altogether or he may land badly and damage himself. Almost certainly he will have to do the fall a number of times before the director is satisfied. The important thing for us to remember, in trying to define the activities of the stuntman, is that whatever the cause of the falls—pure accident in the case of the window-cleaner; to further some dramatic purpose in the stuntman's case—the fall of the stuntman is no less 'real' than that of the window-cleaner. Both falls have an existence within the space-time continuum, both are subject to the same law of gravity and both men land with more or less the same velocity. The falls differ not in themselves, but only in the nature of their cause.

Cycles and motorcycles

The cycle and motorcycle have both been used as stunt vehicles. One of the opening sequences in *The Spy Who Came In From The Cold* (1966) shows a returning spy—played by Terry Yorke—attempting to cross the Berlin East-West frontier at Check-point Charlie on a bicycle. Half-way between Russian and American guards he is caught in a hail of bullets. He is hit in the back. He swerves and finally falls from the cycle on to the wet cobbles.

Because of its comparatively slow speed, the cycle-fall does not present any very great hazards to the stuntman, though it is not without its own peculiar problems. The major problem is the total exposure of the stuntman to the camera. There is nothing about a cycle that allows him to conceal any devices that would help him to fall more safely. The stuntman concealed inside a car can take almost any precautions for his safety that he thinks fit. The cyclist can rely only on his skill and a minimum of body-padding.

A deliberate fall on to wet cobbles requires a good deal more skill than most cinema audiences realise if broken wrists are to be avoided. At speed—a run down a hill into a hedge, for example

—the cycle has a habit of catching the clothing as the stuntman leaves it. Handlebars and brake-levers, bells and pedals all stick out in such a way that clothing can easily be caught on them. The most dangerous effect of this is to interfere with the fall-pattern that the stuntman has planned for himself. Grace gives an alarming example of such interference. Gene Perkins, doubling for William Desmond, had to roll down a roof slope, over the eaves and drop forty feet on to a mattress. As he went over the eaves his coat caught on a projection and checked the momentum of his fall. According to Grace, Perkins missed the mattress and landed on his head.

Roy Scammell has perfected a technique for crashing a cycle into some low obstruction—a hedge, for example, or a low wall or fence, or even the bonnet of a motorcar. As the cycle hits the obstruction Scammell flies over the handlebars with sufficient height to clear the obstruction and lands out of camera view on a prepared rig of boxes.

The motorcycle has a history as a stunting vehicle in the fairground as well as in the cinema. The 'Wall of Death' and the 'Globe of Death' were both fairground spectaculars in the early years of this century. According to Tyrwhitt-Drake[88] the 'Wall of Death' was first brought to Britain from continental Europe in 1928. It consisted of a wooden 'pit' twenty-four feet in diameter and fourteen feet in height. Two or three motorcyclists raced round the internal walls of this structure on machines without silencers, tearing up and down the wooden sides, creating a terrifying noise, their bodies and cycles parallel with the ground. Their speed determined the height that they could climb up the walls, and centrifugal force held them in position.

The audience stood or sat round the top of the structure, staring down into this gigantic 'cock-pit'. A safety wire ran round the top of the structure to prevent any of the performers inside from coming over the top of the wall into the audience. A variation of this stunt was the motorcycle combination in which a doped lion rode in the sidecar and was prodded by the rider from time to time into giving a desultory growl. The 'Globe of Death' was a twelve-foot sphere of steel bands in which two motorcyclists rode round, at times completely inverted, missing one another by a matter of inches.

The motorcycle presents the stuntman with many of the difficulties that we have seen in connection with the bicycle, but all are magnified by the speed of which the vehicle is capable. The motorcyclist is in full view of the cameras and his machine is a mass of 'bits which stick out', adding considerably to his difficulties in getting clear of it in a staged crash. Admittedly more personal protection is possible with the motorcycle than with the bicycle. A crash helmet, for example, is usually an acceptable piece of motorcycle equipment, and more substantial personal padding can perhaps be worn under a leather suit than is possible for the cyclist, but it is doubtful whether such additional protection adequately compensates for the much greater speed and the greater weight of machinery with which the rider might become entangled.

Helen Gibson's remarkable feat of charging through a wooden gate on a motorcycle, leaping through the open doors of a boxcar and landing on a passing train, demonstrates the only real protection the stunt-actor has—absolute mastery of himself and the machine.

Motorcycle leaps

Charles Hutchison, as he showed in *The Whirlwind* (1920) for example, was in the same class as Miss Gibson when it came to motorcycle work. In *Hurricane Hutch* (1921) he did a thirty-foot motorcycle leap across a broken bridge,[89] and in fact leaps are possible with the motorcycle that would be impossible with cycles. They are still part of many military tattoos and police displays where we see motorcyclists going off ramps through blazing hoops in the same tradition as the earlier 'resin-back' riders of the circus did, and the still earlier trick riders of the eighteenth century. Grace gives an account of the way in which Noomis was hurt doubling for Jack Mower in *Manslaughter*, which differs from that given in *Photoplay*[90] and from the account given by Leatrice Joy to Brownlow.[91] According to Grace, Noomis did not drive into the side of a car but by using a small ramp took the motorcycle over the top of a moving car. The leap itself was successful, but Noomis landed badly and broke a collarbone.[92] Miss Joy's account is probably the more accurate since she was on the set at the time, but Grace's account is clearly of a stunt that had been performed with a motorcycle and in all probability by Noomis.

Rémy Julienne, the French stunt actor, did a remarkable leap with motorcycle and sidecar in *Le mur de L'Atlantique* (1954), and Ken Buckle was injured taking a similar machine over the parapet of a race track for *Those Magnificent Men In Their Flying Machines* (1965). But perhaps the most incredible of all leaps was that performed by Shorty Osborne who tried to do a parachute jump by driving a motorcycle over the cliffs at Santa Monica. Unfortunately the parachute failed to open properly and Osborne suffered such severe leg injuries that, according to Grace, he had lost two inches in height after his recovery.

Motorcycle falls

Falls from motorcycles have something in common with horse falls. Indeed to some extent the motorcycle has found a place in the modern cinema that in earlier years would have been occupied by the horse. The chase involving a car and a rocket-firing motorcycle in *Thunderball* is similar to, though a good deal more spectacular than, earlier chases on horseback. Cyd Child's fall off a pillion in *No Blade of Grass* (1970) amongst the wheels of other motorcyclists has echoes of those horse falls by Yakima Canutt amongst the thudding hooves of galloping Indian attackers, and Roy Street used the technique of the 'step stirrup' fall from a horse in the British TV series *The Gold Robbers* (1969). Pushing off with his feet from a fixed bar on the motorcycle, he landed on a concrete road at a speed of some twenty to twenty-five miles an hour.

The analogy between motorcycle and horse cannot of course be carried too far. Nothing in the field of horse stunting can compare with Joe Powell's crash of a motorcycle into a tree for *The Small*

Voice (1948). The speed was something approaching forty miles an hour and he is reputed to have been paid a sum of £25 for two takes.[93]

Ship stunts

Ship stunts tend to be stunts which have already been established elsewhere, adapted to conditions afloat. The ship does not present any very special conditions for the stuntman which he has not already faced in performing the stunt elsewhere. Fights on the decks of ships are much the same as fights on dry land. Dramatic rope-swings, such as we see in *Captain Blood*, do not differ in any fundamental way from the rope-swings of Johnny Weismuller's Tarzan simply because they take place afloat. Many such scenes, in fact, take place on the studio floor and only on the screen do they appear in the context of a ship. Herbert Rawlinson's dive from a moving Los Angeles fireboat (*The Flame Fighter*, 1925) and Alf Joint's spectacular dive in *The Longships* (1963) do present the special problem of leaving a moving rather than a static take-off, but it is a problem that was faced earlier by Gene Perkins, and Harold Lloyd and Eddie Sutherland in their leap from a moving train to a fixed rope during the shooting of an episode of *The Hazards of Helen*. This is not to minimise the dangers of the ship stunt, but simply to point out that the fact that it takes place afloat does not significantly add to those dangers or the skill necessary to overcome them.

The most sensational ship battles as part of an entertainment are still those staged by the Romans. 'One of the most extravagant forms of combat was the *naumachia* or naval battle,' says Grant,[94] writing of Roman gladiatorial displays. 'Huge areas were flooded in order to make artificial lakes for the ships, and gladiators, especially prisoners of war, were trained to fight on board.' The emperor Claudius, to celebrate the successful completion of a tunnel draining Lake Fucine, mounted 'the greatest gladiatorial water-fight of all time' in which nineteen thousand combatants in triremes, quadriremes and a range of other craft took part. The water-borne gladiators fought in earnest and there was 'much blood-letting'.

Nothing that we have ever seen in the cinema can match the spectacle of that horrific battle as we imagine it must have appeared to those present. Even the massive array of the Allied invasion fleet as it first appears out of the morning mist in *The Longest Day* (1961), cannot have impressed its first audiences as much as the fantastic spectacle of the *naumachia* mounted by Claudius. Nor, of course, would we want it to. The cinema, whatever its detractors might say, is an art form. It transmutes reality, it does not simply re-enact it.

The nearest the cinema has come to portraying the kind of spectacle that Claudius's subjects witnessed is perhaps the sea-battle in *Ben-Hur* (1925), between the pirate ship and the Roman trireme, its hull loaded with sweating, beaten galley slaves. Yet even here the cinema has certain advantages over Claudius's real-life spectacle. Close-ups allow us to see individuals in action and watch the tons of water pour down on the trapped galley slaves as the pirate vessel—towed by an unseen motorboat—rams its prow through the timbers of the trireme. There is no doubt about the danger involved to extras and stuntmen in such a scene. When the trireme burst into flames—helped by oil-soaked materials—the fire spread more rapidly than had been expected. Wind fanned the flames. Extras, many of them unable to swim, leapt into the sea. Rescue boats picked many of them up in a half-drowned condition, but there were persistent reports of fatalities which caused the production company (M-G-M) acute embarrassment.

The coach and wagon

The cinema has seen a range of other vehicles employed in spectacular scenes. The stagecoach, as we have seen, is a perennial vehicle in the Western spectacular with its own particular dangers. The roof-fight requires particular skill since a coach moving at any speed at all is perhaps the most insecure vehicle imaginable. It rocks, bucks, tilts and sways at every irregularity of the ground.

The roof-fight 'requires one hand for hitting and the other for hanging on'. The transfer to the coach is a specialist stunt, made particularly hazardous by the enormous size of the back wheels which revolve within a few inches of the door.

Turning over a stagecoach involves the same kind of technical device that we have seen in the car roll-over, except that the stunt driver cannot rely on any of the safety apparatus available to the car driver. Initially, the stunt was performed with the horses still harnessed to the coach, but the intervention of the societies for the prevention of cruelty to animals led to the invention of a device that unhitches horses and coach a moment before the crash. Canutt mentions a similar device which he used on the mass crash of chariots in the chariot race in Wyler's *Ben-Hur* (1959). LeRoy Johnson is one of the more recent specialists in the wagon roll-over. He performed the stunt a number of times in the TV serial *Wagon Train* (1959—) at fees reputed to have ranged from $500 to $2,500 a time.[95]

The wagon and the horse-drawn 'buggy' appear as frequently in the Western as the stagecoach. On one occasion, Canutt drove a buggy off a cliff into water and in *McLintock!* (1964) John Wayne injured the base of his spine when he landed badly on a moving hay wagon after a twenty-foot leap from a roof. In *The Bellhop* (1918) Keaton found a leap from a horsecar on to the back of the horse that was pulling it particularly difficult. The horse was far enough in front of the car to prevent his kicking it, so that Keaton had a leap of about six feet. He did the leap from a box inside the car and he had wrapped the reins around his hands for security. The horse sensed him coming and side-stepped. He hit the cobbled street and was dragged by the reins.[96]

Trams, buses, fire-engines

Trams, buses and fire-engines have all had parts in film action sequences. Harold Lloyd used a bus body mounted on a truck for the alarming sequences in *For Heaven's Sake* (1926). A man, apparently doing a balancing act on the top rail of the bus as it raced through the streets of Los Angeles, was supported by a metal device that went up one trouser leg and gripped his body. This left him free to make whatever wild gestures he wished with his arms, his other leg and the upper part of his body.[97]

On another occasion, Lloyd used a fire-engine. He was to hold on to a hose as the engine tore down a street. The hose was supposed to be connected to the vehicle to prevent Lloyd falling off. The connection, however, had not been made and the actor fell off and was injured.

For Lloyd's street scenes he provided all his own vehicles and pedestrians. The locations, of course, were real: 'We would get a whole cordon of police and rope off probably three blocks.'[98] Keaton's approach to a similar situation has a certain Sennett-like improvisation about it, although Keaton in fact never worked for Sennett. For a location stunt he used 'two or three motor cops to control traffic'. They were never paid for such work 'but we used to give them an extra's check or a stunt check. That was probably $10.'

But we do not have to delve into the cinema's history to find the more hair-raising of stunts with vehicles. In *Where Eagles Dare* (1968), Alf Joint's leap from one alpine cable car to another moving in the opposite direction, together with the fight on top of the car, provide vehicle stunt sequences that can match anything ever seen on the screen.

5 Falls, leaps and jumps

The net fall

'No one can go on turning triple and double somersaults in the air day after day without occasionally falling,' says Manning-Sanders. The fact is of considerable importance in the development of cinema stunting. Were it not for the human fallibility of even the greatest aerialists, it is possible that high falling as a very spectacular aspect of stunting would never have been introduced. The fact that aerialists occasionally fell by accident induced them to take precautions to minimise injury, and these precautions opened up the possibilities of deliberate high falls as a new feature of spectacle.

Illustration: King of Kings (1965). Manuel Gonzelas falling 57 feet.

Falls, leaps and jumps

The Romans used nets as safety devices in their high-level rope dancing, but do not seem to have used them for the deliberate performance of falls as part of their acts. For something over a thousand years after the final disappearance of the Roman spectacles, rope dancers seem to have taken no safety precautions whatever. Jacob Hall, interviewed by Pepys, talks of accidental falls from the tight-rope as if they were not uncommon occurrences which rarely led to serious injury. But when Leotard, in the nineteenth century, extended the range of aerial work to include such features as the somersault, this increased considerably the risk of accidental falls. To minimise possible injury he practised over water and during the performance of his act spread a mattress over the stage. Increased aerial complexity involved increased risk to the performer and finally the net became a standard piece of safety equipment in the high aerial act.

It is perhaps surprising that in the circus the net remained no more than a safety device, despite the fact that Cubanos had demonstrated the spectacular effect of the fall. Cubanos leapt from a platform on to a trapeze thirty feet away. As he grasped the trapeze it broke and he fell. Just before he hit the ground he turned and seized a rope tied to one ankle and arrested his fall. Manning-Sanders condemned the act as 'deception' and it may be that her sense of outrage is shared by the majority of circus audiences. Such a reaction could account for the rarity with which the deliberate fall is performed in the circus. A more likely explanation is that the electrifying effect of the fall depends on the element of unexpectedness. Once high falls had become a regular part of the conclusion of aerial acts the audience would grow used to them and they would no longer hold the same excitement for spectators. Whatever the reason, it was left to the cinema to exploit the full possibilities of a stunt that the circus had introduced.

The earliest high falls performed before the camera were made into nets and one of the most spectacular net-falling sequences occurred in Griffith's *Intolerance*, in which people were pitched bodily from the walls of Babylon. Henabery described the technique of staging such falls in an interview with Brownlow[99] in

1964, and mentioned one of the problems involved. Leo Noomis led the team of stuntmen who were to fall into the nets. Noomis explained the need to land on the back, not on the feet. His own fall was perfect, but some of his team, ignoring his advice and landing on their feet, broke their noses against their knees.

As Henabery discovered, the net is far from being a perfect 'rig' on which to fall. It requires a special technique if it is to be used safely. Manning-Sanders, talking of its use in the circus, admits its advantages over the mattress but points out some of its disadvantages. For example, it sinks on impact and on its return 'throws the artiste up to some height. And, in addition, to fall at a wrong angle results in a broken neck. . . . One of the first lessons the flying-trapeze artiste must learn, therefore, is the art of falling: he must "ball up" and land on his shoulders, with his legs in the air and his knees stiff.'[100]

Despite its other disadvantages—the time it takes to set up, the fact that it must be some six to eight feet from the ground because of its 'give' on impact and the tendency in the cinema for the stuntman to bounce back into frame—it was some time before a more satisfactory rig was invented. Dick Grace performed his first cinema stunt—a forty-foot fall—into a net. Gene Perkins, who later died in an air transfer stunt, was famous for his 'exceedingly high wire and net dives' for which he was paid 'about $75 a week', and in an article published in 1932 Burke[101] mentions a seventy-five-foot fall that Leroy Mason made 'into a net that broke at the crucial moment'.

Early falling 'rigs'

What the net really introduced in the cinema was the *high* fall rather than the idea of falling itself. Comedy had always employed the fall as a technique for producing laughter in an audience—the slip on a banana skin, the accidental trip, the 'prat fall' which landed the comedian ignominiously on his backside. The writings of Keaton, Chaplin and Lloyd are full of references to such falls as an essential part of the art of the visual comedian.

Such falls have been a continuous feature of cinema comedy since the early days of film, but they do seem to have been influenced to some extent by the introduction of the high fall. Where at one time it was sufficient for a comedian to trip over a paving stone and spreadeagle himself in the dust, it now became necessary for him to fall out of windows and off high ledges without the aid of any kind of rig. Arbuckle, says Keaton, 'took falls no other man of his weight ever attempted'; the Keystone Cops 'knew nothing whatever about falling'; and Jimmy Bryant 'kept taking the punishment like some battered old club fighter right to the end of his acting days' because, apparently, no precautions of any kind were taken to minimise the possibility of serious injury. For one stunt Grace fell twenty-five feet without any kind of rig and Perkins attempted a drop of forty feet from the eaves of a roof with nothing to break his fall but a mattress. But such stunts, as Keaton remarks, were bound to have serious consequences sooner or later, and for a fall of more than ten or twelve feet some form of 'rig', some apparatus for breaking the fall, began to be regarded as essential.

The simple flock or straw mattress was the earliest rig and for lower falls it served its purpose. It had the advantage from the camera's point of view of producing no 'bounce-back' so that the frame could be set only a foot or two above the mattress. Its disadvantage was that it still produced a hard landing and required a very high degree of skill from the stuntman. The physical attitude of the stuntman at the moment of impact was crucial for his safe survival.

As the cinema's demand for higher and more spectacular falls increased, the mattress as the sole safety device fell into disuse. Keaton used a pit full of straw for a fall from the second floor of a building in *One Week* (1920), and injured himself. A similar rig which he used in *Hard Luck* (1921) was no more satisfactory. 'He was required to dive from a fifty-foot platform,' says Montgomery,[102] 'missing a swimming pool by a few yards, to crash through a "marble" tiled pavement made of paper, covered with wax. He dived, but his head and shoulders were seriously cut.' For

a high dive in *The Paleface* (1921)—something around eighty feet—
he returned to the net which despite its limitations was still the
only really practical safety device for the high-faller.

But the search for a more satisfactory rig continued and Grace,
writing in 1930, makes what must be one of the earliest references
to the use of the box as the basic element of the high-fall rig which
was ultimately to replace the net. Arthur Seitz, according to
Grace, used 'a huge dry-goods box' to break a fall from a second
floor window. Seitz struck the edge of the box when he hit it and
was permanently crippled, but Grace attributes this more to
Seitz's age which affected his judgement than to any inherent
defect in the rig.

The modern high fall

The modern cinema high fall is a highly skilled stunt and usually
requires a background of high diving and acrobatic work. Grace
classified all falls below fifty feet as 'minor' and only those over
that height as 'major'. This classification is no longer accepted
and it is doubtful whether Grace's measurements are any more
than rule of thumb since no stuntman uses a tape measure to check
the exact height of the fall he is about to perform in case he might
incidentally break a world record. He is concerned with other
more important matters.

Alf Joint, one of the world's great high fallers, considers that
no one should attempt a fall of more than forty feet on to a rig,[103]
though he admits that for suitable cash inducements higher falls
have been done. Bob Simmons, for example, is credited with a
fall of ninety feet and Joint himself has certainly done higher falls
than the limit he himself suggests.

The lower limit of the high fall now would perhaps be regarded
as twenty to thirty feet. For falls higher than this lower limit,
specialist ability in aerial body control is required since the way
in which the faller hits his rig will determine whether he is injured
or not. If the stuntman lands on his side, for example, his knees
bang together and may cause injury to his legs. If he lands with

an arm first he can well dislocate his shoulder or penetrate his rig so deeply as to hit the ground beneath.

Control of a fall is maintained by the head, according to Keaton. The aim of a stuntman landing from a high fall is to spreadeagle himself, if possible on his back, so that his weight is distributed as much as possible over the surface of his rig. The adoption of this landing position must be delayed as long as possible because the film sequence may not require the stuntman to appear spread-eagled on his back at all. It may require him, for example, to appear to be dropping feet first. Roy Scammell is a high faller who has perfected the delayed turn into his final landing position. On a fall of forty-five feet on to a rig some eight feet high, he can fall headfirst for some thirty feet leaving himself only five or six feet in which to turn over on to his back and spreadeagle himself for the landing. Scammell is also reputed to have done a high fall landing face-down on his rig.

The box rig

The modern rig is based on an arrangement of cardboard boxes, each measuring two feet square by four feet in length. The boxes are built up like bricks to the height that the stuntman considers adequate for a particular fall. The ground area covered by the boxes depends not only on the preference of the individual stunt-man but on the nature of the fall. For a forty-foot fall, for example, a ground area varying from twenty feet to thirty feet square would be covered by the erection of boxes, provided that the fall was from a stationary take-off.

In the case of a running take-off, however, in which perhaps a stuntman is chased along a high balcony and has to leap running from the end of it, a much more considerable ground area would be covered to allow for his unpredictable trajectory through the air. For such a fall five layers of boxes might be required, resulting in a rig some ten feet high. Flattened boxes might be placed between each layer to reduce the risk of penetration by the stuntman's body. In most cases, and particularly on a slippery studio floor, the rig will be roped round so that the boxes do not scatter when struck. A tarpaulin is often used over the top of the rig to give the boxes further security. Flock or straw mattresses are laid on top of the boxes so that the stuntman does not injure himself on the stiff edges.

On impact the boxes produce a controlled collapse that dissipates the stuntman's falling energy successfully. Jack Cooper in *Exodus* (1960) and Roy Scammell in the TV series *Catweazle* (1970) both used such a rig for falls of about sixty feet. The rig, of course, adds considerably to the expense of mounting a falling sequence. The price of boxes varies between 20p and 35p each and those that are crushed by the impact of a fall must be discarded. The preparation of each box, the building of the rig, the roping round and the placing of mattresses on top of it—either done by the stuntman himself or under his personal supervision—adds to labour costs. The fall itself might cost the production company a further £250 at least, in fees to the stuntman.

Considering the importance to the stuntman of this rig it is perhaps surprising how little its nature is understood outside the profession. Even after interviews with some of the world's most prominent high fallers, Khan in an article in one of the most respected daily newspapers[104] describes the box rig as consisting of 'an expanse firstly of layers of flattened cardboard boxes, then flock mattresses and then possibly a canvas sheet, covering an area where he reckons he will land'. Since flattened boxes have no ability to absorb falling energy, such a rig would kill any high faller who used it, with absolute certainty.

Even when properly set up it still has its dangers. There is always the possibility of hitting it badly or feeling it slip or scatter on impact because of some defect in the way it has been secured. But the stuntman's worst fear is that he may miss the rig altogether and hit the ground with the full velocity of his fall. All high fallers agree that as they prepare to drop, the rig never looks big enough. 'It looks about the size of a postage stamp,' is a phrase that is constantly repeated in conversations with high fallers. Jack Cooper admits to being frightened,[105] particularly immediately before the fall but when it is too late to withdraw from it. But the momen the has jumped, all the tension disappears. He describes the sensation as 'floating'.

This fear, in particular the conviction that there is something wrong with the rig, is at times unfortunately justified. Cooper did a sixty-foot fall out of a window in *Where Eagles Dare*, and injured himself. During the night the straw mattresses on his rig had frozen solid.

A box rig—similar to that used by the high faller, but of very much smaller proportions—is used occasionally for falls in the theatre. The problem of such falls lies not in their inherent danger—none of them would qualify for the classification of 'major', either in Grace's terms or within the more modern interpretation of that word—but in the fact that they must be repeated at frequent intervals. The cinema fall is a once-for-all affair. It may need to be performed twice or even three times before the director or the stuntman is satisfied with it, but once it is successfully executed and filmed that is an end of it.

In the theatre a fall must be repeated at each performance throughout the run of the play. One of the present writers, in a stage production of *Hamlet*, was required to perform a thirteen-foot fall on to a single cardboard box at each performance for a number of weeks. In the London stage musical, *The Four Musketeers* (1967), Roy Scammell gave a nightly performance of a spectacular twenty-foot fall from a balcony on to a box rig disguised as a large banqueting table.

The problem of disguising the rig is more pressing in the theatre than in the cinema. In the cinema the film can be cut at the point where the rig is about to appear, and an identical set-up can then be shown in which the star, having replaced the stuntman, is seen lying on the floor. Such a technique is impossible in the theatre and usually the stuntman is last seen disappearing behind a piece of scenery or large property where his rig has been set up.

Similar masking has of course been used in the cinema. In William Wellman's production of *Beau Geste* (1939) for Paramount, we saw a spectacular backwards fall from the top of a lookout tower in which the actual landing was masked by a high wall. But in the cinema this is only one of many techniques which can be used to prevent the stuntman's rig from being seen by the audience, whereas in the theatre it remains almost the only one. In a stage version of *Coriolanus* (Stratford, England, 1959), for example, Sir Laurence Olivier in the lead part did a spectacular death fall backwards off a high rostrum, but his landing—understandably—was masked from the audience.

Another method of cinema masking is by using a pit rather like that used by Keaton. The pit is filled with boxes with the usual mattresses on top and the hole in the ground covered by tarpaulin. The tarpaulin itself may be masked so that the appearance to the camera is of perfectly solid ground. One can understand why such a rig is not popular with high fallers. To have the rig look 'about the size of a postage stamp' is bad enough. But for the stuntman not to be able to see any rig at all when he looks down from his fifty to sixty feet of height is a good deal more alarming.

As we have seen, the high fall is dangerous because it is high. Other falls may be dangerous for other reasons. What some of those other dangers are is evident in one of the final sequences from *It's A Mad, Mad, Mad, Mad World* (1963) in which we see a stuntman, doubling for Spencer Tracy, thrown off a wire into a pine tree. He grabs for a branch which breaks—Charles Hutchison, as we shall see later, demonstrated the danger of this particular stunt—hooks on to telegraph wires and slides down them towards a building on the far side of the street. The slide carries him through a glass window into the upper part of an office. As he hits the floor it collapses and we finally see him dropping through it to the room beneath.

Falls through structures

Grace points to the very real dangers of falling through structures in his account of a thirty-foot fall that he and Dick Curwood performed from a swinging cable through a glass roof. Even the glass seems to have been real instead of the 'toffee glass' that the

…ft:

…ck Cooper demonstrates

…w a horse is trained to fall

… the bit'

…e page 67

…ght:

…ree examples of

…en Buckle's versatility:

…u can't win 'em all 1969

…orse fall, note 'cup stirrup'

…e Long Duel 1968

…ddle fall'

…anhoe 1951

…se of the 'jerk harness'

…t:

…e Longships 1961

…nass horse fall staged by

…o Simmons

Five examples of the
art of Yakima Canutt:

Left:
Virginia City 1940
The 'running w'

'Stirrup drag'

'Bulldogging'

Right:
'Bronc riding'

Stagecoach 1939
His greatest feat

Yakima Canutt is the only
stuntman to have received
special Academy Award

ft:
sino Royale 1966
avy Wilding making use
his 'somersault jacket'

ght:
hree examples of first class
ecial effects

e Long Day's Dying 1968
erek Ware in foreground

e Last Grenade 1970
ddie Powell using a
e harness

e Last Grenade 1970
fects devised by
t Moore

t:
sino Royale 1966
vy Wilding pulling down
horse Popsie

erleaf top left:
ose *Magnificent Men in*
ir Flying Machines 1964
n Buckle doubling for
rt Froebe, see page 99

erleaf bottom left:
Blade of Grass 1970
nt girl Cyd Child in
ion

erleaf top right:
e Damned 1961
k Cooper at the Wheel

erleaf bottom right:
nte Carlo or Bust 1967
rc Boyle at 55 mph
oting on to a moving
y

modern special effects man would produce for such a stunt, since Grace, with understandable surprise, says, ' Strange to say, I did not get a cut!' But Curwood, who followed Grace on the stunt, mistimed it and broke his back. It was this injury, as we shall see, that Grace thought led to Curwood's later death when he was unable to hang on to an aerial rope ladder towed by an aircraft.

Another very spectacular fall through glass took place in *The Glass Key* (1942) when Alan Ladd escapes from an upper room by leaping through the window. We see the stuntman fall from the window, drop through the glass roof of a terrace and land across a small table scattering crockery that has been placed on it. The credit for engineering this stunt is given by Hagner to Jimmy Dundee.[106] Perhaps an even more spectacular and dangerous fall took place during the bar brawl scene in the 'Gay Lady' saloon in *Dodge City*. Three stuntmen—Harvey Parry, Cliff Lyons and Duke Green—are fighting on a balcony. The balcony collapses and they are pitched downwards, fall through a lower balcony and crash on to a roulette table beneath. The payment they are reputed to have received for the fall was $485 each.

High falls require precise teamwork if they are to be filmed successfully. Cameras must be placed accurately if as much of the fall as possible is to be recorded without the rig coming into frame. The angle at which the fall is shot is important, since a wrong camera angle can reduce considerably the impression of height that an audience receives. The camera in any case tends to reduce the impression of height and it is possible that falls could be lengthened by some overcranking of the camera so that the slight degree of slow motion that this would produce would give the audience the sensation of a longer fall.

Some falls—the spectacular seventy-foot double leap in *Butch Cassidy and the Sundance Kid* is an example—are the result of collaboration between stuntmen, special effects men and process photographers, and this important kind of collaboration we will consider in detail later.

The high dive

From the cameraman's viewpoint the dive into water poses fewer problems than the leap on to a rig because the audience can be shown the landing. From the stuntman's viewpoint it certainly poses greater problems of height. Whereas a sixty-foot fall on to a box rig is extremely high, stuntmen diving into water for some spectacular film sequence have come close to breaking the world record.

The highest recorded dive appears to be that performed by Mme Andrée Podeur at Brest in France in 1955. She fell 172 feet and 'only recovered consciousness after artificial respiration had been applied',[107] yet in 1970 Alf Joint performed a dive of about 160 feet into the Mediterranean for a TV commercial film. A repetition of the dive caused him injuries which required hospital treatment.

We can understand how easily such injuries can be caused when we remember that the speed at which a human body strikes the water from such a height is approaching seventy miles an hour. Even from lower heights high dives require absolute control over body movement, particularly at the moment of entry. Jack Cooper suffered temporary paralysis after a bad landing from a seventy-five-foot dive into the sea during the filming of *The Crimson Pirate* (1951). And even after the successful completion of a high dive, there is always the possibility that in the final editing of the film it will be rejected. 'I did the 120-foot dive twice for *The Guns of Navarone* (1961)', says Bob Simmons,[108] 'and both shots finished up on the cutting room floor!'

The technique of high diving differs from that of high falling. The high fall on to a box rig requires a stuntman to spread out his body just before impact, so as not to penetrate the rig too deeply. By contrast, the high diver enters the water with as little resistance as possible.

It is perhaps of interest to note that the professional divers from La Quebrada Cliff into the sea at Acapulco in Mexico fall a distance of a little over 120 feet. For these remarkable dives they have justifiably won world fame. The stuntmen who perform no less remarkable feats for the camera, are unknown outside the tight and circumscribed limits of their own profession.

The dangers inherent in many high dives into the sea, and the stuntman's feelings as he uses his skill to avoid them, are perhaps shown most clearly in a dive performed by Grace and recounted by him in considerable detail. The dive, of eighty-six feet, took place from a cliff on the island of Santa Cruz when he was doubling for Henry Walthal in a John Ford film. His first recollection as he is preparing for the dive is of Bobby Dunn, who had earlier been blinded in one eye when in a high dive he struck a match that was floating on the water. As he stands ready to dive he deliberately avoids looking downwards at the spot he is proposing to aim at, until the director has given the signal for the dive to take place. When the signal has been given he takes up his position and gives one deliberate and momentary look at his target below.

In his own words describing this particular dive he says:

I must jump out at least ten feet to clear the part of the cliff that bellied out. Yet I couldn't afford to overbalance. The muscles of my legs tightened as I crouched for the leap. Then the legs straightened and I sprang. For just a moment I thought that I couldn't clear the ledge, and I moved my arms and head to change my course. It meant that I would have to turn a front flip, or what we call a 'full'. I was relieved when I saw the cliff pass by my head! Then I concentrated on making the dive. But I had neglected to take into consideration the deceptive wind which funnelled through the gap. As I struck it, I was thrown off balance, and tried to make a 'one and a half', which means a complete fall and a half, landing on my feet. Dangerous with shallow water, but I was powerless to do better! Now I was nearing the waves, and entirely out of position. It couldn't be helped, so suddenly I gave up trying for the classic one. Just one quick movement and I flopped on my back. It would be a heavy blow I'd get, but better than being dashed on the rocks below! I wondered quickly what would be the result. Well, I wouldn't have long to wait before I found out!—I hit. The spout of water that rose was huge, as I disappeared under the surface. There I turned completely over, just grazing the rocks.[109]

Despite a certain dramatic excess that colours Grace's descriptions of many of his stunts, he does succeed in giving here some indication of the problems of the high diver and high faller and the stream of psychological activity with which he reacts to them. His statement that the whole dive in fact took only two and a half seconds is a further example of his dramatic understatement, unless, as is possible, he is referring to the *screen* time to which the dive was reduced by editorial intervention.

This danger of accidentally hitting rocks, or deliberately striking other obstacles, is common enough amongst stunt high divers. During the shooting of *Helen of Troy* (1956) Jack Cooper faced the very real possibility of hitting rocks in a dive of more than sixty feet into the sea and Paddy Ryan's acrobatic and very spectacular fall into an eight-foot-deep moat in *Ivanhoe* (1952) involved negotiating the wires and hidden scaffolding supporting the property curtain wall of a castle. Ryan was to be paid in cash for the stunt and when asked afterwards if he had been frightened he gave the classic reply of the stuntman: 'Very frightened. I saw all those faces looking up at me but I couldn't see the cashier anywhere.' In the history of cinema stunting, and particularly in the field of high dives, Ryan has a permanent place of honour. He is an Englishman who has been in films since the late twenties and whose work transcends the national boundaries of film making, linking him with such great American innovators as Leo Noomis and David Sharpe.

But perhaps the most remarkable dive in connection with dangerous obstacles is that performed by David Sharpe, the stuntman doubling for Ross Martin in *The Great Race* (1965). Here we see the stuntman turn on the window ledge of a castle interior and dive through the window into the waters of the moat beneath—

a distance, perhaps, of thirty feet. But on the water floats a rowing boat with a man at the oars. We see the stuntman plummet towards the boat, strike it and go straight through the bottom. The real achievement here is not the daring required of a stuntman to pitch himself head-first at the structure of a moving boat, however frail that structure has been made by the work of the property department. Such daring is an essential part of the make-up of all stuntmen. Rather it is the sheer physical skill and the precise sense of timing that allow him to hit a small boat in just the right place and at the same time miss the man who is sitting in it. 'What would have happened if?' is a question that all stunts pose for us. It is part of their compulsive attraction for an audience. One cannot help wondering what would have happened in this case if the diver, dropping from some thirty feet, had struck the firm edge of the boat instead of the weakened floor, or more disastrously, had landed head-first on the man sitting in it. The fact that neither of these things happened was entirely due to the skill of the stuntman in being able to do exactly what was required of him.

The water drop

The feet-first drop into water can at times look more spectacular than the dive. We expect a diver to hit the water hands first, and since he is a diver we expect him to know what he is doing. His obvious skill and experience in some way reduce for us the element of danger. But the feet-first fall suggests a certain amateurishness, a certain lack of skill and experience, which for the audience enhances the sense of danger. 'That,' we seem to say to ourselves, 'is exactly how I would fall in similar circumstances.' The apparent lack of skill produces a greater feeling of identification.

Yet the jump feet-first into water cannot be performed from the same height as the dive. We must regard Francis McDonald's seventy-foot jump from the top deck of the coastal steamer *Yale* for an episode in *The Voice on the Wire* (1917) serial as being quite exceptional. Frequently for such a jump the stuntman will tape his legs together from ankles to knee to prevent them separating on impact, and protect his genitals with soft rubber padding. Some of the more spectacular feet-first jumps into water were performed in *Where Eagles Dare*, which Alf Joint has described as 'certainly one of the most dangerous films I have taken part in'. 'At one point,' says Joint,[110] 'four of the team, including a woman, had to drop out of the cable car forty feet into the river below.' The woman was Gillian Aldam, the English stuntwoman.

The problem of getting any really accurate impression of the heights that high fallers and high divers cover is highlighted by another account of Gillian Aldam's part in this particular multiple fall. 'For a leap of seventy feet into a narrow freezing stream from a cable car in *Where Eagles Dare* she earned £350,' says McDowell.[111] The height of the drop has gained thirty feet in the telling and the 'river' that Joint mentions has become 'a narrow freezing stream'. Flynn, too, contributes to the general confusion by stating that his friend Buster Wiles did falls of two hundred feet into water.

The high slide

A variation of the high fall is the high slide. The spectacular slide down a cable performed by Bob Simmons in *Holiday in Spain/ Scent of Murder* (1960), is an example. We saw Simmons hook an umbrella on to a cable attached to the three-hundred-foot Malaga radio tower and slide down it to the twelve-foot-wide wall of a castle. It took him six days to set up the stunt and he tested it first with sandbags to get the right speed of slide. Finally he did the stunt himself nine times in front of the cameras.[112]

The stunt is adapted brilliantly to the particular requirements of the cinema, and the preparation that Simmons describes is typical of the way in which all top stuntmen now tackle difficult and dangerous problems. Yet this stunt has a long tradition. Holinshed[113] mentions the death of a 'rope-flyer', a man who gave public displays of his ability to slide down a rope, anchored at one end to some high point and at the other to the ground. The usual technique employed by the 'rope-flyer' was to come down the rope head-first balanced on a wooden board. Hogarth's picture, *Southwark Fair*, shows Cadman, perhaps the greatest of rope-flyers, in action. Cadman was killed in 1740 when attempting to 'fly' down a rope stretched from 'the top of a church steeple in Shrewsbury across the Severn to the meadows on the other side'.[114]

Stairfalls

The staircase fall, which we have seen in innumerable films and occasionally in the theatre, presents none of the dangers of the high fall, in the sense that a miscalculation is likely to lead to death or severe injuries. It is not, however, without its own special difficulties. We must remember that in this as in all stunts the stuntman has two jobs to do. He has to fall downstairs without injuring himself and he has to do so in such a way that his performance is effective for the camera. The staircase fall can usually be shot more 'tightly' than most high falls and high dives, so that the detailed behaviour of the stuntman during the fall is more readily visible to the audience. The high dive, if it is executed successfully, leaves the stuntman unscathed, whereas even the most successful stairfall can leave him severely bruised because at every point of the fall he is in contact with hard surfaces.

Harvey Parry pointed out many years ago the fallacy of regarding some stunts as intrinsically more dangerous than others. There is, he said, no such thing as the 'most dangerous stunt'. All stunts are dangerous unless they are properly planned and prepared for. 'The only time I was ever injured was in a fall of less than six inches.'[115] The film was *The Call of the Wild* (1935) in which as a drunk he had to step off the sidewalk. As he took the necessary step he slipped, fell backwards, and broke his back on a stake that was hidden under the snow.

Most stuntmen prefer to fall down a straight flight of stairs with banisters on either side. The banisters can be used to direct the fall. The way in which the fall is started is important since it determines its shape and to a large extent its speed. Many stuntmen prefer to launch themselves backwards so as to get the step of a stair under their necks and then direct the rest of the fall from that position. In some cases this backwards starting position fits naturally in with the preceding action. For example we might see an actor climbing the stairs. As he reaches the top he may be struck by someone, or he may see a terrifying apparition which causes him to fall backwards. In either case, when stuntman is substituted for actor he can start his backwards fall as a logical consequence of the preceding sequence. On other occasions the stuntman can reach his required starting position by his own reactions to the preceding sequence. An actor, for example, standing at the top of the stairs facing down them may be shot from below. When the stuntman is substituted he can decide to react to the shooting by taking the bullet in his side, spinning round and again starting his stairfall backwards.

There are, however, stairfalls in which a back-launch is not possible. In the case of an old man walking downstairs, tripping and falling the rest of the way, the stuntman is compelled to begin his fall with a forward somersault and then direct himself sideways when he has made contact with the stairs. An additional difficulty will be introduced if the director decided that the old man, killed in the fall, must be seen in close-up lying face-upwards. The stuntman in this case must direct his fall so as to finish in this position so that for the following close-up the actor playing the old man can take up exactly the same position.

The fall without banisters is more difficult. Banisters are useful for directing the fall during its progress and they have the additional advantage of preventing the stuntman from rolling off the stairs altogether and falling to the floor below. A particularly spectacular stairfall of this kind took place in *Robin Hood* (1938), in which we see Hood in manacles pitched down a flight of stone steps without a banister into the dungeon below.

Since speed is important in the stairfall if the stuntman is to control his downward movement, stairs with low risers—some flights that have been used in film sequences have risers of only four and a half inches instead of the more usual eight—present special problems. Such a staircase is little more than a ramp with an irregular surface and requires a considerable launching speed if the stuntman is to stay in complete control of his direction.

Speed, of course, brings its own problems. There have been cases where the stuntman in trying to get the necessary speed on launching has struck the banisters with such force that they have broken, leaving him to cope with a totally unexpected fall to the floor beyond. We can see the importance of speed when we consider falls down curved staircases. The spiral staircase is almost impossible to fall down because before he has built up sufficient speed to direct his fall properly, the stuntman finds himself jammed tight against banister or wall. Perhaps the most successful fall down a curved staircase took place in *A Night at the Opera* (1935). Its success, like the success of all stunts, lay in the way it had been meticulously planned and prepared.

We get an indication of the dangers involved in some of the longer stairfalls from the fact that for their execution the stuntman will wear more padding than for many other stunts. He needs to protect all vulnerable points from the raps that they will take from the hard edges of stairs and banisters. Elbows and knees are of course protected and football shinguards are pushed down socks or tights. Some protection is necessary for hips, kidneys and the base of the spine, and usually ankle straps are worn. Where contemporary dress allows it the shoulders too are given some protection, but the modern close-fitting suit frequently makes this difficult. In most stairfalls the stuntman will rap his ankles, the base of his spine and his shoulders.

There are, of course, certain parts of his anatomy that the stuntman cannot protect however much he would like to. Gillian Aldam mentioned her particular worry, in an interview with Eric Random, in connection with a stunt she had been asked to do which involved falling 'backwards down a double flight of stairs with her hands tied behind her back': 'I'm glad the job went to someone else because although it can be done, it's dangerous. If you tuck your head in too much you'll hit your face on the stairs, and if you go too slow you stand a chance of breaking something. You have to go as fast as possible and remain relaxed and detached from the job. Personally, I'm always scared of smashing my teeth. That's my ever-present fear. But I try not to let myself worry, because it's fatal.'[116]

Leaps

Stunt leaps, as opposed to falls, may or may not involve problems of height. Alf Joint's incredible leap from one alpine cable car to another, passing one another in opposite directions fifteen hundred feet above the ground, during the shooting of *Where Eagles Dare*, had a height factor which added enormously to the danger of the stunt. John Sullivan's leap in *The Vikings* (1958) in which he cleared some fourteen feet over an eighty-foot chasm on to axes thrown into the gateway of a castle is little less remarkable, and Paul Baxley and David Sharpe did similar spectacular leaps on to a rising drawbridge in *Richard and the Crusaders* (1954), complicated by the fact that their landing point was not stationary.

Leaps of this kind are not of course a recent cinematic innovation. In the nineteen-twenties Dick Grace did a leap of some thirteen feet from the top of one nine-storey building to another, and similar stunts have appeared in many films since. Perhaps the most remarkable of the early stunt leaps is that attempted by Charles Hutchison in *Double Adventure* (1921). He leapt from the top of a fifty-foot oil derrick to the branches of a tree below. Accounts vary as to what happened then. According to one his hold slipped and he fell sixty feet on to another branch. Another suggests that the branch broke, and a third says that he collided with the branch and fell. Certainly he broke both his wrists and the production of the film was held up for two months. After that, because of the possibility of his damaged wrists failing to hold him as securely as they had done on similar previous leaps, he tended to use a stuntman to perform such sequences for him.

'Bulldogging'

That special kind of leap which we know as 'bulldogging' reached the cinema by way of the rodeo. Originally it involved dropping from a horse on to a running steer, manhandling it to the ground and securing it in the shortest time possible. We saw an example of the term's more modern meaning in *Colt .45* (1959), when two Indians drop from the balcony of a saloon on to one of the villains moving beneath. Another example occurred in *Robin Hood* (1938) when Mutch the Miller drops from the branch of a tree on to a Norman horseman riding below.

In the rodeo the term is narrow, but in the cinema it has been widened to include many drops on to other actors where an element of movement affects the landing. It might be applied now to Wayne's leap from a moving jeep on to Kirk Douglas during the production of *Cast a Giant Shadow* (1965). Wayne and Yakima Canutt helped to pioneer the 'bulldog' in the cinema. 'One dangerous stunt Duke [Wayne] and Yak performed together,' says Tomkies,[117] 'was where Yak had to gallop down a steep hill on a horse, dive from his mount and "bulldog" Duke off a moving railway handcart and roll on down the hill with him.'

In such stunts, of course, the leaping man cannot aim to hit his opponent 'square-on', since to do so might cause him severe injury. His aim is to miss the opponent fractionally and carry him with him to the ground. Such a sequence is usually followed by some ground wrestling and finally a cut to a close-up of the stars who have now replaced the stuntmen. We see this for example in *The Plainsman* (1937) when Wild Bill Hickock leaps from a cliff on to an Indian riding below, carries him out of the saddle and wrestles with him on the ground; and a review of *The Son of the Sheik* (1926) which appeared in the *New York Times* talks of Rudolph Valentino showing 'no more hesitancy in hurling himself off a horse dragging another man from his mount than he would in diving into the deeply cushioned bed in his desert tent'. The impeccable timing required for leaps of this kind is perhaps shown at its best in *The Great Race* when David Sharpe, doubling for Tony Curtis, does a diving leap of some sixteen feet on to a crowd of fighting men.

Keaton's leaping ability

The ability to leap accurately on to stationary or moving targets requires a good deal more than simple physical skill. It requires a highly developed sense of distance and timing. Talking of Keaton's superb leaping ability in *The General*, Lebel[118] says, 'He leaps from the truck attached to his locomotive to the tender, and from the tender to his driver's cabin with a graceful curve that brings him with an almost teleguided precision to his destination. The unequal length of the successive leaps proves that the certainty of his trajectory owes nothing to tricks and everything to his muscular mastery.' It was this lack of 'teleguided precision' that brought disaster to Silvertip, a stuntman mentioned by Grace. Doubling for Ruth Roland he mistimed a leap from a fast-running train into a lagoon and killed himself when he hit the bank instead of the water.

Rope work

The rope has frequently been used in connection with leaps and jumps. We associate it perhaps most closely with the many Tarzan films that have been made and with such names as Elmo Lincoln, Jock Mahoney and Johnny Weismuller. The rope swing and leap from one perch to another was almost the backbone of Tarzan's action sequences. As a means of transportation in the jungle the rope might almost be seen to perform the same function as the horse in the Western. It is always available. It can carry the hero into action quickly, silently and with the required amount of spectacle. It can be used for short journeys—the perch to perch swing—or for much longer ones, the hero flying from rope to rope in a continuous series of swings. It requires, of course, tremendous agility and strength. Elmo Lincoln, who died in 1952 at the age of sixty-three, created the screen Tarzan with *Tarzan of the Apes*. In an interview[119] he said he had once been insured for $150,000. Of his rope-swinging stunts he said modestly, 'There's nothing to it, providing you hold on and let go at the right time.'

Falls, leaps and jumps

Similar perch to perch swings have been used indoors to carry men into or out of action. The swing across a theatre auditorium in *Scaramouche* (1952) is an example. So too is the swing over the top of the bar room brawl in *Destry Rides Again* (1939). Flynn's haul up the castle gateway in *Robin Hood*, although done with the help of Kirby flying harness, can also be regarded as a rope stunt. We see the actor hacking at the rope holding up the portcullis. As the rope parts, Flynn—or more probably Don Taylor, Flynn's double at that period—catches hold of it and is dragged up the wall of the gateway, apparently by the weight of the descending portcullis. In the same film we see a repetition of the stunt pioneered by the early Tarzans, when hordes of 'Merry Men' drop from the trees on ropes to attack the retainers of Sir Guy of Gisbourne.

6 Work in the air

Early air stunts

Manned flight, at first in lighter-than-air and later in heavier-than-air machines, opened a new dimension to the stuntman concerned with work in the air.

The first ascent in a tethered hot-air balloon, by Jean François Pilatre de Rozier on October 15th, 1783, was itself regarded as a stunt though it was motivated more by the desire to experiment in a new and fascinating medium than by a wish to entertain. The popular attitude to the early pioneers of heavier-than-air machines was similar. Blériot performed a 'stunt', according to the press,

Illustration: Hogan's Alley (1926). Monty Blue performing.

126

when he won the prize offered by Lord Northcliffe's *Daily Mail* for being the first man to fly the English Channel in an aeroplane.

The parachute, which we have seen used so dramatically in films on aviation and modern war, has almost as old a history as the balloon and indeed its conception first began with da Vinci in the fifteenth century. J. P. Blanchard, a Frenchman, is reputed to have dropped a dog on a parachute in 1785 and to have broken a leg in a parachute jump he made himself in 1793. The parachute jump, in fact, became a regular feature of aerial displays during the later years of the nineteenth century and the early years of the twentieth.

Closer to our concept of stunting are the exploits of men like the Italian Brothers, mentioned by Frost,[120] and Clem Sohn. In 1854 in London's Vauxhall Gardens, the Italian Brothers gave a public display of trapeze work suspended from the car of an ascending balloon, a display which was later prohibited on the direction of the Home Secretary because of its 'perilous nature'. The American Clem Sohn built a considerable reputation for himself during the thirties as 'The Bird Man'. His act consisted of leaping from an aircraft, performing elaborate aerial acrobatics and simulated flight with the help of fabric 'wings', and finally completing his drop by parachute. He was killed in the Bois de Vincennes, Paris, in the summer of 1936, when both regular and emergency parachutes failed to open.

The air circus

The 'air circus' was a regular feature of summer outdoor entertainments in both America and Europe during the twenties and early thirties. In America in particular it produced brilliant stunt-pilots whose aerobatic skill has never been surpassed, men like Dick Curwood, Al Wilson, Frank Tomick, Omar Locklear, Dick Grace, Len Povey, Cliff Bergere, Art Goebel and Al Johnson. Inevitably, many of them combined 'air circus' stunting with stunt flying for the cinema. 'The greatest of them all', in the opinion of William Wellman who directed *Wings* (1927), was Dick Grace.

Grace had none of the physical attributes popularly associated with the stuntman. By contrast with the magnificent athletic physique of Frank Merrill—who claimed the title of 'The World's Most Perfect Man'—Joe Bonomo and Johnny Weismuller, Grace was small, dapper and slim with hair parted centrally in the fashion of the early thirties. Phillips, writing of Grace in 1932, described him as 'a frail little man in the late thirties'.[121] Grace was commissioned as a flyer in the First World War and saw service, though apparently not action, in France and Italy. On his return to the States he took to 'barnstorming' in old ex-service aircraft and on the west coast met Locklear who was already gaining fame as an aerial stuntman.

Locklear, in fact, was something of a model for aspiring aerial stuntmen. Cliff Bergere 'watched Locklear like a hawk' and finally entered films himself as an aerial stuntman. Locklear seems to have been no more like the popular image of a stuntman than Grace himself. There was something of the compulsive daredevil in him that drove him to do stunts that were increasingly dangerous. From Grace's account of him one forms the impression of a highly strung-up personality who found relaxation difficult if not impossible. At times he was hard to approach as if hidden behind a preoccupation with the next stunt or the danger inherent in it. There is an aura of destiny about him, as if he had a premonition that stunting would in the end kill him. He was a pioneer of wing-walking and mid-air transfers, which he performed both before the cameras and over San Francisco before live audiences.

Grace witnessed the aircraft crash in which Locklear was killed. Grace had some premonition that took him out to the airfield that night. Locklear's plane, piloted not by Locklear himself but by the experienced 'Skeets' Elliot—Milton Elliot—was already airborne. As it circled at 5,000 feet, phosphorus flares were ignited on the wings to give the impression that it was on fire. As Grace watched, it went into a 'deliberate spin' from which it never recovered. It hit the ground and burnt. The cause of the crash remains a mystery. 'Skeets' Elliot was an experienced pilot. Recovery from a spin can with some aircraft involve difficulties, but with most small planes application of full opposite rudder together with a forward 'stick' position is sufficient to bring them safely out of the manœuvre.

It is of course possible that in the night conditions, and with visibility from the cockpit made more difficult by the phosphorus flares on the wings, Elliot misjudged his height from the ground and allowed the spin to go on too long for him to be able to recover from it before the aircraft crashed. But such a gross misjudgement seems unlikely by an experienced pilot, a pilot who presumably knew the aircraft and its pattern of behaviour in a spin and who had certainly performed much more demanding stunts before. It seems particularly tragic that Omar Locklear should have met his death after all not performing one of his own stunts about which, according to Grace, he had premonitions of disaster, but in an aircraft that slipped out of the control of another aerial stuntman.

The mystery surrounding Locklear's death is intensified by the recent publication of a photograph showing the aircraft after the crash.[122] The machine appears to have hit and damaged a car on impact and does not lie in the attitude that one would expect after a crash resulting from a spin. Certainly there is no sign of its having caught fire, as Grace said it did.

Wing-walking

Wing-walking was another stunt that the development of the aeroplane produced. Locklear and Grace, together with Dick Curwood, must have been amongst the earliest stuntmen to perform it. Grace also talks of 'running' on the top wing of a biplane in flight, a stunt he considered laconically to be 'not easy'. His casual comments on some of the problems involved are hair-raising in themselves. 'When you strike a bump,' he says, 'you are left in mid-air for a few seconds, and just hope that the ship won't travel clear from under you, before you start coming down.' Grace, we should remember, is talking of the days before it was accepted practice to wear a parachute!

Agility and precision of movement were as important for the successful wing-walker as for the trapeze artist. Burgess, an early wing-walker, was 'fifty pounds too much for quick, nimble walking on wings' and was killed when he fell from a plane on to high-tension cables. High-tension cables, which were already beginning to spread an increasingly complex net over the Californian coastal region, were in fact a constant hazard to low-flying stuntmen. Al Johnson was another stunt flyer who was killed when he hit them on his approach run for a stunt in *Hell's Angels* (1930).

The aerial fight

It was a logical step from the wing-walk to the wing fight on an aircraft in flight. Maurice Murphy is one of the men with whom Grace helped to pioneer such fights. They were dangerous, not because of any intrinsic difficulty, but because to make them look effective meant making moves and taking falls which, had they not been perfectly judged, would have led to certain death.

The aircraft which Grace and his colleagues used had a cruising speed of perhaps eighty miles an hour, and this made possible stunts which would be quite impossible on more modern planes travelling at perhaps two hundred and fifty miles an hour. Again, the two wings of the biplane of the period were laced together by a series of metal braces which provided holds for men fighting one another on the lower wing. This in no way detracts from the skill of men like Locklear and Grace, but it does just make credible stunts which would otherwise appear to be little short of magical.

Mid-air transfers

The transfer had been established in the early Westerns by the stuntmen who changed from galloping horse to stagecoach, or from car to train. Some of these transfers Grace regards as only 'minor' stunts. But he classifies as a 'major' stunt the aerial transfer, the change from one aircraft to another in flight that had brought Locklear his early fame. In a biplane the technique itself, while calling for superb skill and absolute confidence, was not particularly difficult. The stuntman climbed out of his open cockpit when the aircraft to which he was going to transfer had reached a position a few feet above and a little to one side of his own machine. He stepped on to his lower wing and walked along its leading edge, steadying himself on the metal struts until he reached the last of them at the wing's extremity. From this final strut the stuntman climbed on to the top wing and from that position he was able to reach up and grasp the wing-skid of the other plane—'the only tense moment in a change'.

Even in modern aircraft, less susceptible than the early biplanes to sudden upcurrents of air, close precision formation flying requires intense concentration and a good deal of skill. One can imagine the concentration of the early biplane pilot, flying low enough to be affected by every rising current of air, watching every minute variation of his wing tip in relation to that of the other machine no more than two or three feet above his own, waiting for the signal from the stuntman that told him the transfer had taken place safely and that he could drop his own machine clear of the other. It is not difficult to understand why the stuntmen referred so regularly to their pilots as 'one of the shrewdest pilots on the west coast'—of Frank Tomick—and 'one of the greatest of stunt pilots on the coast'—of Art Goebel.

The stunt could be performed the other way round with the transfer plane above instead of below the second aircraft. The transfer was made via a rope ladder hanging from the first aircraft. The stuntman climbed out of the cockpit and reached the ladder from the lower wing. From the bottom rung of the ladder he made an inverted transfer to the plane below him. Unlike the change to an aircraft above, Grace considered this transfer difficult, 'hanging by your knees from an unstable rope ladder and waiting until the other plane gets below'.

The forward movement of the plane—something between seventy and eighty miles an hour perhaps—created a wind of hurricane force which tore at the clothes of the stuntman and swung and twisted the ladder quite unpredictably. It was impossible to wear either helmet or goggles because the wind tore them off the face. The hair was 'whipped and beaten until you can't even comb it for days after . . . during one picture eleven shirts were torn from my back in making wing tricks.'

Air-to-ground transfers

Locklear helped to pioneer the transfer from a plane to the roof of a train using a rope ladder. Certainly no less dangerous was the transfer performed by Reg Kavanagh when he hung from the undercarriage of a plane by his hands and dropped feet-first on to the roof of a car. At the time he was 'doing about eighty miles per hour'. The car roof was six feet below him. As he struck it with his feet he began to fall off. Fortunately it was the practice of motor manufacturers in those days—the thirties—to fit some of their models with a luggage rail that ran round the edge of the car roof. Kavanagh managed to cling to this and save himself from falling to the ground.

Hal Needham performed what we could regard as a transfer of sorts when he dropped from an aircraft on to a galloping horseman, a feat of spectacular 'bulldogging' which he regarded as his 'most dangerous stunt',[123] a view reflected in the fee of $1,500 that he was paid for it. The short film time that such stunts occupied and the way in which they were piled one on top of another in the early cinema is seen in *The Eagle's Talons* (1923), a film in which Al Wilson did the stunt flying. In the very first episode the heroine, played by Ann Little, dropped from the wing of an aircraft on to a moving car, climbed on to a second aircraft from the car, and finally did a mid-air transfer back to the first aircraft.[124]

The technique of undercranking the camera, as we have seen, allowed many stunts to be performed at slower speeds than those at which they finally appeared on the screen. This increased the safety factor for the stuntmen involved. Undercranking, for example, allowed a jump from a train apparently travelling at fifty miles an hour to be performed with the train *actually* doing no more than twenty-five or thirty. The danger of injury to the stunt-man in the event of a fall was therefore reduced. But a major problem of the aircraft stunt is that undercranking is of little help.

A train or a car can travel at any speed from stationary to top speed. This is not true of an aeroplane. An aeroplane flies only when its forward speed is such that the speed at which air flows over its flying surfaces gives it the necessary lift for it to become airborne, and it remains flying only as long as this minimum speed is maintained. If the forward speed drops below this critical point, the aeroplane falls out of the sky.

In some light aircraft—the German Fieseler Storch FI 156 of the Second World War is one of them—this critical speed may be as low as thirty miles an hour, but this is exceptional. The critical speed is more likely to be something approaching sixty miles an hour and since this speed leaves little in the way of a safety margin above the stalling speed, most stunts, which naturally require the pilot to stay in absolute control of the machine, must be performed well above this speed.

Cliff Bergere throws light on the speeds at which some of the early air transfers took place.[125] The ideal transfer takes place with both transfer and receiving vehicle travelling at the same speed so that both vehicles are stationary relative to one another. Bergere made an unsuccessful attempt to transfer from the end of a rope ladder attached to an aircraft, to a train travelling at twenty-five miles an hour. Only when Al Wilson, the pilot, had landed and persuaded the engine driver to raise the speed to fifty-five miles an hour—something much closer to the speed at which the aircraft had to fly—was Bergere able to perform the stunt. 'I got down on the ladder and no sooner found my feet on the bottom rung than I landed in a sitting position right on top of the train.'

The aircraft-to-train transfer has always been coloured by the death of Gene Edward Perkins at the age of twenty-four. Perkins was regarded at the time as one of the greatest stuntmen in or out of the cinema. Clarence Brown, who directed Valentino and Garbo and has been responsible for many splendid film action sequences, mentions Perkins's coolness and self-control, his sense of timing and body control. Grace, who knew Perkins well, calls him quite simply 'the greatest double in pictures'. His earnings at the time of his death were about $75 a week. There are many accounts of

Perkins's death, all of which differ in detail. The account given by Grace[126] is the most credible. Grace was involved personally in the stunt because he had been approached first to pilot the aircraft from which Perkins was to make his rope ladder descent. He was ultimately rejected in favour of an inexperienced pilot who was prepared to do the stunt for considerably less money than Grace required.

The stunt took place at Riverside, California. Two attempts were made and both were unsuccessful because of the incompetence of the pilot. Paul Malvern—another stuntman known to Grace—was on top of the train and Perkins was to drop on him and start a fist fight. In fact, Malvern's real job was to help Perkins land safely. Finally a third attempt was made, with Perkins no doubt rather tired after being buffeted on the end of a flying rope ladder for some time. He was on the bottom rung of the ladder, hanging by his hands. If the strength of his arms failed him he would be lost, because there was no way to safety except by pulling himself back up the ladder. He had no safety wire securing him to the ladder or the aircraft, although according to Grace this was quite usual at this period.

The third run ended in tragedy. Perkins, dangling from the rope ladder, swung into the side of the train and struck one of the coaches. Malvern stood on the train roof unable to do anything to help. As Perkins passed him, still managing to cling to the ladder, Malvern could see that he had been hurt. Grace thinks the ribs in one side of his chest had been broken. Whatever the damage was it was too severe for him to be able to climb back up the rope ladder and into the comparative security of the cockpit. He shook his head at Malvern and dropped to the ground. Malvern dropped off the moving train and went to Perkins. According to Malvern who reported the details of the disaster to Grace, all Perkins said to him was, 'I—I couldn't hold on any longer—Paul.' He died in hospital a day or two later.

The unfortunate pilot of Perkins's plane seems never to have been named publicly and has always carried a certain implied responsibility for Perkins's death. All commentators on the incident agree that he was inexperienced. Grace says that he only got the job because of the low fee he was prepared to charge. But in extenuation it must be said that the difficulties for the pilot in such a stunt are considerable. In a crosswind, such as apparently existed on this occasion, an aircraft does not fly in the direction in which it is pointing. The crosswind blows it off the line of its fore-and-aft axis. Its real movement over the ground is crabwise, dependent on its airspeed and the direction and speed of the crosswind. Not only must the pilot gauge exactly the height of his dangling colleague on the ladder above the roof of the train, but he must also compensate with absolute accuracy for the effects of the crosswind. Since the width of the train roof is no more than ten feet, he must in effect fly an absolutely accurate course for some considerable time that deviates less than five feet on either side of a given line of flight. This flight line will not necessarily coincide with the longitudinal axis of the train since the crosswind will prevent the stuntman from hanging directly under the aircraft. Even for a highly experienced pilot such precise flying demands perhaps more skill than any other manœuvre he is called upon to perform during the whole of his flying career.

Aerial rope-work

Dick Curwood died on the flying rope ladder, though under more mysterious circumstances. Curwood had broken his back on an earlier stunt and never fully recovered from the injury. On this occasion he was to do some rope ladder stunts and had Frank Tomick as his pilot. Tomick was a very experienced pilot and sensed that something had gone wrong with the stunt. When he checked the rope ladder there was no sign of Curwood. He had simply fallen off without being seen by anyone. 'Personally,' says Grace, 'I think his broken back gave way at a crucial moment.'

Grace considered all stunts of this kind to be 'major' and highly dangerous. The facts certainly support him. He talks with admiration of Bob Rose's 'cool and mathematical calculation of the situation' when he allowed himself to be dragged through the sea on the end of a flying rope ladder. Ladder stunting is extremely hard work, particularly when the stunt has to be performed a number of times. Both Perkins and Curwood were killed because for one reason or another their strength gave out.

But the rope ladder, in Grace's view, is at least preferable to the single rope. It is possible with the ladder to snatch an occasional rest. The feet can support some of the body-weight, or an arm can be pushed between the rungs so that some of the weight is taken by the shoulder. None of this is possible with the single rope. Once on it, the stuntman must hang on by his hands until the completion of the stunt, without any possibility of rest.

The helicopter

The helicopter is a comparatively recent innovation as a vehicle for cinema stunting and it has opened up further possibilities for aerial stunts. Its advantage over the aeroplane is that, like the train and the car, its forward speed can be reduced to a stationary hover. Its principal disadvantage from the stuntman's viewpoint is that of downdraught from the rotating blades. The windforce on two stuntmen fighting on the struts of a hovering helicopter, for example, is so great that half their energy needs to be used simply to hold themselves on the machine, even though they may in some circumstances be able to use safety harness wired inconspicuously to the aircraft. Apart from this downdraught, and therefore the added difficulty of take-off, the drop from a hovering helicopter into water poses no more problems for the stuntman than the high fall from any other fixed launching point.

The aircraft crash

But whatever new aerial innovations we have seen in the cinema recently, the most spectacular air stunt from the audience viewpoint remains the crash, and associated with it are such names as Dick Grace, Paul Mantz and Frank Tallman. Even as early as 1932 Grace had survived 'thirty-seven deliberate crashes for films'[127] but the three for which he is particularly remembered are the ones he performed for William Wellman's *Wings*. They are remembered, as Wellman himself says,[128] even by people who are too young ever to have seen the film, because *Wings* and Grace's flying stunts have passed as it were into folk memory.

Grace was to perform four major stunts on the film, but in fact was only able to complete three of them. His first stunt was the crashing of a Spad fighter in No-Man's-Land, an area already scarred by craters and barbed wire. For this he took certain precautions. He saw that the posts sticking up from the ground to support the barbed wire were made of balsa in the area in which he intended to crash. He also fitted a new and more substantial type of safety belt because he had found with the old lap belt that his head snapped viciously on impact. He seems, in fact, to have decided on a new technique altogether, since in some earlier crashes he had relied on being thrown clear of the cockpit on impact, removing goggles in case they shattered in his face, releasing his safety belt and drawing up his feet in case the engine was pushed back into the cockpit. He was apparently averse to padding round the cockpit rim because he felt it might get in the way of his team of rescue workers.

He calculated that his speed on impact in the Spad crash was ninety-five miles an hour. The aircraft tripped on its fixed undercarriage, turned over on its back and left him hanging upside down suspended from his safety harness. Like all flyers Grace had a dread of his aircraft catching fire as it hit the ground and finding himself trapped in a blazing cockpit. He had his own rescue squad standing by in case such a disaster should happen and he minimised the fire risk by reducing the amount of petrol carried in the tank. But as with all precautions taken by stuntmen, this last one brought its own particular problem. Once committed to the crash the stuntman had to go through with it since if he decided to abandon it on the first run, circle the area again and make a second approach, the possibility of engine failure through lack of fuel was very high. Such a failure would put him in no less dangerous a position than the crash itself.

The second *Wings* stunt performed by Grace was the crashing of a Gotha bomber into a building. This particular stunt presented no new problems for Grace. He had performed it before. On a previous occasion he had crashed an aircraft into a barn and evolved a technique for 'sighting' it so that the cockpit itself would receive minimal damage. For the barn crash he built a large window in the side of the building with glazing bars in the shape of a cross. This cross he used to guide the aircraft precisely on to the part of the target that would cause himself and the machine least damage.

This degree of precision, as we saw in the case of the aircraft rope ladder transfer to a train, requires absolute control by the pilot over the machine's movements. Very rarely do conditions exist in which the air is completely still, conditions in which the aircraft's movement over the ground is perfectly in line with its own longitudinal axis. Some compensation for sidewind is usually necessary. Again, the building itself will affect the direction and strength of the sidewind so that a moment before impact the machine might change course sufficiently to crash in such an unpredictable manner as to cause severe cockpit damage.

Grace survived the Gotha crash but was less fortunate with his third major stunt on the film. In this he was to crash a D7 Fokker, powered by a two-hundred horsepower Liberty engine, nose-first into the ground immediately after take-off. Stunting apart, this is perhaps the most dangerous situation in which any flyer can find himself. Engine failure on take-off, which produces in real life a situation for the pilot identical with that faced by Grace, usually results in a severe crash.

High altitude engine failure gives a pilot plenty of opportunity to select the best site for a forced-landing and to note wind direction. He can assess all the difficulties of his chosen landing area—the disposition of trees, for example, and irregularities in the ground—long before he makes his final approach to it, and take whatever action is necessary to avoid them. But engine failure on take-off gives him no leeway of any kind. If he has only just left the ground then his speed is only a little above stalling point.

He must drop the nose at once in order to maintain what little airspeed he has or his machine will fall out of the air like so much scrap metal. He has no room whatever for manoeuvre. He can simply go forward in a straight line, letting the aircraft settle back towards the ground and hoping that when it does so it will not run nose-on into a tree or the side of a house. The situation is similar to the one that Grace deliberately faced with the Fokker.

Of course, Grace was meticulous in his preparations. If he made sure that the wire posts in the Spad crash were made of balsa, then he certainly made sure before the Fokker crash that no obstacles lay in his path that would have added unnecessarily to the danger of the stunt. He had a minimum of petrol whereas in the real-life situation the tank is carrying its maximum. And yet there was an unavoidable problem that the real-life situation does not present to the pilot: he had to crash the aircraft exactly where the director wanted it crashed. He was not free, as would be the ordinary pilot caught in such a situation, to select his own moment and place for putting the aircraft down. We should remember too that with the real-life situation the pilot's sole aim is to land his aircraft with as little damage to himself and it as possible. Grace's aim was quite the opposite: he was being paid to cause maximum damage to the aircraft by deliberately crashing it in front of the cameras, and if possible surviving with minimum damage to himself.

On this occasion he failed. The reason, in Wellman's opinion,[129] was because instead of taking the aircraft right over on its back, he took it half over. The result was a severely injured neck. He was taken to hospital and his neck put in plaster. He was supposed to keep the cast on for a year, but six weeks later Wellman saw him dancing in San Antonio. He had become tired of the cast, smashed it with a hammer, and left the hospital by way of a window.

Dick Grace

Grace is important in the development of cinema stunting because he established patterns of air crashes on which much later aerial stunts have been based, and he has left in his autobiographical writings, perhaps the best documented account of the life of a major stunt actor that exists. We know, for example, something of the conditions under which he and other stuntmen in the early cinema worked. When he was injured making a picture for Famous Players Lasky, the company quite voluntarily paid him half his salary during the six months he was unable to work. His contract for *Wings* contained a clause specifically releasing the production company from any claims arising from his death during the performance of a stunt. He was, however, guaranteed hospital treatment and the payment of his funeral expenses. Additionally, his next of kin would be entitled to $5,000 under the workman's compensation law in the event of his death. The same law gave some financial help in the event of permanent disability.

Grace has been followed by many first-class aerial stunt actors. We remember the brilliant flying in *Those Magnificient Men In Their Flying Machines* and *The Battle of Britain* (1969), the near-suicidal stunt in *Twelve O'Clock High* (1949) in which Paul Mantz crash-landed a Flying Fortress single-handed for a fee of £2,000,[130] the spectacular crash of a single-seat fighter on to the deck of an aircraft carrier in *Wings of the Eagle* (1957), and the way Frank Tallman flew his aircraft through a bill board in *It's a Mad, Mad, Mad, Mad World*. But none of this later aerial stunting surpasses Grace's work. He has been matched but never overshadowed. His most dangerous stunt, in his own opinion, was crashing an aircraft into the sea in *The Lost Squadron* (1932), a largely autobiographical film for which he provided the story. The simplest and safest aircraft crash, again according to Grace, was that from a side-slip in which the wing tip strikes the ground first and the crumbling wing absorbs much of the impact.

William Wellman

Historically, *Wings* is a very important picture for another reason. Wellman was asked to direct it because he had been a pilot and had experienced aerial combat.

Work in the air

Wings established the fact that an action-orientated director is essential for the successful filming of action sequences. It seems, perhaps, self-evident, but it is a fact which is still not fully realised. Many potentially first-class action sequences, crucial to the development of a film, have had their effectiveness minimised or destroyed during the years that have passed since Wellman made *Wings*, by directors who simply did not understand the problems faced by stuntmen and fight coordinators. The introduction of the second-unit director was one answer to this problem but, as we shall see later, it is not the final one. Wellman was the ideal director for *Wings*. He had been a member of the Lafayette Flying Corps in the First World War and had seen action as a Spad pilot with the Chat-Noir escadrille based on Luneville in eastern France. He knew *as a practitioner* what problems a particular flying sequence posed for a pilot. On *Wings* he demonstrated his complete understanding of the stunt pilot's position. On one occasion, when he was dissatisfied with the work of a particular pilot, he took the aircraft up himself and crashed it.*

His understanding of the problems of action extended to crowd work on the ground. When some of the extras were afraid to lie on the ground for fear of being trodden on by others who were to retreat over the top of them, Wellman lay down with them. Even today, most stuntmen—and certainly those involved with television action—would regard the appointment of a director only half as action-orientated as Wellman, as little less than a godsend.

The mid-air explosion

The aircraft crash tends to be regarded as the most spectacular

* Wellman is not the only director to have involved himself directly in action. Josef von Sternberg, in his book *Fun In A Chinese Laundry*, mentions his involvement with Special Effects in the making of *Exquisite Sinner* (1926): 'When I had to, I had even taken a rifle out of the hands of a marksman who had refused to shoot an egg from under a hen because he insisted it could not be done at thirty paces without killing the bird, and without a second thought I had taken aim to have the surprised chicken rise from the splattered egg.'

and dangerous form of aerial stunt work, but other highly spectacular work has appeared on the screen and in terms of danger the mid-air explosion from which Dick Curwood miraculously escaped matches any aircraft crash that has ever been performed.

Curwood, who had only just recovered from severe spinal injuries, accepted an invitation to blow up an aircraft in mid-air for a fee of $3,500, by detonating explosives in the front cockpit and in the petrol tank. The stunt had been rigged so that after he had pressed the firing device a ten-second delay fuse would come into operation. This delay was sufficient to allow him to leave the aircraft and drop well clear of it before pulling his parachute ripcord. But the delay fuse failed and as he pressed the firing device the explosive charges fired instantaneously. The explosion caused temporary loss of consciousness. Fortunately he recovered in time to use the parachute.

Aerial stunting continues to be one of the most dangerous forms of action. Grace conceived the somewhat bizarre notion of a 'Squadron of Death', a squadron which all aerial stuntmen joined sooner or later. 'Of his [Grace's] twenty-two professional rivals,' said Phillips in 1932,[131] 'eighteen are dead and four will never fly again.'

7 Combat

Combat as entertainment

The idea of combat as a form of entertainment is, as we have seen, very old indeed. It existed in pre-Christian Egypt and Greece and reached its most spectacular form in the arenas of Rome. The Roman gladiator was a trained professional entertainer in exactly the same way as the modern circus aerialist is. The medieval joust, whatever its origination in the Christian concept of chivalry may have been, became a lavish spectacle of combat, at times only marginally less bloody than earlier gladiatorial contests. Even such modern equivalents of the original joust as those organised by the

Illustration: Manhunt (1970). Terry Walsh on trampoline take off.

British Jousting Association, although ostensibly designed 'to bring back the colour, pageantry and chivalry that was once "Olde England" ' have an element of high risk which is their principal audience appeal: 'It is unfortunate if injuries occur but these cannot always be avoided as this is one of the most dangerous of medieval sports and requires skill and courage not only from the rider but from the horse.'[132]

Sword spectacles given by professional Masters of Arms appeared as part of the entertainment at the itinerant fairs of medieval Europe, despite the fact that in England at least the teaching of fencing was illegal except under the most special circumstances. In Elizabethan England the Masters of Defence, organised at last into a legal gild, fought their 'prizes' before audiences of enthusiastic Londoners. The 'prize' was ostensibly an examination. Those who passed the examination by demonstrating their ability publicly with a wide range of weapons, were admitted to membership of the gild.

But the entertainment possibilities of such examinations were soon realised and the 'prizes'—usually fought outside the City limits because of the opposition of the City Fathers—were preceded by public notices and parades to the accompaniment of martial music. Ben Jonson gives an example of a Bill of Challenge issued by a Master on behalf of a student in one of his plays:[133]

Be it known to all that profess arms that we, A.B., Master of the Noble Science of Defence, do give leave and licence to our Provost, C.D., to play his Master's Prize against all Masters in their subtile mysterie at these weapons, vis: long sword, sword and buckler, Morris Pike, and rapier and dagger. These are to give notice that our said Provost will be present the . . . th day of the present month to perform and do his uttermost for the achievement and bearing away of the prize. God Save The Queen.

Such announcements 'were posted freely about the streets of

London and Westminster for the information of the world at large'.[134]

Occasionally the City Fathers relented, usually under pressure from such eminent figures as Ambrose, Earl of Warwick, who complained in 1582 that John David, a servant of his, had been prevented from playing his Provost's prize in the yard of the Bull Inn in Bishopsgate. Then prizes were fought inside the limits of the City of London, not only at the Bull, but also at the King's Head at Pye Corner and in the yard of the Belle Sauvage on Ludgate Hill. But more usually sites had to be found outside the City and beyond the jurisdiction of the City Fathers. Ely Place in Holborn and the Artillery Garden in Bishopsgate Without were popular meeting places for the 'prize fighters', but so were the 'Theatre' and the 'Curtain' in Holywell, and this is a good deal more significant from our point of view. The 'Theatre' and the 'Curtain' were more usually used by actors for the performance of plays and there seems little doubt that the drawing power of public combat of the kind mounted by the Masters of Defence did not go unnoticed by the men of the theatre.

Certainly the growth of prize fighting coincides with the introduction of combat sequences into the plays of the period. The plays of Shakespeare, for example, contain some of the most spectacular action scenes that have ever been seen in the theatre. *Hamlet* contains a rapier and dagger fight, the outcome of which is critical to the play's dramatic development. *Twelfth Night* has a comic fight that when it first appeared before its ebullient Elizabethan audience, must have had them in tears of laughter. *Macbeth* and *Julius Caesar* introduce whole armies to the stage. Combat, then, as a significant element in dramatic entertainment, has a long pre-cinema history.

Theatre combat

We do not know for certain how the early stage fights were conducted and what exactly the weapons that were used were like. But we can conclude for two reasons that they must have been spectacular and competent affairs. In the first place there is ample evidence that the actors and playwrights knew a good deal about the use of the contemporary Elizabethan weapons, rapier and broadsword. Richard Tarlton, whom we described earlier as perhaps the first stuntman to whom we can give a name, was not only one of the most distinguished of Elizabethan actors but also a Master of Defence. With such a qualification, he might well have been the first fight arranger, and in the case of the battle scenes which appear in many of the plays of the period he was probably the first fight coordinator, at least since the gory days of Imperial Rome.

In the second place it is inconceivable that the Elizabethan theatre men, who in so many ways had shown their ability as business men, would have allowed their performances to contain fight scenes unless they were convinced that such scenes would bear comparison with the actual fights mounted by the Masters of Defence in their prize-fighting. Again, the audience itself was specialised. Not only had it seen the prizes that were fought in the same buildings as those in which the plays themselves took place, but references in the plays—particularly in those of Ben Jonson, who himself faced the severe processes of law for having fought and killed a man with the sword—suggest that the published works of such fencing masters as Carança, Narvaez and Silver were widely read, and that references to them and to such English fighters as 'abbot Antony' and 'Blinkinsops the bold' were immediately appreciated by the audience.

The weapons used were almost certainly those of the period, 'production' weapons that had been blunted at the point and along the cutting edges of the blade. For a theatrical fight to be meaningful and exciting an audience must be prepared to believe that the weapons used are at least capable of inflicting the damage that the playwright has credited them with. In the fight in the last act of *Hamlet*, for example, in which Hamlet and Laertes fight and are killed, the rapiers that are used must be sufficiently realistic to convince an audience that they are capable of inflicting the deaths that are required of them. If an Elizabethan audience was accustomed to the daily sight of the rapier, as indeed it was, then it seems unlikely that anything but the real weapon would have appeared to it convincing when used in the theatre.

The fight arranger

It might well have been this need to use a real weapon of the period, blunted where possible but still retaining its essential lethal quality, that created the fight arranger as we still know him. A real weapon is dangerous, whatever attempts are made to minimise that danger. A real rapier or broadsword, however it is treated, will still put out an eye or break a wrist. It cannot be used with any degree of safety in the theatre unless the movements to be made with it are known to both participants in a fight and have been rehearsed by them until they have become second nature.

It is the function of the fight arranger to choreograph the fight in such a way that it contributes to the intention of dramatist and director. He must work out not only the overall floor pattern of the fight, bearing in mind the disposition of scenery and other actors, but also each individual move. The individual moves must be in keeping with the nature of the character who is fighting and within the capabilities of the actor playing the part. The fight arranger will train the actors in the use of a particular weapon where necessary, though in the case of the sword he will hope that the actors have had some experience in its use as part of their earlier training. Finally, with the general floor pattern established and the individual moves agreed, the fight arranger will be responsible for the adequate rehearsal of the fighters.

The relationship between a successful stage fight and a successful dance routine is very close. 'Although I specialise in arranging fight sequences with arms, most often swords, all I am, in effect, is a choreographer,' says William Hobbs, Fight Director for the National Theatre.[135] There is, however, one important difference between the stage fight and any other form of dance. If a performer forgets his moves in a *pas de deux* he will simply embarrass his partner and make himself look ridiculous, but if he forgets his moves in a stage fight he risks serious injury either to himself or his opponent.

Rehearsal of a stage fight is absolutely crucial, if the performance is to be effective and the dangers involved kept to a minimum. Even amongst professional stuntmen this fact is still not entirely accepted. Max Diamond, talking of the public performances mounted by the British Jousting Association, says[136] 'You have to play it by ear. Any stuntman will explain that you can work out a routine for two or three minutes . . . and then it's impossible to remember any more'. The result is predictable: 'Somebody is going to be injured. There's going to be some bodies flying about and some blood spilled.'

Film combat

Combat in the theatre has severe limitations. Some of these limitations arise from the need for actors to remember fight 'routines' in precise detail, routines which in the case of the Hamlet-Laertes sword fight, for example, last for several minutes and require not only high-class sword play but the preservation of character as well. Other limitations rise from the nature of the theatre itself. Shakespeare acknowledged these limitations of theatrical combat in the Prologue to *Henry V*—'Can this cockpit hold/The vasty fields of France? Or may we cram/Within this wooden O the very casques/That did affright the air at Agincourt?'

The cinema knows no such limitations. Only financial considerations place any restrictions on what it can show its audience. If the battle of Agincourt requires us to see 'the vasty fields of France', they can be provided. Even the weapons used in the battle do not present the problems that the theatre faces. In the theatre if a sword fight, for example, is to be credible to an audience, not only must the weapons *look* capable of creating the mayhem required of them but when they touch they must also *sound* like real weapons. If the audience has been asked to believe that they are made of steel, then when they touch one another they must have the ring of steel. If they sound like wood or plastic, then the whole illusion is destroyed. The cinema knows no such problem. Sound can be divorced from sight and dubbed on later during further processing of the film. The noise of a plastic battle axe striking a plastic shield can be made to sound like the most thunderous onslaught of metal on metal.

The spectacular possibilities of sword play in the cinema are beyond the wildest dreams of the most ambitious fight arranger in the theatre. The spectacular sword play that we associate with Flynn in the cinema, the sabre fighting in the various film versions of *Prisoner of Zenda*, the brilliant rapier play of Stewart Granger and Mel Ferrer in *Scaramouche*, the duel in the cathedral with hand-and-a-half swords that we saw in *El Cid* (1961), are all examples of sword combat which would be almost impossible in the theatre. One reason is the difficulty mentioned by Max Diamond of remembering a rehearsed 'routine' for more than a limited time, a difficulty which is considerably greater for an ordinary actor than for the specialised actor—the stuntman— whom Diamond had in mind.

A second reason is the complexity of the set against which many cinema sword fights take place. In *The Three Musketeers* (1949), for example, Gene Kelly brings to bear all his brilliance as a dancer and combines it with the required movements of the sword to carry out a fight sequence lasting a full five minutes—at that time the longest on record—that takes him up flights of steps and in and out of statues and fountains in such a way that the weapons of his opponents miss him by fractions of an inch. It is just possible that Kelly, with his dance training, could have performed a similar fight in the theatre, but it is doubtful whether any other actor could have done so. In some of the sword play in *Robin Hood* (1938) the fight moves from one set continuously into another, a technique which presents no special difficulties in the cinema but is quite impossible in the theatre.

The third, and perhaps most important reason for the far greater spectacle that we see in cinema sword play—and in combat generally—than we see in anything mounted in the theatre, is the fact that for much of a sequence the fighting can be carried out by an action specialist, a stuntman skilled in sword play and doubling for the principal. Doubling has been used as a theatre technique, but it is extraordinarily difficult to handle. In a theatre production of *Romeo and Juliet* for example, there is no way in which doubles can be substituted for the principals in the fight sequence between Mercutio, Tybalt and Romeo, and yet, according to Benvolio's account of it it must be fought with a high degree of skill:

> . . . he tilts
> With piercing steel at bold Mercutio's breast,
> Who all as hot, turns deadly point to point,
> And with a martial scorn, with one hand beats
> Cold death aside, and with the other sends
> It back to Tybalt, whose dexterity
> Retorts it . . .

In consequence the film fight has a quality of spectacle that the theatre cannot hope to match. The question of memorising a long sequence of complex movements presents no real problem to the cinema actor since the fight is broken into a series of very short scenes and given the necessary continuity at a later stage by the editor. In many cases the actor himself hardly needs to fight at all. The 'master' shot, in which the fight is fought in its entirety, is usually filmed with stuntmen doubling for the principals. Into this are inserted 'cut-ins' of the principals in close-up making at most two or three parries or a particularly significant thrust. Surprisingly perhaps, even Flynn talks of letting the stuntmen take over 'if there was swordplay'.[137] In his view, the function of the actor in sword play is not to be a brilliant fencer but to know 'how to make it look good'.

The real credit for the spectacular effect of most sword play in the cinema must go to the fight director and the stuntmen, as Flynn generously recognises: 'A good stuntman, if you know him, you can trust, and you will come out of your duel with him with your mouth still in front of your face, with teeth still in it, your ear still on the side of your head, and your nose where it was to begin with.'[138] This was not true, in Flynn's experience, when one fought with other actors. On one occasion he almost lost an eye and on another he was struck in the mouth with a sword point.

Flynn's view of sword play as something haphazard and dangerous is in contrast with that of a modern professional fight director like William Hobbs. 'Good movement,' says Hobbs, 'is the whole secret behind stage fighting.'[139] Training, planning, choreography and rehearsal are of the utmost importance to him and his views are shared by most modern fight directors.

Flynn gives one actor's view of sword play and we should not generalise too much from what he says. The impression of disorganisation bordering on chaos that he gives is, to say the least, an exaggeration since without detailed planning, training and rehearsal the kind of fights that we see in *Robin Hood*, for example, could never have been realised.

As long ago as 1920, according to Rudy Behlmer,[140] Henry J. Uyttenhove had been brought in to help with the sword play in Douglas Fairbanks's *The Mark of Zorro* (1920). Behlmer regards this as possibly the first time that an expert swordsman had been brought in to help with the fencing sequences of a film, because before that date screen sword play had been no more than 'knife sharpenings'. Again, we have here another example of the cinema's refusal to acknowledge the work of the theatre, for a fight arranger had become an established part of theatre fighting many years earlier. Laking,[141] for example, writing of the production of *Richard III* at the Globe Theatre in London in 1889, mentions 'Mr Egerton Castle's finely arranged fights'.

The Belgian fencing masters

Uyttenhove was a Belgain by birth, a product of Belgium's Military Institute of Physical Education and Fencing. When Fairbanks retained his services for *Zorro*, he had been fencing coach at the Los Angeles Athletic Club for fifteen years. Uyttenhove went on to advise on a number of pictures in the early twenties—*The Three Musketeers* (1920), *The Prisoner of Zenda*

(1922), *To Have and to Hold* (1922), *Robin Hood, Trifling Women* (1922), *Monte Cristo* (1922), *Rupert of Hentzau* (1923) and *Scaramouche* (1923). Not only did he help to establish the fight arranger as an essential figure in cinema sword-action scenes, but he was the first of a line of Belgian swordsmen who have dominated this aspect of films during most of Hollywood's life.

Fred Cavens, although born of French parents in 1887 was another product of the Belgian Military Institute. He was, in Behlmer's opinion, 'chiefly responsible for bringing style and technique to the duels in Hollywood films'. Fairbanks, impressed by the sword play in Max Linder's *The Three Must-Get-Theres* (1922)—a satirical comment on the Fairbanks tradition—for which Cavens had been responsible, engaged him to train actors, double for them where necessary, and arrange sword fights.

Cavens is largely unknown outside the small circle of specialists concerned with action. Yet he is perhaps more responsible for the style and visual effectiveness of screen sword play than any other single person. All sword play in the cinema had, in his view, to be larger than life. It had to be as large and obvious as possible— within the limits of 'correctness' and credibility—otherwise its pattern would not be comprehensible to an audience. It had, in short, to be the very opposite of competition fencing.

The point needs stressing in view of a widely held belief that not only will a top competition fencer make a first-rate film fencer but, reciprocally, a first-rate film fencer must necessarily be a top fencer in competition terms. The view, understandable though it is, is quite wrong. Indeed almost the opposite is true. Douglas Fairbanks, for example, was not a brilliant fencer. Nor was Flynn. Rathbone, although in Cavens's view 'better than the best fencer in the world'[142] for cinematic purposes, would not have made a competition fencer.

Cavens regarded the 'routine'—the planned series of moves that go to make up a film fight—as crucial. It should be logical in the way it developed, yet it should contain attacking and defensive moves that were as spectacular as they could be made. It should be above all 'a fight and not a fencing exhibition', and it should be rehearsed by the participants until it could be performed almost unconsciously.

Not only was it necessary for the fight to be effectively fought, but the whole cinematic treatment of it had to be effective. Behlmer[143] mentions the John Barrymore fight in *Don Juan* (1926) as an example of this, where camera angles, dramatic close-ups and imaginative editing all play significant parts in the final cinematic achievement. It is of interest to note that when the same actor fought ten years later in *Romeo and Juliet* (1936), he was called, 'a dangerous son-of-a-bitch with that sword'.[144]

Cavens not only arranged sword fights and trained and rehearsed the actors in them, he also doubled for the principals when necessary. So too did other action specialists. In *The Sea Hawk* (1940), for example, Flynn and Henry Daniell were doubled in Cavens's sword routines by Don Turner, Ned Davenport and Ralph Faulkner.

Faulkner in fact is particularly interesting in the development of this particular type of action in the cinema since, contrary to what we might expect in view of Cavens's comments, he had been a top competition fencer. In 1928 and again in 1932 he was American Olympic champion in sabre and épée play, and he coached not only actors for film purposes but also potential Olympic champions for competition work. Perhaps the work for which he will always be best remembered is the sabre fight between Douglas Fairbanks Junior and Ronald Colman in the 1937 remake by David O. Selznick of *The Prisoner of Zenda*. For this 'the actors were coached, routined, and, for many set-ups, doubled', by Faulkner.

Albert Cavens, who worked with his father for many years, carried on the tradition established by Fred after his death in 1962. The Belgian tradition was also continued through Jean Heremans who had followed Uyttenhove at the Los Angeles Athletic Club. He is perhaps best known for what are probably the two longest and most spectacular sword sequences on film, the acrobatic sequence from *The Three Musketeers* with Gene Kelly in the role of D'Artagnan, and the six-and-a-half-minute

fight between Mel Ferrer and Stewart Granger in *Scaramouche*—
'the longest, most elaborately mounted, and one of the finest,
duels ever seen on the screen.'[145]

There are, in Behlmer's view, seven stages in the mounting of a
film sword fight. As soon as the actors who will be engaged in the
fight have been cast, they embark on a course of instruction in
sword play under the fight arranger. The producer and director,
in the meantime, decide the general requirements of the fight
sequences, then discuss these in detail with the fight arranger. In
the light of this discussion, the fight arranger prepares a 'routine'—
a continuous plan of the sword play—which he submits to the
director for his approval. When the routine has been agreed, the
fight arranger rehearses it with the men who will be doubling for
the principal actors in certain sequences. When the routine is
polished, it is shown to the actors who are involved in the fight.
The actors learn the routine in 'phrases', a phrase being made up
of a number of single movements which Behlmer calls 'counts'.
Finally, the routine as fought by the actors receives the approval
of the director. 'After which, the duel routine is broken up into
master shots, close-ups, special angles, etc., and photographed
with either principals or doubles, depending upon the actors'
capabilities and the specific shot.[146]

Medieval combat

The sword, although the classic weapon of personal combat, is
by no means the only one to have appeared in cinema fights.
Indeed, it is possible that a greater variety of weapons has been
used for combat on the screen than has ever been used in real life.
Although the general approach to the mounting of such contests
remains the same whatever weapons are used—the establishment
of a general movement plan and the working out and rehearsal of
specific movements—each weapon has its own peculiarities which
make particular demands on the stuntman using it.

That alarming weapon the ball and chain, for example, has been
used in many medieval sequences, the best remembered of which

is perhaps the jousting sequence in *Ivanhoe*. It consisted in its original form of a short staff to which a spiked metal ball some two or three inches in diameter was attached by a length of chain.

In the cinema, of course, much of its lethal quality can be minimised by making it of plastic and dubbing the sound on later, but its ability to cause considerable damage cannot be entirely removed if it is still to behave in a credible way. Attempts to use a rubber ball, for example, have never been really successful. When a rubber ball strikes a shield or body armour it doesn't behave in the way a steel ball would and at once the illusion is broken. If the audience no longer believes that the weapon is what it is supposed to be, it no longer believes in the fight itself, and the whole intention of the spectacle is destroyed.

The technique of using such a weapon consists in keeping the chain under tension by moving the ball through a series of circles or arcs of circles. The centrifugal force acting on the ball during such movements keeps the chain straight and allows very heavy crushing blows to be struck. If a blow is attempted without the chain being in tension the ball will almost certainly strike the arm of the user. Against a shield the weapon presents no particular difficulties, assuming the movement has been properly rehearsed, since it is not difficult to construct a shield for film use which will withstand the force of a specially prepared ball and chain. But when the defence is conducted by another weapon the problem becomes more complex. In the *Ivanhoe* sequence the fight develops into one in which the ball and chain is opposed by the battle axe. The flexible nature of the chain prevents the kind of parry with the battleaxe that would be effective against a stiff weapon. As soon as the ball and chain is opposed in the conventional way the tension of the chain collapses and the ball wraps itself around the opposing weapon and possibly round the knuckles of the defender.

Other aspects of the medieval joust have their own particular problems. Nothing that the cinema can do technically can alto-gether remove the danger of two stuntmen galloping towards one another and coming to impact with wooden lances. Max Diamond has made this abundantly clear in his jousting displays on behalf of the British Jousting Association. In the Fairbanks *Robin Hood* the opening tournament sequence contains a joust between the Earl of Huntingdon (Douglas Fairbanks) and Sir Guy of Gisbourne (Paul Dickey) in which Sir Guy is lifted clear of his saddle by Huntingdon's lance, although he had previously taken the precaution of strapping himself into it. Even admitting that the straps did not really secure Gisbourne to his saddle and that camera angles and speeds were adjusted to produce the maximum spectacle with the minimum of danger, this remains a remarkable and highly risky stunt.

The quarterstaff

The quarterstaff has also been widely associated with medieval action scenes in the cinema. Perhaps the best remembered encounter is that between Flynn (Robin Hood) and Alan Hale (Little John) in the 1938 *Robin Hood*. Flynn and Hale find themselves at opposite ends of a tree trunk spanning a stream. Each denies the other's right to cross first and they meet in the middle of the trunk with quarterstaffs. The camera is obviously undercranked to give an impression of a faster fight than actually took place but the effect is none the less remarkable, particularly when one considers the highly insecure foothold that both men had.

This version of *Robin Hood* is in fact something of a standard work on stunting in the cinema, needing only aerial combat to complete it. It is a film that holds its position in cinema history almost entirely on the strength of its brilliant action sequences. Philip Jenkinson sums up the views of many people towards it:

> I have championed this classic movie for so long, my natural sense of reserve compels me to minimise the superlatives. If I therefore appease my enthusiastic feelings by simply stating that it is beyond question the best-photographed, best-designed, best-acted and best-directed adventure film for boys and girls of all ages ever to leave Hollywood, then I don't feel I have betrayed my instinctive need for restraint.[147]

Combat

This sequence is in fact a good deal more important in the development of stunting than it must appear to audiences viewing it, because the quarterstaff is really the prototype of very many weapons which range from the early medieval period to the present day. Close combat with the short pike, the two-handed sword, the glaive and the halberd owe a great deal to play with the quarterstaff. The use of the point and the butt-stroke in modern bayonet fighting can be traced directly back to quarterstaff combat and the very ingenious spear fight in *The Hidden Fortress* (1958) owes a good deal to quarterstaff play. Even Samurai sword play such as was seen in the spectacular fight sequences in *Rashomon* (1951) and *The Seven Samurai* (1954) uses moves similar to those in play with the quarterstaff. The ability of a stuntman to use a quarterstaff without having his knuckles crushed at every blow, opens up to him a whole range of weapons which appear constantly in film combat.

Knife-fighting

Combat with the bow and arrow and the spear is really more the responsibility of the special effects team and the specialist archer than of the stuntman. So are effects like the throwing of axes and knives at particular targets. But combat with the knife is certainly handled by the stuntman and requires a great deal of care in the planning and accuracy of movement in the execution.

Knives are usually of some stiff plastic material, replaced by authentic weapons of steel for close-up shots. The rubber knife is satisfactory unless it actually comes in contact with some object and bends. Knives with retractable blades are generally thought to be too dangerous for fighting purposes and certainly for actually stabbing. A stuntman using such a knife expects it to work. He expects that when the blade touches its target it will automatically be pushed up into the handle against the gentle pressure of a spring. Naturally he delivers the blow with a good deal more force than he would in the case of a fixed-blade knife. If in fact the blade retracts as the designer and manufacturer intended it to, the blow can be both effective and harmless. If, however, the retraction mechanism fails, then the blow is likely to be lethal.

Knife-fighting is highly mobile and tends to move in a circular pattern as each fighter tries to gain the 'blind' side of his opponent. In the case of right-handed fighters, this general circular movement is usually clockwise, each combatant moving towards his left. The left hand is held forward to seize the opponent's knife hand or parry a cut or thrust when it is delivered. More effectively, the left hand can be protected by material of some sort—a jacket or a cloak perhaps—and its defensive possibilities in that case are very considerably enhanced. Knife-fighting in its modern form is probably best known through James Bowie who evolved a general purpose heavy knife in the early years of the nineteenth century and has appeared as a semi-fictional character in a large number of films. One of his more memorable appearances was in *The Alamo* when, in the guise of Richard Widmark, he created more mayhem with the famous knife than one would have thought possible with half a dozen Gatlings.

The dagger, as an early form of knife, we associate particularly with period films. A good example of its use occurs in the Flynn *Robin Hood* when Much the Miller drops from a tree on to a Norman horseman, pulls him out of the saddle and finally dispatches him with the dagger.

Unorthodox weapons

There remains a range of weapons that demand more skill from the props, make-up and special effects departments than from stuntmen. A bicycle-chain, for example, can be made of light plastic so that it can actually be used in a fracas without causing damage to anyone struck by it. Bricks and stones are usually of felt so that they can be seen to strike an actor without causing him real injury. Bottles are of 'sugar glass' and furniture of balsa wood, scored so that it will break immediately on impact. A blow over the head with a real chair would lay any man unconscious, but the balsa wood chair disintegrates. The stuntman—or actor—

struck by it is perhaps bruised, but not seriously damaged. Only the use of balsa wood furniture allows the performance of that semi-comic stunt that we have seen on so many occasions in the Western or the 'back-woods' film in which a giant of a man is struck full across the head with a chair or table. The piece of furniture disintegrates about his shoulders, he shakes his head and after the briefest of pauses continues his bear-like advance upon his adversary.

The short whip, with its felt lash, and the cosh which is to strike a real blow, are again more dependent for their safe use upon the work of the property men who make them than upon the actors who wield them. An effective cosh, for example, which can be used safely with a considerable amount of force upon the more bony areas of the skull, can be produced from a length of cardboard roll covered down its length and over its ends with electrician's tape. In addition to its visual effectiveness it produces a sound which is acceptable to an audience as that produced by a real cosh. A more sophisticated cosh would be of hollow moulded plastic painted to produce whatever visual effect was required.

The slash with the knife, sword or razor requires first-class timing on the part of the actors together with a high degree of competence on the part of the make-up team, since the effect obviously has to be faked and falls therefore outside the real terms of reference of the stuntman. The actor receiving the blow has the wound it is to produce created on him by the make-up staff, before the scene is shot. During the shooting he masks the wound from the camera by his body position. As he is apparently struck by the cutting weapon he turns into camera and reveals the wound as if its cause were in fact the blow from the weapon. A particularly effective example of this appeared in Peter Watkins's *Culloden* (1964).

The punch-up

If anything gives the lie to the popular view of the stuntman it is close combat. The image of a man with close-set eyes, narrow forehead and ears bloated with clotted blood from innumerable heavy blows—an image suggesting an intelligence capable of little more than dumb obedience to authoritarian direction—is not one that we can reconcile easily with that physical dexterity and precision timing that close combat before the camera requires. Yet it is an image that even Flynn perpetuates in his autobiography. During the making of *Gentleman Jim* (1942) Flynn went through a sequence with Jack Loper, who had at one time been a sufficiently good boxer to have fought Joe Louis. Loper agreed a routine with Flynn, but promptly forgot it when the rehearsal started and hit Flynn on the chin. According to Flynn he was unconscious for two hours. Further rehearsals produced no better results. Flynn threatened to hit Loper with a champagne bottle and he became so docile as to be useless. To revive his 'fighting spirit', Flynn struck him in the testicles and was promptly knocked unconscious once more.

Loper, of course, was a boxer not a stuntman. A stuntman is an actor with a special skill. As such, he understands the requirements of the situation Flynn describes whereas a boxer does not. According to Keaton, Sennett had taken this view years earlier. This was why his Keystone team was a team of actors rather than trained acrobats. The trained acrobat can execute magnificent acrobatics but he cannot immerse himself in a character, and this immersion is essential to the kind of comedy Sennett was filming.

It is of course in the comic unarmed combat sequence of which Keaton was a master that we see the real conflict between the popular image of the stuntman and the fact. Such combat makes the greatest demands on the stuntman as an actor. It requires absolute precision of movement, split-second timing if injury is to be avoided, and an ability to portray character in a convincing way. It requires, too, an understanding of the nature of film, of what the camera can and cannot do.

If we were to give credit to one man for developing the punch-up into a totally credible form of film action, that man would be John Wayne. In fairness, of course, we cannot do this. A number of actors and stuntmen before and after Wayne struggled to evolve forms of unarmed combat that would be increasingly credible to film audiences. But Wayne is something of a watershed in this development. He had been a stuntman in his early cinema days and he had brought a considerable intelligence to the problems of screen action. He had, for example, invented a device for giving a naturalistic movement to reins 'when you're pulling them for a camera but there's no horse there'.

In the days of the silent cinema two problems militated against the success of unarmed combat scenes. In the first place, they communicated exclusively in visual terms. The sound of a punch striking could not be heard, nor could the grunts and growls of the combatants. In the second place the way in which camera angles could be used to 'fake' a punch was not understood. When two men were required to punch one another that was exactly what they did. Of course they pulled their punches as much as they could within the limits of credibility, and they aimed punches at shoulders, chests and arms rather than at heads. For much of the time they simply mauled one another.

The introduction of sound answered the first problem. Wayne and his friend and collaborator Yakima Canutt answered the second. They realised that by placing the camera in a particular position and moving in a particular way it was possible to give the impression of a tremendous punch at the head while in fact missing by inches. Later actors who have stood up to Wayne in film bar rooms must have been grateful to him for the technique that he and Canutt evolved, since, according to Ralph Volkie—Wayne's trainer and the trainer of five champion boxers—'Duke's got the hardest right hand punch of any man I've ever seen, including Dempsey.'[148]

This kind of unarmed combat requires good acting ability together with an understanding of the nature of film. The punch itself is adjusted to meet the requirements of the medium. It is not the punch of the boxer or the punch of the real brawl. 'A film fight is the opposite of a real fight,' says Wayne, 'because the camera has to see everything. You have to reach way back and sock out and make a big show. In a real fight you hit short and close. You don't get *time* to pull your punches back so far.'

Stunting in the cinema

It is Wayne, too, who stresses the vital importance of 'reaction' in action scenes. The recipient of the punch is almost more important than the deliverer, since it is his reaction to the blow that tells the audience how powerful and effective it has been. 'The difference between good acting and bad acting is the difference between acting and reacting,' says Wayne. Good acting is the ability of actors to '*react* in a logical natural way to the situations they're in'. Such statements might conceivably have been taken from Stanislavski or Boleslavski. They are cornerstones of acting theory. In their particular context they are of the greatest importance since they identify the stuntman with the rest of the acting community. 'I've many times heard it said that John Wayne doesn't *act*, he just plays himself in film after film,' says Tomkies. 'Anyone naive enough to believe any actor could stay at the very peak of such a ruthless profession and become the biggest box office draw the world has ever known—or conceivably ever will know—merely by being himself, needs his brains examining.'

Wayne's theory and practice of unarmed combat are now generally accepted. Fights are shot from a number of different camera set-ups, the set-up being changed as soon as the fight ceases to be visually interesting. Each set-up in a properly directed fight, records at most three or four punches. Punches at the head can miss by almost six inches depending on the angle from which they are shot. Only punches at the stomach, which are usually shot in profile, need to establish contact between fist and body. Such punches are of course 'pulled' and in any case a fit man can take such a punch without suffering any real damage. Blows with other parts of the body—kicks, for example—are delivered in accordance with the same principles. A kick to the crutch, such as we saw delivered by Paul Newman in *Butch Cassidy and the Sundance Kid*, must of course be faked by camera angle, body positions and the reaction of the recipient.

Mass combat

A great deal of combat that has appeared on the screen has involved masses of participants rather than a single pair. *Intolerance* is an early example of such mass combat. Of the battle scenes in *Napoleon* (1927) the director, Abel Gance, said, 'I had so many extras at Nice that I couldn't fit them all into one frame!' Mass combat occurred too in *Wings*, *All Quiet On The Western Front* (1930) and the various versions of *Robin Hood* and *Ben-Hur*. We remember the bar room brawls in *Dodge City*, *Destry Rides Again*, *Shane* (1952) and a dozen other memorable pictures.

Such scenes required more than a couple of experienced stunt-men. Many required hundreds. They created the Stunt Co-ordinator to plan and interlock the various individual actions. They created the second unit director with his experience in directing action sequences. They threw greater demands on the property department than it had known before and they brought into prominence the Special Effects Man. These people are an essential part of the modern film action sequence and we will need to look at their particular contribution to that sequence in more detail later.

8 The team approach to action

The need for a team approach

Like any other actor, the stuntman is dependent for the success of his work on the support of many other people. He is part of a team whose corporate effort alone can produce the kind of spectacle we associate with the cinema. It is not a new problem for the actor. In the theatre the actor cannot act and at the same time operate the lighting switchboard. Nor can he play his own part and that of other characters on the stage at one and the same time. For such essential support he is dependent on other people. The stuntman is in the same position. He can build his rig and secure his padding,

Illustration: Khartoum (1967). Mass horse fall staged by Joe Canutt.

but he cannot both jump and operate the camera that will record his jump.

The growth of this dependence has produced in the cinema a range of specialists each with his own particular contribution to make to spectacle and action. When we look back over the development of film action, it is not difficult to see how this has come about and what the factors were that created such men as the Action Coordinator, the Second Unit Director and the Special Effects Man. When we remember such exciting spectacles as the mass action scenes in *Intolerance* and *Ben-Hur* (1926), the banqueting brawl and the mass broadsword fighting in *Robin Hood* (1938), we can see that the individual stuntman cannot act in isolation. He needs some outside authority to direct the pattern of his work within the much more complex shape of the overall scene.

The fist and furniture mêlée that smashed up the 'Gay Lady' saloon in *Dodge City* involved 105 extras, according to George May,[149] including such top stuntmen as Cliff Lyons, Duke Green and Harvey Parry. Pay to some of the stuntmen was as high as $850 for one day's work in the scene. No film company, however prosperous, can afford to pay such money to individuals involved in mass action scenes without making sure that as much of their work as possible is made use of in the final version of the film. And this can only be guaranteed if the action is planned in detail beforehand, properly coordinated on the set, directed by a man with a special understanding of action, and backed by men who can devise furniture and properties that will do what is required of them.

Arranging and coordinating action

The idea of appointing a man to arrange and coordinate action is not new. Grant[150] makes reference to Narcissus as the man responsible for coordinating one of the water displays mounted by the Roman Emperor Claudius in which gladiators fought one another on pontoons, and in the theatre the idea of a 'fight director'—a man who would design the fights and train and rehearse the actors in them—can be traced back for at least a hundred years.

But in the cinema, as we have seen, many established theatre traditions were either unknown or unacceptable, and the arranger of fights in the theatre seems never to have had any influence in the cinema until comparatively recent times. Nowadays we have a top theatre fight arranger like William Hobbs arranging the fights in Polanski's *Macbeth* (1971), but earlier references to mass action in the cinema suggest a very haphazard state of affairs. According to Henabery,[151] the extras on the walls of Babylon in *Intolerance* were armed with spears, bows and arrows and 'magnesium bombs'. They fired at the attacking Persian army below them apparently indiscriminately. They seemed to find particular satisfaction in hitting a 'dead' Persian lying on the ground and making him get to his feet and run away. It is surprising that Henabery mentions only one extra visiting the first-aid tent because 'an arrow had pierced the side of his head and come out on top of his scalp'.

Yet even at this stage of the cinema's development there was at least the realisation that effective action required something more than the casual arming of masses of extras and letting them pitch missiles at one another, for it was on *Intolerance* that Leo Noomis was asked to instruct and organise the team of high-divers employed to fall off the walls of Babylon into nets. Such instructing and organising is the function of the man we would now call a fight arranger or fight coordinator, though, as Hobbs himself says, there is more to it than that: 'You can't get away nowadays with all that Hollywood stuff, Errol Flynn and Rathbone; people would just laugh if you put it on stage. It's repetitive. I think the actors had a much easier time then. Now every single movement is planned to make an effect. You're like a choreographer, making pictures. That part of the play's yours.'[152]

It was, of course, some time in the history of the cinema before the fight coordinator could really regard any part of the final film as 'his'. Indeed, the relationship between the man responsible for choreographing the fight sequences in a film and the film's director is still one which cannot be clearly defined. It is a flexible relationship, very much dependent on the degree to which the director is 'action-orientated'. Hobbs throws light on the relationship between himself as fight arranger and Roman Polanski as director on *Macbeth*. 'When he [Polanski] tried to tell me how I should deliver a blow, that got my goat a bit, having him poking a sword in my eye,' he says. And again: 'Where the director took over and where I stopped was a very moot point, something the audience will never know. In fact, where I did the fights and the combatants are covered in blood and gore, that's Polanski, it's not me.'[153]

We cannot trace any clear line of development from the early haphazard days of cinema action to the modern days of men like Hobbs. At one time or another almost everyone has had a hand in action sequences. Men like Keaton arranged and coordinated all their own stuntwork. Actors like Flynn suggested fight 'routines' to their stunt doubles. In the case of William Wellman, we have a director who not only was able to conceive and coordinate stunts, but when necessary could do them himself.

Nevertheless, there are early references to men whose function it was to coordinate the movements of large numbers of extras in mass action scenes, and these men do fulfil at least one of the essential functions of the modern action coordinator. Allan Dwan[154] makes reference to such men in the handling of the crowds of extras used in the 1922 version of *Robin Hood* which he directed. These crowds were divided into small groups and each group was given a leader. These leaders became Dwan's assistants and were directly responsible to him. Such a delegation of authority, without which the scenes could not have been managed at all, was helped considerably by the fact that all the men with whom Dwan was working had had military training during the recently concluded World War. Such training, in Dwan's view, produced men who could work together under a coordinator, and such an ability is essential if mass action sequences are to be handled successfully.

Dwan refers to his coordinators as 'assistants'. William Wyler was also given the title of assistant director for carrying out the same function under Fred Niblo on the 1926 *Ben-Hur*. He was one of thirty other assistants that Niblo had about him for the crowd scenes. He was given a costume and directed the group of which he was a part by means of prearranged visual signals.

To some extent Wyler's statement supports Chaplin's view of the way in which scenes of mass action are managed. The big spectacular was never a cinema form that appealed to Chaplin. In his view, the only thing needed to mount it successfully was money. 'With the glorification of glue and canvas,' he says,[155] 'one can float the langorous Cleopatra down the Nile, march 20,000 extras into the Dead Sea, or blow down the walls of Jericho; all of which is nothing but the virtuosity of building contractors. And while the field marshal sits in his directorial chair with script and table chart, his drill sergeants sweat and grunt over the landscape, bawling out orders to the divisions; one whistle meaning "10,000 from the left", two whistles "10,000 from the right", and three, "All on and go to it".' Nevertheless, if scenes of spectacle and crowd movement were to be presented on the screen they had to be organised. They had to be planned and coordinated by someone, whether he be given the name of assistant director, like Wyler, or referred to dismissively by Chaplin as a drill sergeant.

Indeed, the name of this planner and coordinator is still not generally agreed. In the credits on *The Heroes of Telemark* (1965), Gerry Crampton appears as Stunt Adviser. Tex Fuller is referred to[156] as Stunt Arranger on *No Blade of Grass*. Theodore Taylor mentions the use of a 'Stunt Coordinator' to choreograph large action scenes.[157] Brownlow[158] refers to Al Raboch as 'handling the crowds' during the burning trireme scene in the 1926 *Ben-Hur*, Mickey Wood is credited with having 'arranged the fights' in *Simba* (1955), *Brighton Rock* (1947) and *High Treason* (1951),[159] and William Hobbs is still called 'the best fight arranger in the theatre'.[160] Such men fulfil a vital function in action sequences, whatever title they are known by. They bring a specialist knowledge to bear on the planning of action scenes, on the training of the participants in them, and on their coordination before the camera. They are choreographers working in a special field of movement, and 'Fight Coordinator' or 'Action Coordinator' might be more accurate titles for them than those they are more generally given.

In such bar room brawls as those we saw, for example, in *Shane* and *Destry Rides Again*, or for the tremendous punch-up on board ship that appears in *The Roaring Twenties*, the work of the fight coordinator is crucial. He must design a fight that is in keeping with the characters involved in it: 'We always remember to keep the character of the person involved in any stunt in mind,' says Bob Simmons.[161] 'Bond, for example, always punches straight—in the British style. An American roundhouse punch would look more impressive but would be completely out of character for him.' He must, of course, design a fight that is in keeping with the director's view of the entire film and of the place of action within it. He must operate within the physical framework that he is given. If the scene is a Western bar room with a central staircase and a fixed iron stove placed centrally, then he must accept these physical limitations and perhaps even try to capitalise them. He cannot ask for them to be removed because they restrict the action he has in mind.

Within the physical shape he is given for his brawl he will block out the various areas in which specific aspects of it are to take place—a leap from the balcony on to a deputy sheriff, the pitching of the town drunk over the bar on to a prepared box-rig masked by the bar itself, the bringing down of the villain by breaking a prepared balsa-wood chair across his head. The action which is to take place within each area must be worked out in detail and rehearsed with the stuntmen or extras who are to carry it out.

From the fight coordinator's point of view, the need to have a director and a cameraman who understand his work is crucial, for it means nothing for him to produce a highly spectacular piece of action in the studio unless it can be translated into film terms. Such a translation depends on the degree to which other members of the team are aware of the problems posed by action sequences, and their ability to overcome them.

The second unit director

Awareness of this need to translate action into effective film terms has of course been recognised since the early days of the cinema. Some directors—B. Reeves Eason was one of them—learnt their trade on early low-budget pictures which were crammed with action sequences. When it became obvious that some small unit, largely independent of the main film unit working on a picture, could best handle the action scenes, it was only reasonable that directors like Eason should be approached to run such units. They had cut their teeth on action, very frequently in the old silent serials, and they knew how to film it so as to extract its maximum effect.

This Second Unit arose more out of an economic need than an artistic one. It was expensive to have a star waiting for action sequences to be filmed in which his part was taken by a double. It was expensive, too, to have a top director employed in shooting action instead of concentrating exclusively on what were considered more important scenes. A Second Unit solved these economic problems.

Despite the fact that in the past the Second Unit director has rarely been given a credit for his work, the scenes he created are frequently the ones that we remember most clearly in retrospect. The chariot race and the naval battle in the 1926 *Ben-Hur*—the work of B. Reeves Eason—are still the most talked-of scenes in that picture. The same is true of the chariot race in the *Ben-Hur* of 1959, directed by Yakima Canutt. The massive Indian battle scenes in *The Plainsman* which were directed by Arthur Rosson, are perhaps more immediately remembered than any other part of that picture. The same is true of James Basevi's earthquake sequences in *San Francisco* (1936) and Canutt's jousting scenes in *Ivanhoe*. Yet to the vast majority of filmgoers the Second Unit director is nameless and his task not even vaguely comprehended. His 'forte is action' and action, although it has produced some of the most memorable moments in the cinema for us, is not regarded as really significant.

Many Second Unit directors, as one would expect, have

graduated from the ranks of stuntmen. Canutt and Arthur Rosson are examples. So is Richard Talmadge who in the twenties 'modelled' for Fairbanks on such films as *Robin Hood*, but who is now better known for his Second Unit direction in *The Real Glory* (1939), *Garden of Evil* (1954) and *The Egyptian* (1954). A more recent example is Cliff Lyons—'one of the finest stunt riders' and probably the last man to take a horse off a cliff in front of the cameras—who directed the action in *The Comancheros* (1961), *The Conqueror* (1956) and of course *The Alamo*. According to Amaral[162] *The Alamo* contains a stunting record established by Lyons for 'staging the fall of the largest number of horses (12) in a single scene'. But stunting is not the only area from which Second Unit directors—or Action Directors as they are sometimes known—have come. Fred Guiol, who did the Second Unit work on *A Place in the Sun* (1951) and *Shane*, had at one time been a property man with Harold Lloyd. And Eason's background was highly individual.

B. Reeves Eason

Eason, who died in 1956 at the age of sixty-five, was born in Fryors Point, Mississippi, and worked with Thomas Rickett's American Film Company in Santa Barbara as 'writer, actor, stuntman, property man'. He had experience in directing low-budget, all-action Westerns and he worked during the early days of sound with Nat Levine's Mascot Pictures directing serials. His work here brought him into contact with some of the great stuntmen of the period. On the twelve-episode *Vanishing Legion* (1931), for example, the cast contained both Joe Bonomo and Yakima Canutt. On *Mystery Mountain* (1934) he and Otto Brower are given direction credits and Eason is also given a credit for his work on the original story. He directed the *Law of the Wild* (1934) serial with Armand Schaefer and wrote the screenplay for it with Sherman Lowe. He was in many ways an all-round man of the cinema, yet he remains a shadowy figure emerging from time to time with some new action achievement of near genius. The 1926 *Ben-Hur* chariot race is his; so is the *Cimarron* (1931) land rush sequence and the charge in *The Charge of the Light Brigade*. He did the jousting work in the 1938 *Robin Hood*, the burning of Atlanta scenes in *Gone With The Wind* (1939), the battle scenes in *Sergeant York* (1941) and the stallion fight in *Duel in the Sun* (1947). Faced with such a list, no one can question Goodman's statement: 'The second-unit director is a creative moviemaker in his own right.'[163]

Yet the credits given to this remarkable man are niggardly in the extreme: 'Directorial Associate' on *Ben-Hur*, 'Director of Horse Action' on *The Charge of the Light Brigade*, 'Joust Scenes Director' on *Robin Hood*. There is little wonder that, like most of his present-day counterparts, he is unknown to the millions who have been almost lifted out of their seats by the spectacles that he has brought to the screen. (It is possible in fact that the first full credit to an action director did not appear until 1936 in connection with *Under Two Flags*, when the words 'Battle Sequences directed by Otto Brower' were shown on the screen.)

Eason operated almost as an independent force within the larger framework of the particular film he was employed for. He had his own budget and his own crew. He virtually wrote his own script, based perhaps on the flimsiest of action suggestions in the screenplay. According to Goodman, the wrecking of the train in *Duel in the Sun* covered one page in the screenplay. Eason expanded it to a shooting script of fifteen pages.

Armed with such a script he could begin shooting. He shot the complete action in long-shot first. This provided a permanent record of the whole shape and continuity of the sequence. Then from a series of different camera set-ups he would film close-ups—a fist, a face, the nostrils of a horse, the terrified reaction of a single member of a crowd, a spinning chariot wheel.

Eason understood the problem faced by stuntmen in brawl scenes. He picked camera angles that would allow a punch to miss in reality, yet look as if it had landed square on a jaw. He was keen on low-angle and high-angle shots of action, which he could intercut with other shots to create his 'action tempo'. And nothing was too much trouble for him, if it gave him the result he was after. In both *The Charge of the Light Brigade* and *Sergeant York* he dug long trenches across the field of action and ran a truck on rails along them. From cameras mounted on the truck he could get shots from low and high angle levels and from eye level.

Eason's own views on directing action explain his methods and what he was trying to achieve. 'You can have a small army of people charging across the screen, and it won't matter much to the audience. But if you show details of the action, like guns going off, individual men fighting or a fist hitting someone in the eye, then you will have more feeling of action than if all the extras in Hollywood are running about. That is why real catastrophes often look tame in newsreels. You need detail work and close shots in a movie. Only then does it come to life.'[164]

Special effects

As with any other form of corporate artistic creation, it is impossible to compartmentalise the work of any one member of the team. Its frontiers are not clear-cut. The work of the individual stuntman overlaps the work of the fight coordinator. Similarly the work of the Second Unit director can involve fight coordination, and in the case of Eason frequently did. William Wellman was an action team in himself. Not only did he direct *Wings* and take part in the crashing of aircraft, but he combined the jobs of action director, action coordinator and special effects man, personally detonating the explosions in the big battle scene.

Today it is difficult to imagine a director engaging himself so fully, not because directors have changed but because the whole process of Special Effects has become so much more complex. Pat Moore, of P. Moore & Co., is a typical Special Effects man. He has a background of training in chemistry and worked at one time for a chemical firm. Such a background is useful to him since a good deal of Special Effects work requires some ability to think chemically. In fact, as Moore himself says, 'Special Effects isn't a training, it's a way of thinking.'[165] 'You don't need to be a specialist in the field of space engineering, or electronics or chemistry,' says Moore, 'but the Special Effects man must have some general knowledge of all these subjects—and of course a good many others.'

The job of the Special Effects man is almost impossible to define, since its range if so wide and is extended with each film he makes, because each new film poses new problems. On one occasion he may be required to show a tombstone being split by a thunderbolt, on the next he may have to show the streets of San Francisco being split by an earthquake. He needs an understanding of materials and what can be done with them, and he must keep informed about the new materials which are being produced all the time. He needs a thorough understanding of film—of what it can and cannot do as a medium. Above all he needs to understand the problems of stuntmen since these are the actors with whom he usually works most closely.

The relationship between stuntman and Special Effects man is very much the same as that which existed between earlier performers and the property men who backed them up—between Harold Lloyd and Fred Guiol, Keaton and Fred Gabourie, Houdini and Jim Collins. It is a relationship of complete confidence in one another's ability.

Toffee glass

One area in which we see how this cooperation has been built up is in the use of glass in stunts. It does seem that when we saw glass being used in connection with stunts in the early days of the cinema, the material was indeed glass. In 1929, Cartwright mentions how Emil Jannings cut his hand badly during the making of *The Street of Sin* (1928) when he pushed it through a real glass window.[166] This was no accident apparently. Jannings had rehearsed the action with celluloid and only transferred to glass for the actual 'take'.* One can only presume that at the time no satisfactory

*In connection with this we should perhaps bear in mind the comments made on Jannings in Josef von Sternberg's book, *Fun In A Chinese Laundry*: 'To direct a child is one thing,' says von Sternberg, 'but when the youngster weighs close to three hundred pounds it is not easy to laugh at all his pranks.'

substitute had been found for glass. Kavanagh,[167] too, refers to a stunt he was involved in in which a splinter of glass hit his fore-head and Grace's surprised comment that 'I did not get a cut!' on the stunt in which he dropped thirty feet from a swinging cable through a glass roof, indicates that the glass to which he is referring is indeed real enough.[168]

This was one of the many problems in the cinema's early life that affected not only stuntmen but the technicians who worked so closely with them. In fact, like so many stunting problems, it was a dual one: how could the glass be made safe for the stuntman, and how, therefore, could glass stunts be made more spectacular? Again, like so many answers to stunt problems, we shall probably never know who the technician was who first hit on the idea of using 'sugar' glass or 'toffee' glass. Cinema spectacle is as indebted to him as it is to the man who first used cardboard boxes as the basis of a falling rig, because his discovery opened up a new dimension in stunting. Without the discovery, the spectacular scene in *The Glass Key* in which we see Alan Ladd's stunt double dropping through a glass roof and on to a coffee table beneath, would have been impossible. So too would the scenes with horses—in *Pinto Ben* (1924) and *Jesse James*, for example—in which we see horses and riders going through enormous windows amidst what appears to be a shower of broken glass. 'For *Pinto Ben*,' says Amaral,[169] 'Fritz and Hart (William S.) galloped across a bar room and jumped through a large window. The glass was actually clear candy.'

This 'candy' was in fact manufactured for the Special Effects man by confectionery firms. In front of the camera it looked like glass. It could be set into a balsa wood frame and turned into the window of a shop or a barroom. When it was struck it shattered in very much the same way as glass. Moore can remember the days only a year or two ago when it was usual for extras to gather round a window of 'toffee' glass when a stuntman was about to go through it. They did so not to marvel at the stuntman's ability but to seize the largest pieces of glass and eat them.

This bizarre interest in windows has recently disappeared

because of a change in the nature of the glass used. 'Toffee' glass had one disadvantage. Although it would not cut, certain of the slivers were in fact sufficiently stiff and sharply pointed to be able to penetrate flesh if they were fallen on in a particular way. The replacement of 'toffee' glass by a modern resin has removed even this danger. The new resins can be crushed between finger and thumb into a powder without showing any sign of penetrating the skin.*

Glass shots

A further area of cooperation between Special Effects and stuntmen is in the field of high falls. George Roy Hill who directed *Butch Cassidy and the Sundance Kid* has given details of how the two principal actors—Robert Redford (the Sundance Kid) and

---

* It has proved surprisingly difficult to trace any early manufacturers of 'toffee' glass in the United Kingdom. We are, however, particularly grateful to R. W. Parry of the Experimental Department of John Mackintosh and Sons Limited—now part of Rowntree Mackintosh Limited—for the following information given in a letter dated 26th October 1971: 'We have never made this material for the film industry but it is true that we once made some sheets of "glass" for Anglia TV over ten years ago. I have no record of the precise details, but the procedure was roughly as follows:—Take some corn syrup (i.e. liquid glucose, approximately 20% water), and boil this rapidly (preferably under vacuum to avoid discoloration) to around 5% water. Remove any scum, after allowing air bubbles to rise to surface, pour carefully on to lightly oiled metal slab with metal bars forming the shape required. Allow to cool and finally wrap in waxed paper (i.e. keep airtight) until shortly before required. This material will rapidly become sticky on the surface if the humidity is on the high side. This is the way we adopted for TV but the firm who made this material probably had far more sophisticated methods!' K. W. De Witt of Fox's Glacier Mints Limited—also now a part of Rowntree Mackintosh Limited—has also been most helpful in contributing the following information: 'Presumably, the glass itself was boiled sugar syrup as we use for Glacier Mints. This consists of a mixture of sugar and "liquid glucose" (called "corn syrup" in the United States) which is boiled up with water to a temperature of 275–300° F. The boiled syrup can be poured on to a cooling slab to make a sheet or into a mould to make a bottle, and when cool, looks and behaves like glass. It will, of course, deteriorate rapidly when exposed to moisture in the atmosphere.'

The team approach to action

Paul Newman (Butch Cassidy)—appeared to jump from a cliff top into a river to escape a posse.[170] The water on this particular location was too shallow for the stuntmen to do the actual jump, so the stars did a jump off the cliff on to a platform erected just below the cliff face.

The jump itself, in which we apparently see Redford and Newman falling from the cliff top into the river, was done several months later by stuntmen at the Fox Ranch at Malibu, miles away from the original location. 'We put our two stuntmen up on a seventy-foot crane. We stirred up the water with a dozen outboard motors to simulate the rapids.' The Special Effects man had a sheet of glass painted to represent the cliffs of the original location and the stuntmen were filmed through the glass and panned down to where they hit the water. But this new location required the stuntmen to move from left to right of the screen when they jumped, whereas Redford and Newman for whom they were doubling had jumped from right to left. So the filmed version of the stuntmen's jump was finally reversed and cut into the end of the stars' jump. For such an effect the Special Effects man is essential. Without him the location, which had presumably been chosen with great care by the director, could not have been used. Alternatively, some other method of escape from the posse would have had to be introduced since the stars could not be shown leaping into that particular river from that particular cliff top.

Explosions

Butch Cassidy and the Sundance Kid is also memorable for the sequence in which an excess of dynamite is used to blow up a railway boxcar during a robbery, and explosions of this kind have always formed a central part of the work of the Special Effects man. In a film like *The Bridge On The River Kwai* (1957), the final blowing up of the bridge is almost the mainspring of the plot, and the Special Effects explosive work on *The Longest Day* is almost more important than any other single aspect of the film. Such effects, of course, must be handled by explosives specialists.

G

Dynamite, even when used to enhance the most fictional of film episodes, is still dynamite.

For *Butch Cassidy and The Sundance Kid*, Hill had a 'dynamite man' in attendance. As one would expect, of course, such a precaution has not always been taken. In the early days of the industry, the general haphazard way in which explosives were used makes somewhat alarming reading. Montgomery[171] refers to 'a premature explosion in the big tank' in which Chester Conklin, one of the Keystones, was blown through the air. 'He was severely shaken, but unbroken. The bottom of the tank, however, was blown clean out, and the studio was flooded with water.' Conklin, 'the cross-eyed cop with a walrus moustache', not only survived the explosion but lived to be eighty-three. He died in Hollywood in October 1971. In 1919 Lloyd's career almost came to an end when, in the taking of a publicity still, he was handed by accident an explosive bomb instead of a property one. Predictably, the bomb went off in his hand, severely damaging it. His face was badly burned and his eyes seemed as if they might be permanently injured. For nine months he was out of commission.

The French director Abel Gance[172] recalled a similar disaster during the shooting of *Napoleon* when an inexperienced armourer was being employed. Plugs of burning paper were being fired into camera and one fell into a kilo of magnesium that the armourer had left at Gance's feet. Everyone was set alight. Such occurrences, though undoubtedly alarming, cannot have been entirely un-expected since Gance mentions a special burn ointment that he had available. Gance admitted that he regarded injuries as unavoidable in battle scenes, and held the view that the cinema was something for which one should be quite prepared 'to risk one's life'.

It is fortunate that Gance's attitude is not one that need nowadays be held by the director of action sequences. Improved techniques for handling explosives, developed by the Special Effects man, have made scenes of devastation like those arranged by John Fulton in *The Heroes of Telemark* where bridges, large buildings and wooden houses all disintegrate during an Allied bombing raid, not only possible but comparatively safe. Hill points to the safety factor that was constantly borne in mind in making the action sequences of *Butch Cassidy,* when he mentions that in the boxcar explosion the car itself was built of balsa wood to minimise the danger to the stuntmen.

But perhaps we get our deepest insight into the activities of the Special Effects man involved in mounting explosions, from an account[173] of Lee Zavitz's work on Frankenheimer's *The Train.* Zavitz and his crew of fifty worked for six weeks preparing a square mile of railway marshalling yards at Gargenville near Paris for demolition. The aim was to recreate the actual destruction of a similar yard by Allied bombers in the Second World War. Explosive charges were planted in a hundred and fifty separate holes. 'Wires were run throughout almost two miles of trenches to a control bunker from which demolition men, linked by telephone with Zavitz, but unable to see the marshalling yards, made the electrical contacts which set off the detonations. Through 60 switches and more than 20,000 metres of cable, 140 individual explosions were set off in just over fifty seconds. In order to duplicate, as nearly as possible, the concentrated Allied bombing raids of 1945, charges of dynamite and large plastic containers of high-octane petrol were placed in the trucks, buildings, sheds, control towers, and a 22-car train which were to be blown up. In all, the destruction required nearly two tons of TNT and dynamite and some 2,000 gallons of petrol.' The result, as one would expect, was one of the most spectacular Special Effects sequences ever seen on film.

Yet from the Special Effects viewpoint, these massive and spectacular sequences are not necessarily the most difficult. They require endless thought and planning but they do not necessarily involve real danger to human life. By contrast, the blowing up of a stuntman by a landmine does involve such danger and adds an element of difficulty and anxiety for the Special Effects man that many more spectacular explosions would not pose for him. Such a stunt requires the Special Effects man to know exactly what a given weight of explosive laid in a particular way will do. He needs to know how to lay the explosive so that the main blast will pass to one side or other of the stuntman whilst still appearing to an audience to be directed squarely at him.

A not uncommon stunt which we see is one in which a soldier is apparently blown clean into the air by an explosion directly beneath him. The effect—and the safety of the stuntman in his soldier's uniform—is dependent on the split-second timing of the Special Effects man responsible for detonating the charge already set in the ground. A frequent way in which the stunt is performed is for the stuntman to jump on a trampoline—or its smaller version the trampette—which is set just below the level of the ground or masked by some object between it and the camera. As the trampette throws the stuntman into the air, the Special Effects man fires the charge. To the audience viewing the scene later, the cause of the sudden upward movement of the stuntman apparently out of control, is the explosion beneath his feet. Jerk harness in conjunction with block and tackle has been used in the case of the soldier who falls on a hand grenade in order to protect his comrades. As the grenade explodes beneath him he is pulled upwards by the harness and again the cause of the sudden upward movement appears to be the explosion beneath him.

Another problem that both stuntman and Special Effects man face is in connection with the explosion that takes place very close to the stuntman. The explosion is of sufficient force to damage property, yet must avoid harming the stuntman. One of the present writers, for example, had an explosion detonated within feet of him during the shooting of *The Long Day's Dying* (1968). He was briefed by the Special Effects man—in this case Pat Moore—to stand in a particular spot with his back to the explosion. When the charge was detonated it demolished one of the main supporting timbers of a large building, but because of the way in which it had been placed by Moore it left the stuntman unharmed.

There are of course many other ways in which the Special Effects man can use explosives in connection with stuntmen. In some cases it is possible to use compressed air instead of a chemical explosive. But even the most effective explosion poses problems for the director. 'You have to overcrank the camera for an explosion, otherwise it looks too fast,' said George Roy Hill in discussing the boxcar explosion in *Butch Cassidy*. The explosion was filmed with a number of cameras running at different speeds. The normal running speed is twenty-four frames per second, but the main camera in this particular explosion was running at sixty-four frames.

To some directors the real explosion, however it is shot, is less effective than the fabricated one. Rotha[174] mentions the work of V. I. Pudovkin in connection with an explosion in *The End of St. Petersburg* (1927):

> In order to render the *effect* of this explosion with absolute fidelity, he caused a charge of high explosive to be buried and had it detonated. The explosion was terrific, but filmically it was quite ineffective. So by means of editing, he built an explosion out of small bits of film, by taking separate shots of clouds of smoke and of a magnesium flare, welding them into a series of images, he cut a shot of a river that he had taken some time before, which was appropriate owing to its tones of light and shade. The whole assembly when seen on the screen was vividly effective, but it had been achieved *without employing a shot of the real explosion*.

We should remember, however, that Pudovkin was working on a silent film. His explosion was therefore entirely visual and as such lacked one of the principal factors which make the modern film explosion credible—noise.

Fire stunts

Harvey Parry has declared that there is no such thing as the 'most dangerous stunt'.[175] Nevertheless there are many stuntmen who would regard 'playing about with fire' as being an activity with more than its fair share of hazards. Nowadays the Special Effects man is essential for helping the stuntman to handle fire. This has not always been the case. Houdini, for example, was once rash enough to allow some Boy Scouts in Los Angeles to build a fire, tie him to a stake in the middle of it and set fire to the thing. He intended to do one of his famous escapes from the flames before there was any real danger of his being burnt. What he had not anticipated was that the Scouts, in their enthusiasm to get the thing blazing quickly, had poured paraffin on the fire before setting light to it. Under the circumstances he was fortunate to have escaped severe burning.[176]

Grace credits Gene Perkins with spectacular fire stunts during the twenties, but it was Grace himself who perhaps suffered more from this particular stunt than anyone else. This is surprising when one bears in mind that, according to Phillips,[177] fire was Grace's 'greatest dread'. But it was not in Grace's temperament to avoid a particular stunt simply because it terrified him. Perhaps his 'dread' might have been less if he had been backed by a modern Special Effects man, because his misfortunes in connection with fire stunts seem all to have arisen because of inadequacies in this area. He was burnt on a film being directed by Bernard Durning when he was required to do a sixty-foot jump into a fireman's net from a five-storey studio set that had been set on fire. Because of a lack of proper Special Effects work the rate of burning was faster than had been expected and in fact reached explosion point.

In that case Grace was fortunate. But he was far less fortunate on another occasion when he was doubling for a ballet dancer in a fire stunt. According to his own account of the incident[178] he was set on fire after having been sprayed with a mixture of 'gasoline and alcohol'! It is not surprising that he was severely burnt. According to medical calculations 786 square inches of body surface were burned, 'in places half an inch deep'. After months of slow recovery from his terrible injuries he discovered that 'the wounds left under my arms by the fire had webbed in healing. My doctor said I would never again be able to lift my arms high over my head.' Such a medical opinion was not to be taken too literally by Grace: 'I stood before a mirror and cut the webs with a razor blade. Now I can raise my arms as high as anyone.'

The function of the Special Effects man in connection with fire stunts is to devise ways in which they can be done, so that they will be both safe and effective. A highly spectacular fire stunt, requiring the closest possible cooperation between Special Effects man and stuntman appears in *Patton* (1971) in which we see the stuntman—in this case Joe Canutt, son of Yakima—hit by a flamethrower. Paul Baxley performed a similar stunt in *Tobruk* (1967). The flame suit in which the stuntman is clothed must of course be able to stand up to such treatment. The greatest care must be taken by the Special Effects man in deciding how long the flamethrower can be directed at its human target, since although the suit will offer protection from the flame it cannot for long prevent the stuntman from beginning to blister inside his suit from the general heat with which he is being surrounded. One of the present writers, performing a fire stunt in Peter Watkins's *The War Game* (1965), discovered that although an asbestos lagging kept him reasonably free from the flames, the heat generated inside the lagging caused the flesh to blister. The effect was reminiscent of baking a chicken wrapped in aluminium foil.*

The flame suit and asbestos lagging are only two of the devices that can be used to reduce the danger of fire stunts. Fans are sometimes used to blow the flames from burning garments away from the body of the stuntman. Staff are of course standing by to smother the flames the moment the shot is completed. Since human hair burns very quickly, for some fire stunts wigs are worn which have a base of asbestos material.

The inflammable mixture used by the Special Effects man to set fire to the stuntman has of course been very carefully prepared. The days of rule-of-thumb mixtures of 'gasoline and alcohol' have fortunately gone. Paraffin is a more common base and was in fact used for the *War Game* sequence. Usually some oil needs to be

---

* A new material, FPT, which is now being manufactured by Fire-Proof Textiles AG of Zug, Switzerland, might well help to produce still more spectacular fire stunts in the future. In a correspondence with the authors, Fire-Proof Textiles AG state: 'Two layers of standard type FPT fabric are sufficient to protect human skin from direct flame action for more than one minute, even at flame temperatures of over 800° C.'

added since flames tend not to be seen on the screen unless they have a certain smoky 'body'. Increasingly a petrol-based jelly is used when a stuntman has to appear on fire.

The Special Effects man gives a good deal of thought to ways in which these dangerous stunts with fire can be made both safer and more effective. The Bowie Flame Harness, produced by Bowie Films, is one of the results of such thought. The device consists of a gas burner mounted on harness and worn under the jacket. The burner is connected to a tiny butane gas bottle which will fit in a pocket. The jacket is impregnated with inflammable jelly. By operating a hand-held switch, the stuntman can set himself on fire at will.

Bullet strikes

Apart from producing the massive explosions necessary to decimate a town in a simulated aerial bombardment, the Special Effects man is required to produce the minor explosions associated with the discharging of bullets. Where we see a bullet from the Sheriff's gun smashing its way through a table, we are seeing one of the results of the Special Effects man's work. Many such bullet effects appear in *Butch Cassidy*. 'In any sequence involving guns, of course, you've got to rig the hits,' says George Roy Hill, the director.[179] Explaining the way in which tables appear to be struck by bullets, he says: 'Our Special Effects man here is wiring the table for the first bullet hit. He's drilled a hole in it, he's stuck a charge in it and he's wired it to his battery and his assistant has another set of wires running from the battery to his finger tips. In the scene the guys (Paul Newman and Robert Redford) sit down at the table to get served their dinners and on cue he sets off the charge with one hand and fires the gun with the other.'

A similar technique can be used for showing bullets striking a wall. Small holes are drilled in the wall, filled with tiny explosive charges, wired, and finally detonated in a pre-agreed order. Alternatively, as Hill says, 'mostly we use these airguns fired by Special Effects crew off-camera. They can fire "blood" pellets and "dust" pellets and you'll obviously save a lot of time with them rather than setting individual charges. They're amazingly accurate.'

A version of the gun that Hill is mentioning is the 'Universal Capsule Gun' made by Ken Morris. In general appearance it looks like a submachine-gun. It is operated by compressed air fed to it by a tube from a cylinder. The pressure of this air can be varied so that the muzzle velocity of projectiles can be altered according to the distance they need to be fired. A pressure of some forty pounds a square inch, for example, is needed to fire a pellet at a target two feet away. For a distance of six feet a pressure of about fifty-five pounds a square inch is necessary.

The gun fires either 'dust' pellets or 'blood' pellets. The former, made usually of some Fuller's Earth mixture, are used to simulate real bullets striking walls. When they are fired by the Special Effects man from off-camera, they disintegrate on impact. The little puff of dust given off is sufficient to give the illusion to an audience of a real bullet strike. The 'blood' pellets contain a concoction which has the appearance and texture of blood. They are fired directly at actors by the Special Effects man and on impact they leave a blood-coloured stain on flesh or clothing which suggests the penetration of a real bullet. Where such pellets are to be fired at an actor, the Special Effects man tries them out on himself first. If they do not hit with sufficient force to give the effect required, the air pressure is increased. If on the other hand the Special Effects man finds the impact too painful, the air pressure is reduced. A further type of pellet occasionally in use is one which can be fired at glass. When it strikes a shop window or a car windscreen, for example, it gives the impression of having produced a hole in it surrounded by radiating cracks. The impression is of a real bullet having penetrated the glass at high speed.

There are other ways in which the impression of bullet strikes can be given. In the case of that popular scene in which we see an aircraft diving down on a column of refugees and firing its machine-guns, the ground is previously primed and wired by the Special Effects man who on a signal can detonate his line of small charges in such a way as to give the impression of a burst of machine-gun fire. Equally, for a bullet strike on a stuntman, an explosive cap can actually be fired on his body. This is placed by the Special Effects man over the top of a metal shield that the stuntman wears on his body. Over the top of the cap is a thin rubber capsule full of synthetic blood. The explosive cap is then wired so that it can either be fired by the Special Effects man or by the stuntman himself. When it explodes the metal plate prevents any of its force going towards the stuntman's body. As it explodes outwards it bursts the blood capsule and gives the impression of a bullet strike on the stuntman.

The effect has one disadvantage. The explosive movement is outwards, whereas a bullet strike is inwards. Understandably, stuntmen and Special Effects men who are totally bound up in their profession find this lack of authenticity unsatisfactory. They are, for example, much more in favour of the shot in which we see the back of the stuntman who has been hit from the front by a bullet. In such a shot the explosion outwards of the cap is consistent with the passage of a bullet from the front and out through the back. Perhaps the most remarkable achievement of the Special Effects man in this particular area are the deaths of Bonny and Clyde in Warren Beatty's production of the 1967 film directed by Arthur Penn. In this case the credits list Danny Lee as being responsible for Special Effects.

Props

The line which separates the work of the property man and the Special Effects man is no easier to define than that which separates other members of the action team. The work of Fred Gabourie for Keaton clearly covers both fields. In a crude sense we may say that the property man supplies properties—five-barred gates, swords or Victorian washstands. The Special Effects man, by contrast, produces specialised filmic effects with properties. As Pat Moore puts it: 'You film in Pinewood, we transport you to the Taj Mahal.' 'I'll produce a property,' the props man seems to say.

'I'll transmute that property,' seems to be the attitude of the Special Effects man.

Goodman[180] quotes from the production notes of *Six O'Clock Low* (1951), a satirical comment by Mono-Grant Pictures on *Twelve O'Clock High*: 'Special Effects—To help keep costs down, many special effects were used. The English countryside was cleverly duplicated by photographing Pasadena through a monocle. In those scenes involving Nazi aircraft, a German lens was used.' Like all satire, the statement contains a grain of truth. It is understandable that we are at times confused by the fine line of demarcation separating the work of the Special Effects man and the props man, since in some areas their responsibilities impinge very closely on one another. Our confusion is not important, so long as we realise that both men make essential contributions to film action.

Whereas the arrow and the spear are likely to be found in the property department, the flick-up arrow that suddenly appears sticking from the breast of a prospector and the spear that flies unerringly on to its target are creations of the Special Effects department. The flick-up arrow is a spring-loaded device that can be sewn into the clothing of the stuntman who is to use it. On a signal he can release the spring-retaining mechanism and the foreshortened arrow which has been concealed will fly upwards. The impression is of a man suddenly struck by an arrow. If the stuntman is on horseback, he may complete the sequence by doing a saddle fall.

An interesting variation of the flick-up arrow appeared in *Custer of the West* (1966), in which a stuntman is seen taking an arrow in the neck. The arrow in this case is double. When the mechanism is released by the stuntman, not only does the tail of the arrow fly up, but also the head. The impression is of an arrow having gone clean through the stuntman's neck. A variation of the flick-up arrow is the telescopic one. The intention again is to give the impression of an arrow having suddenly embedded itself in a stuntman. But the mechanism here is more complex and the arrow is not particularly satisfactory.

The use of a thin wire or 'fishline' to direct missiles was an invention of considerable importance. In the case of the arrow, for example, the technique consists of drilling a very small hole down the whole length of the arrow and threading the fishline through it. The exact place on the target that is to be struck by the arrow is also drilled and the fishline threaded through it. Both ends of the fishline are secured. When the arrow is placed in the bow and fired towards the target, the fishline, invisible to the camera, will guide it on to the exact place it is to hit. The technique is useful in such scenes as that in the various versions of the Robin Hood story in which Robin displays his skill as an archer, finally splitting the arrow of his nearest rival. It is equally useful in the William Tell legend in which Tell unerringly splits an apple on the head of his son with a crossbow bolt. The use of a fishline to direct the flight of a missile is not restricted to arrows and crossbow bolts. Spears can be directed along lines on hidden runners and in *Long Day's Dying* fishlines were used to direct the flight of commando knives that were being thrown at dogs.

Special Effects and the props department supply a range of other weapons. Rubber bayonets are safer in mass infantry action than the real things. Retractable bayonets have been produced, but, like retractable-bladed knives, there is always the danger that the retraction mechanism will fail and produce a lethal weapon. David Niven recalls that rubber lances were used during the shooting of *The Charge of the Light Brigade*.[181] Bowie Films have produced entire rifles of rubber 'so that actors wouldn't hurt themselves if they fell awkwardly on them'.[182]

The gorilla who dominated New York City in *King Kong* (1933) was at that time a marvel of Special Effects work. Mass cavalry battles require a supply of dummy dead horses. The human dummy that is not required to move poses no particular problems, but the moving dummy, particularly the one who is to take the place of a stuntman, must be produced by a specialist. Henabery seems to have been one of the first men to have worked seriously on the movements of dummies in film action. In the walls of Babylon sequence in *Intolerance* he was anxious to use dummies for some of the falls, but he discovered that even in long shot ordinary dummies were unconvincing. After a great deal of work he produced a dummy whose limbs couldn't bend the wrong way and so destroy the illusion.

The props man faces both the safety problem and the problem of authenticity of appearance in providing weapons for action scenes. It is possible in a sword fight, for example, to dub on the sounds of clashing weapons and heavy-breathing combatants afterwards. But it is not possible to change the visual image. A sword that looks as if it is made of pliable plastic in reality will look like pliable plastic on film. The point is an important one. If in some of Flynn's more swashbuckling sword play one did not believe that the weapon he was carrying was capable, at least within the screen convention, of killing, then the whole myth would collapse. The 'willing suspension of disbelief' is no less essential in action sequences than in any other aspect of dramatic entertainment.

There is, of course, a problem here for the props man. In some cases a sword that looks too authentic is too heavy for the actor who is to wield it. Geraldine Farrar complained that in *Joan the Woman* (1916) 'the sword alone was almost impossible to handle'.[183] A more potentially disastrous example of authenticity in weapons is mentioned by Brownlow in connection with the shooting of *Ben-Hur* (1926). The film's director, Fred Niblo, found that sharp swords had been provided for the naval battle and that the extras who were going to use them had been divided into pro- and anti-fascist groups.

Keaton, discussing his brief appearance in *Hollywood Cavalcade*, mentions the care that went into the manufacture of what must appear to an audience to be one of the simplest of properties—the custard pie. The missile was constructed with a double crust so that it did not collapse during the delivery. Flour, water and whipped cream were the basic ingredients of the filling. If the target was a blonde, blackberries were added to give a contrasting colour on impact. For a brunette, lemon-meringue was used.[184]

Sound effects

The sound effects man, as we have noticed in the case of sword play, makes a considerable contribution to the stuntman's effectiveness in some action sequences. The bar room brawl is an obvious example of this. Originally the sound of a fist slamming into a face was done during the take. Harry Miller, the first British sound effects man, used a face-slap device consisting of two hinged boards which were snapped together to coincide with the visual image being picked up by the camera.[185] Nowadays, of course, such sounds are dubbed on after the scene has been shot. For the sound of a punch, various techniques have been tried. Punching a cabbage in the vicinity of the microphone is one of them. A more effective and authentic sound is produced simply by driving the clenched fist of one hand into the open palm of the other. Alf Joint talks of throwing punches so as not to hit an opponent, 'and having someone thump a leg of lamb on the soundtrack afterwards'.[186]

Costume and make-up

Costume and make-up staffs also play important parts in the production of successful action sequences. Both contribute to the credibility of such sequences. They make it easier for us to believe in the characters involved in them and in what those characters are doing. Lahue underlines the importance of this when he complains of Joe Bonomo's performance in *Perils of the Wild* (1925): 'Bonomo put on a fine display of the prodigious feats for which he was well known, but his histrionic range was rather limited. . . . But the most jarring note in the whole item was the fact that his natty striped shirt seemed impervious to dirt or water.'[187]

Allan Dwan stresses the need in designing and making costumes to bear in mind the needs of the men who are to wear them. The 'chain mail' used in *Robin Hood* (1922), for example, was in fact made of canvas because real mail would have been too heavy for the actors to wear. The only mail used was in close-ups where Dwan wanted to show it being struck by a sword.[188] Flynn refers to the drawbacks of wearing real armour in *The Private Lives of Elizabeth and Essex* (1939). The weight was so great that he had to be lifted on to his horse with block and tackle.[189]

If we doubt the importance of make-up in lending credibility to action, then we need only recall the scenes of carnage in *Soldier Blue* (1971), the facial effects produced on Kirk Douglas in *The Vikings* after his eye has been torn out by a falcon, and the appearance of Marlon Brando after his savage beatings in *On The Waterfront* (1954) and *The Chase* (1965). Such effects can absorb hours of skilled, specialist attention. Gay Search, discussing make-up in connection with television action, says: 'Swellings can be done simply with make-up, but a severe swelling has to be built up carefully with wax or latex and is a fairly long process.'[190] Even the blood that is used to add authenticity to wounds is no simple concoction. The blood used, for example, in making up wounds for first-aid and rescue training, is 'a mixture of food dyes, syrup and custard powder'.[191]

Specialist services

Stuntmen, Second Unit directors, Special Effects men, make-up, costume and property men all make their regular contributions to the work of the action team, but there are occasions when the services of an outside specialist are needed. A stuntman will in many cases have some ability to ski, but it is unlikely that he will have that high degree of competence required, for example, for the final sequences of *Mortal Storm* (1940), in which we see the two principals attempting to escape from the Gestapo on skis. Equally, some stuntmen have had parachute experience, but for the parachute attack on Ste-Mère-Église in *The Longest Day* it is not stuntmen we see pouring out of the aircraft. For such sequences specialists are usually employed, men whose professional skill in a particular activity is so great that it overrides their lack of acting ability. As Flynn says, the parachute jump for the star and for the professional parachutist are two very different things. The parachutist steps out of the plane and drops two or three thousand feet.

The star steps out of the plane, drops out of frame and lands on a mattress.[192]

Flynn, who 'liked to have them about', was aware of the numbers of specialists in this or that skill who hung on the periphery of the film world. 'I found Hollywood to be a circus-land of experts at this and that. There are people who are specialists with the whip, who can flick a fly or a cigarette out of your mouth. . . . There are specialists in every form of danger, like Howard Hill with the bow and arrow, a man who can put out the flame of a candle with his arrow at thirty or forty feet.'

Specialists like these, of course, had always had a place in entertainment. Coryate, writing of his trip to Venice in 1608,[193] mentions a specialist reminiscent of the purveyor of fake medicines that we have seen in so many Westerns:

Also I have seene a Mountebank hackle and gash his naked arme with a knife most pitifully to beholde, so that the blood hath streamed out in great abundance, and by and by after he hath applied a certaine oyle unto it, wherewith he hath incontinent both stanched the blood and so thoroughly healed the woundes and gashes, that when he hath afterward shewed us his arme againe, we could not possibly perceive the least token of a gash.

McKechnie,[194] quoting from the seventeenth-century work *Hocus Pocus Junior, The Anatomy of Legerdemain, or The Art of Juggling*, describes a trick for cutting one's nose half off: 'For the effecting of this feat you must have a knife for the nonce, made with a gap in the midst of the blade. You must conceal an inch with your finger, and then wring it over the fleshy part of your nose, and your nose will seem as if it were half cut off with the knife. Note that in such feats as this, it were necessary to have a piece of spunge with some sheep's blood in it to be retained privately.'

Houdini, on his visit to Chicago in 1893 for the World's Columbian Exposition which commemorated the four-hundredth anniversary of the discovery of America, met similar specialists. He saw swordswallowers, which he discovered, 'actually let the solid steel blade slide down their throat; they had conquered the "gag reflex". He learnt that fire eaters may put in their mouths awesomely blazing materials, so long as they never forget to breathe out gently to keep the heat away from the soft tissues of the roof of the mouth.'[195] Later, he was fascinated by the specialist skill of a Japanese 'swallower' who could apparently swallow ivory balls and then regurgitate them. He could in fact half-swallow objects and keep them half-way down his oesophagus. Other 'swallowers' used watches, fish and even small animals. Houdini was told that if he wanted to master the technique he should practise with a small potato on a string.

Such specialists still exist in entertainment. As recently as January 1971, Mr Robin (Robbie) Robertson, stage manager of the Octagon Theatre, Bolton, England, a fire-eater, was fined £20 'for driving a motor-cycle with more than the permitted limit of alcohol in his blood'. Mr David Duckworth, defending Mr Robertson, is reported as saying:[196] 'I am going to give his secret away. He contains an amount of methylated spirits in his mouth. The vapour emitted gives the delusion of fire coming from his mouth. A certain amount of methylated spirits would trickle down his throat into his stomach. Also a quantity remains in the mouth and with the heat of the mouth, evaporates, goes into the lungs and then into the blood stream. He was unaware of this at the time.' This plea was taken into consideration by the magistrates and Mr Robertson was not disqualified from driving, as he might otherwise have been.

The specialist archer

Such men are not, of course, stuntmen. They are specialists who are already in the field of entertainment or are brought into it to contribute to some specialised action sequence. Howard Hill is an example. He was at one time perhaps the best-known professional archer in America, and he has the credit of 'Captain of Archers' in the 1938 *Robin Hood*, on which of course he worked with Flynn. His work on the film is obvious to anyone who has seen it. The arrow-shooting sequences bear all the marks of a world-class specialist's hand controlling them. In the banqueting scene in which Flynn, in the character of Locksley, begins his abuse of Prince John's authority, we see knights shot in the breast by arrows, and in the later chase horsemen are picked off their horses by arrows shot into them. For scenes like these—not only in this particular film but in many others that have both preceded and followed it—trick camera shots are not possible beyond a certain point. In most cases, where we see a man actually struck by an arrow he was in reality shot.

In 1925, 'Earl B. Powell, a professional archer, was retained to supervise the archery sequences' in *The Green Archer*, a ten-part serial issued by Pathé.[197] It is of course inconceivable that archers like Powell and Hill should have been given responsibility for certain aspects of action pictures without their specialised skill being called upon. Both were employed because their ability with the bow was so great that they could safely shoot arrows at stunt-men without causing fatalities. Peters[198] mentions the technique in referring to George Brown as 'the best archer in British studios'. The stuntman who was to receive an arrow fired at him by Brown was protected by a 'small back or breastplate of beechwood lined with thin steel'. However proficient an archer a man may be, it requires considerable self-confidence to load a bow with a thirty-inch arrow and fire it at the body of another man. The archer cannot really see his target, since the beechwood protection has to be concealed under the clothes. But though one marvels at the coolness of the archer, prepared to shoot under such circumstances, one marvels a good deal more at the stuntman who is prepared to receive the arrow.

In America, Taylor[199] mentions Dick Farnsworth and Carl Petti as being the top stunt archers at the time he was writing (1967). The stuntmen receiving the arrows shot by these specialists were protected by steel plates covered in balsa wood. The arrows that were fired were ordinary production models with steel heads. Farnsworth, says Taylor, has 'picked men off moving horses, and has hit fellow stunters with flaming arrows in the back or chest'.

For each arrow that he fired at a stuntman he was paid $200. By contrast, 'the extras willing to be targets,' according to Peters, 'are paid an extra £5 a day.'

Naturally there have been occasions when the specialist has shown a certain human fallibility. On the filming of *Richard III* (1956), for example, no less an actor than Sir Laurence Olivier was hit in the leg by an arrow during an action sequence. Equally, there have been occasions when a specialist has misunderstood the nature of the cinema. During the filming of *The Covered Wagon* (1923), Lois Wilson was to be hit by an arrow. An old Indian, hearing of this, offered to shoot an arrow clean through her shoulder: 'Not hurt much. Not break bone. Go right through.'[200]

The specialist marksman

The use of guns to fire real bullets on screen also calls for a specialist. As we have seen, bullet strikes now are usually produced either by a device like Morris's 'Universal Capsule Gun', or by the electrical detonation of explosive caps. This has not always been the case. In the twenties and early thirties George Daly argued that it was safer to use real bullets when bullet strikes were required, than to continue with the technique of firing blanks and faking the hits. Daly, to support his contention that the copper explosive cap could be dangerous, mentioned Gaylord Lloyd, one of the directors of *Scarface* (1932), as having lost an eye through a splinter from one. Daly's technique consisted simply of firing a gun loaded with live rounds to produce the bullet strikes required. In *Public Enemy* (1931), for example, he used a machine-gun to fire live bullets round the actors in the action scenes. In *Little Caesar* (1931) he was responsible for firing the submachine-gun that produced the line of bullets along a billboard and gave the impression of killing Edward G. Robinson.[201]

There have been occasions when stunt actors have learnt a special skill for a particular purpose. John Wayne, for example, learnt to throw knives and tomahawks for Raoul Walsh's *The Big Trail* (1930). But it is more usual under such circumstances for the actor to give way to the specialist. Even such a physically skilled actor as Keaton accepted his limitations when certain specialist skills were required. On *Cops* (1922), for example, instead of attempting a pole leap into a second-floor window he hired Lee Barnes, a pole-vault champion, to do it for him.

Camera work

Action work poses special problems for the cameraman. He must shoot fairly wide, for example, in work with horses, because no horse will perform whatever is expected of it on exactly the spot chosen by the director. Unlike the stuntman, it does not measure distance in inches. The high fall, as we have seen, requires the proper positioning of the camera if we are to see it all. A fall can lose perhaps ten feet if the cameraman is not sensitive to the problems of action work. Again, many high falls appear on the screen to be shorter than in fact they are. There is certainly a case here for some overcranking in order to lengthen them.

Varying the camera speed, of course, is a technique that is of particular importance in action work. In this connection, under-cranking—shooting at a slower speed than that at which the film will be projected so that the action on screen appears faster than it was in reality—is more widely applicable than overcranking. It can be used to increase the speed at which a man draws a gun from a holster, or the speed at which men go at one another with swords. It is important in stunting since it reduces the danger of stunts performed at speed. In weapon play particularly the use of undercranking increases the safety factor, since the actual movements of weapons can be a little slower than they would otherwise have to be, and even a slight reduction in speed allows a much greater accuracy of movement.

Where such weapons as swords, knives or bayonets are concerned, accuracy of movement and personal safety are directly related. For cowboy action sequences cameramen used the 'Western 18', a speed of eighteen frames a second which was particularly suitable for that kind of action. In the days of hand-cranked cameras the speed could be made infinitely variable. The cameraman contributed to the effectiveness of a stunt by the speed at which he decided to shoot it. He could, for example, undercrank to cover up a certain slowness in the action or to heighten a comedian's effectiveness. The technique of undercranking has its limitations of course. Beyond a certain point the action appears so fast as to be no longer credible. Examples of this occur in some of the sword play in *Prisoner of Zenda* (1937) and more particularly in *Captain From Castile* (1947).

At times the cameraman exposes himself to some of the dangers that face the stuntman. In order to get the kind of close-ups that Eason has said are essential, the cameraman must get amongst the action. Joseph August filmed William S. Hart in the saddle from another horse riding beside him; and in the boxing sequences of *Body and Soul* (1948) James Wong Howe got into the ring with a hand-held camera and moved around the boxers on roller skates.[202]

The bar room brawl, which can be covered very largely by good camera angles and good sound effects, requires this kind of physical involvement between cameraman and stuntmen. Reciprocally, as Alf Joint says, the professional stuntman, in planning his approach to a particular stunt, will take into consideration the camera movements that are going to be used to film it.[203] Surprisingly, perhaps, this involvement of the cameraman with dangerous action has very rarely led to disaster. William Hornbeck can recall only one such disaster, when Al Jenkins was killed by a car whilst filming the Santa Monica road race.[204]

Editing

Hornbeck, of course, is one of the great editors and the work of the editor in action sequences is crucial. Brownlow[205] considers the *Ben-Hur* (1926) chariot race, the *Tumbleweeds* (1925) land rush and the battle scene from *The Big Parade* (1925) to be 'supreme examples of the editor's art'. Eason saw editing as an essential part of his theory of action. What produced pace and excitement was not the amount of action in a particular shot but the way shots were assembled and juxtaposed in the cutting room. Keaton too stresses the relationship between the final pace of film action and the editorial process it has been through.

'As a cutter,' says David Lean,[206] putting his finger on the real power of the top-flight editor, 'you decide what an audience shall look at and when.' And in action sequences, what an audience looks at and when is crucial in determining the effect that the whole sequence will have.

Directing

Supreme, of course, in the action team should be the director. 'The director's job is to give everybody help,' says Lean, and certainly a director who is able to do this in the area of action is not as common as one might expect. This is unfortunate, since the stunt-man is no less grateful for directorial help and understanding than any other actor. Nor is he necessarily in less need of it. The point needs making, since whatever contribution to a film other members of the action team make, the director's stamp is ultimately what decides the consistency and quality of the work. The director who is sensitive to the requirements of action will produce work from the action team of a quality that might well amaze them. The director with little understanding of the problems of action can minimise the team's work to the point where it makes little contribution to the film as a whole.

This dichotomy is seen in reverse in a film like *Colt .45,* where brilliant action scenes are almost demolished by a script of breath-taking banality. We see a leap from a cliff on to a moving stage, a forward somersault fall from the stage, a stuntman on horseback lifted bodily out of his saddle by a rope tied across a road. We see the 'bulldogging' of one of the villains by two Indians dropping on him from a balcony, and we see brilliant special effects sequences of bullets and arrows penetrating doors. But juxtaposed to these exciting visual images, we hear 'Indian has ways—make prisoner talk', 'Till sunrise—help friend' and 'Indian always quiet'. The effect is not to lift the language to the level of the action, but to devalue the whole film.

Similarly, where we have banality of action it is not simply ignored by an audience. Its effect is to diminish the credibility of every other aspect of the film. Action must be seen as an integral part of the whole creation, not something which can be handed over to a special team and then injected into the body of an already coherent film, with the intention of providing an otherwise too intelligent piece of work with a certain crude mass appeal. Such an attitude, however cynical it might seem to us to be, is not entirely unheard of in the film industry. It is, in fact, surprisingly common to hear action denigrated by comparison with the spoken word, and Cole talks of 'a society which condemns all forms of visual communication'.[207] The callous verbal battles that we have seen on the screen between husband and wife who have grown to hate one another, are thought somehow more civilised and intelligent than physical battles. It is difficult to see why, when the effect in both cases—and certainly in the former—is to damage and possibly destroy. What the action-orientated director does in effect is to see the significance of both activities. To see them both as being a part of human life, neither being in any sense 'superior' to the other, each simply being 'different'.

This 'wholeness' of view is of course what a stuntman hopes for in the director with whom he is to work. He does not necessarily want a William Wellman who, if the need arises, can do his own stunting. But he does expect a man with an understanding of action and its place in the cinema. Over the years there have been such men. Wellman of course; Griffiths and Dwan are two other obvious giants from the early days; and Gance, with his attitude to action so reminiscent of Eason's. And more recently, John Ford, Anthony Mann and John Frankenheimer, George Roy Hill and Arthur Penn, Ralph Nelson and Sam Peckinpah.

9 Modern stunting

Television

The history of stunting is as long as the history of entertainment, and as entertainment continues to develop so does the stunt aspect of it. Stunting has changed to meet each new demand created by changes in entertainment, changes which have been the result of shifting fashion on the one hand or of developments in entertainment itself on the other. As the film opened up a vast new area for developments in stunting, so television has created new problems for the stuntman and at the same time shown him new possibilities.

Illustration: The Daredevil Men (1971). Marc Boyle being electrocuted.

Modern stunting

The problem, from the stuntman's viewpoint, that still dogs television action is the fact that technical advances have outpaced human advances. There is still a tendency on the part of some television directors to lag considerably behind technological advances, though this is much more the case in Europe than it is in America. The result has been the growth of a belief that there is something in the nature of the medium that militates against action sequences.

Nothing could be further from the truth, though there are aspects of the medium that do pose special problems for the stunt-man. For example, video tape recording tends to make actors look heavier than they are. It has in fact been suggested that ten pounds is the average weight increase that an actor appears to undergo as a result of having his performance recorded on video tape, as opposed to being recorded on film or appearing in the flesh. Coupled with this apparent increase in size, video tape recordings have the effect of slowing down action. This is particularly true in the case of sword play. 'No matter how fast you're moving, you're still going in slow motion,' is a typical stuntman's comment on sword play recorded on video tape. The introduction of 625 lines has helped to readjust this, but something of the problem still remains. It is not, however, insuperable. Video tape can be edited so that the fast cutting that we have seen is necessary to action on film is still possible. Sound can be dubbed on to video tape after-wards, and we have seen that in filmed action this technique adds considerably to its effectiveness. Again, the speed at which video tape runs can be varied, so that the under-cranking and overcranking techniques of film are now available to television.

Early television action

In the early days, television was dogged by the belief that action was something outside its scope. One wonders how this belief arose in the first place and why in some quarters it still exists. The reason is perhaps twofold. In the first place it is technical and in the second place financial. The earliest television broadcasts were 'live', since there was no method then known by which they could be recorded. In the live show, action must be continuous. If the show is of a play, for example, then the play must be played from beginning to end without a break, in the same way as it would be played in the theatre. It could not be stopped half-way through for a complete change of location. The first part of a scene could not be removed because of some defect in it, and replaced by a second performance, any more than it could in the theatre. More important from the stuntman's viewpoint, a partial fall by an actor could not be completed by a stuntman, as is perfectly possible in film through competent editing. But then, early television was not concerned with action but with much more restricted and unadventurous entertainment forms. The newness of the medium was itself sufficiently adventurous and exciting for the early pioneers.

Where a significant break with the theatre tradition was possible was in the use of a number of cameras. In the theatre an audience sees the whole of an action. It sees, for example, nothing in close-up. In television, by contrast, the use of a number of cameras allows a number of different aspects of the action to be taken. The director can select which of these pictures will reach the viewer at any one time, simply by the use of a switch on a control panel. In this way he has some directorial control over the programme *as it is being performed*. In this particular function he is much more in the position of the film director than of the theatre director. What he cannot do which the film director can, is reshoot the action and by careful editing change the pace of a scene and at times actually change its meaning.

Video tape recording

The introduction of a method of recording from television cameras by the use of video tape, did not at first have any great effect on this established television 'method'. Directors still seemed to prefer to run action continuously and to use a number of cameras at once, selecting from each the particular aspects of a scene that seemed to be most significant. This is far from an ideal way of working for the stuntman. Most television fights, according to one of them, 'come out like amateur night in Dixie'. To try to record a fight continuously, as is necessary with this kind of approach, is courting disaster. As Max Diamond has said, in connection with the jousting tournaments mounted by the British Jousting Association, it is impossible for even a professional stuntman to fight a continuous routine lasting more than a few minutes.[208]

Diamond, of course, is talking of a spectacle which most members of the audience view from a distance of some thirty or forty yards. By comparison, television action is in direct competition in the minds of the viewers with film action, and the television technique of 'continuous' shooting from a number of cameras cannot begin to match the achievements on film. Such achievements, as we have seen, have been secured by dozens of different 'set-ups', each perhaps recording no more than a couple of blows, and by meticulous cutting afterwards. We have only to compare the 'continuous' shooting approach which has its roots in early television production and its later development in video tape, with the principles of action laid down by Eason, to see why so much early television action is almost unbelievably banal.

The economics of television action

The second reason for the apparent ineffectiveness of action on television has been financial. This may on the face of it seem surprising, since the early cinema produced highly effective action scenes on almost no budget at all. The extras on *Intolerance*, for example, got 'their carfare, their lunch, and a dollar and a quarter a day'. For five dollars they dived off the top of the Hotel Bryson in down-town Los Angeles into a tub of water. The reason of course was economic. A simple question of supply and demand, with thousands of extras queueing daily for a score of jobs.

Stunting in the cinema

Even at a much later date, during the depression of the thirties, Wayne recalls the appalling social conditions that many Americans experienced: 'The poverty was incredible. They were breaking up boxes and building fires in the streets to keep warm, selling apples from their gardens for money. Ruined men were leaping from windows.'[209] Under such conditions, any kind of payment for any kind of work is preferable to the only alternative—starvation.

Fortunately, television has on the whole known only the more affluent days of this century. Men—even stuntmen and extras—can no longer be urged to risk their lives simply by the threat of starvation. They demand, quite rightly, a reasonable reward for their work. And so do all the other people involved in action sequences—the action director, the special effects man, the cameraman, the property man, the make-up man. Action is expensive and it is precisely in the field of action that television, until comparatively recently, has been prepared to economise. We have seen the unfortunate results.

Television film

Surprisingly perhaps, the field of television film—film made specially for showing on television—has until recently owed very little to the cinema. Its roots have been in the television tradition, so that the possibilities of film have been largely ignored and the limitations of video tape work adhered to. Perhaps it is this as much as anything that has led to the belief that there is something in the nature of television as a medium that militates against action, despite the fact that when we see the classic action movies on television—*Stagecoach*, Flynn's *Robin Hood*, *Destry Rides Again*—their action sequences are not only entirely acceptable but as stirring as ever.

The film produced specifically for television continues to suffer the same financial restrictions that have hampered video taped action. A film fight on a feature film, for example, that would be alloted three days' shooting time, would be shot in a morning for a television film. When we compare this time with the weeks that Eason spent in photographing the details he considered necessary to give that roaring authenticity to the chariot race in *Ben-Hur* (1926), or the five months that Canutt and his team spent on the second version in 1959, we can see why so many results on television have been disappointing.

Again, with a budget severely restricted for action sequences, the use of doubles in television is a comparatively recent innovation. This is surprising when one considers that in a television series the first two episodes are frequently being screened before the last few episodes have been shot, and an injury to a star in the later episodes could have the most disastrous effects on the series. An example of this occurred in the British Broadcasting Corporation's *Maigret* (1960). Ewan Solon, one of the principal actors in the series, broke his leg in one episode jumping from a wall. The incident affected the remaining scripts in which he appeared. The fact that in the later episodes he appeared suffering from some obvious damage to a leg, could clearly not be ignored. The scripts themselves had to be re-adjusted to account for a genuine disability. If the actor had suffered some much greater damage, one wonders how his sudden disappearance from the series would have been accounted for. If the episode had been shot as part of a feature film, the chances of such an accident happening would have been very much more remote. Either a double would have been used for the jump, or it would have been set up in such a way that there was no risk of the actor's injuring himself.

The possibility of television action

In fact, of course, television, whilst admittedly placing restrictions on certain types of action sequence—very high falls, for example, cannot adequately be seen on television—have opened up possibilities too. *Culloden* (1964) shot on 16mm and directed by Peter Watkins for the BBC, is an example of a film made exclusively for television. Even for the widest battle shots, a maximum of forty-five people effectively represented the two opposing armies which in reality had comprised some 15,000 soldiers. The same scenes, projected on to a 16mm screen instead of through a television set, lose their credibility. It does seem, then, that one of the virtues of television is its ability to show mass action scenes which bear favourable comparison with similar scenes in feature films for a fraction of the cost. Only comparatively recently have such action possibilities of television come to be exploited.

What the action specialist used to complain about in television was the low priority given to action. He found it difficult to understand why this was so. Television, he argued, claimed to be essentially a visual medium and action is the supreme visual form. The fight arranger complained of the lack of adequate consultation between himself and the rest of the production team. He complained that he was rarely invited to production meetings, and didn't even meet the designer or the man supplying the horses, for example, until just before shooting began. The results of such a lack of consultation were apparent on television until comparatively recently.

In America, such a state of affairs has largely disappeared, but in Europe—and certainly in Britain—it still to some extent continues. In American television, doubles stand by where necessary, an action director is kept under contract for the whole of a series requiring specialist action, and a section of the budget is specifically set aside to cover the cost of such action. In British television, by contrast, an action director is still usually an afterthought and in general doubles are only brought in at his insistence.

The modern stuntman

The stuntman is now recognised as a specialist in his own right, with his own techniques, his own specialist terminology and his own rates of pay. He is no longer an extra on the one hand, wanting another $5 a day, nor a star on the other, able and willing to do his own action sequences. He exists in his own right, and his work

Modern stunting

in the context of the modern cinema is indispensable. Yet as a professional he is surprisingly unorganised. Such organisations as he might belong to are very loose and do not require him to conduct his professional activities in any very rigid way. His fees, for example, are arranged as a result of personal negotiation between himself or his agent and his immediate employer. They are not negotiated for him by a professional body, although the American Screen Actors Guild does lay down a *minimum* scale of fees for employing a stuntman. Some years ago British Equity also negotiated a minimum daily rate for stuntmen of £10, but this has never been revised to keep pace with the rise in almost all other fees.

One can of course understand the difficulty of laying down fee structures for stuntmen, since every job a stuntman is called upon to do is different from every other job he has done before. But there is also some quality of irrepressible individuality in the stunt-man that militates against his allowing any organisation to get a firm grip on him. He might well have done better for himself and his kind if he had relinquished some of his individual autonomy in favour of a tighter professional organisation which could perhaps have improved his conditions of work and his pay. But he has not done so, and the fact that he has not done so is part of his being a stuntman.

He is to be compared much more with the medieval craftsman, jealous of his own individual skill and the mysteries surrounding it, than he is with the modern skilled worker. He sees any professional organisation to which he might belong, not as a tight professional body with wide powers to negotiate on his behalf, but more as a medieval guild—a much looser organisation of peers, sharing the same mysteries but preserving absolutely their own separate autonomies.

Becoming a stuntman

Entry into the profession has in fact much in common with the way in which an apprentice was initiated into the mysteries of a medieval craft. There is no published body of material on stunting that the apprentice may study. The knowledge of the craft can only be handed down from an experienced stuntman to a novice, either by word of mouth or by demonstration. Experience is the principal tool of study. Even the basic facts that in almost any other subject could at least be grasped intellectually, vary according to situation and stuntman. It is not even possible to say, for example, how many cardboard boxes are required for every ten foot in height in a jump. It depends. It depends on the stuntman using the rig, it depends on the angle of launching, it depends on the particular circumstances.

Many of the specialist techniques are jealously guarded. Such secrecy can only add to the popular misconceptions about stunting and isolate the stuntman still further from his audience and from other members of the acting profession. To shroud the simple facts of the high-fall rig, for example, in secrecy is to imply that if they fell into the hands of people outside the profession the world would be full of human beings leaping off high places into piles of cardboard boxes. It is also to imply that the essence of stunting is not skill, experience, courage and judgement, but simply having access to a body of technical know-how. The stuntman, by preserving a secrecy about the details of his work, does himself less than justice.

'Stuntmen—there are about 150 of them—form a small, cliquey, jealous world with a low opinion of anyone outside it,' says Khan[210] of the British stuntman. 'Jackie Cooper who is one of Britain's foremost stuntmen, said candidly: "There are very few stuntmen who are really interested in the others." ' Again the image projected by such statements is inaccurate, for within the profession a great deal of help and kindness has been shown by some of the top stuntmen to young newcomers. 'Malvern Cornelli and Eddie Tacoma, the best tumblers on the coast,' says Grace, 'took infinite pains to teach me their tricks.' Les White acknowledges the help he had from Paddy Ryan,[211] Gillian Aldam mentions the help she had from Frank Maher: 'He showed me how to take punches and how to fall in any given circumstances,'[212] and Jack Cooper benefited from the experience of Alan Pomeroy, 'one of the old-time stuntmen from Hollywood'.[213]

The special skills of the stuntman

Yet the analogy between entry into a medieval craft and into modern stunting cannot be pushed too far. The medieval craft required only an apprenticeship. Modern stunting requires a high degree of general skill before the apprenticeship itself is embarked upon. Yakima Canutt was a brilliant horseman before he applied his skill to the particular needs of the cinema. Dick Grace was a professional flyer before he adapted his special skill to the needs of *Wings*. Gillian Aldam has a background of circus trapeze work, and Alf Joint was a competitive swimmer at seven. Bob Simmons has had Army boxing experience. Les White had been a boxer, a paratrooper and a steeplejack before entering stunting and to fit himself for the rigours of his new work he embarked on a training programme designed to give him some of the necessary new skills: 'Mondays and Wednesdays I went fencing . . . Saturday afternoons I went diving. Tuesday and Thursdays I did gymnastics. Saturday mornings I learnt pro-wrestling . . . Sundays I went to archery classes.'[214] One wonders what on earth he did on Fridays.

Such general training is necessary, when one considers the wide range of physical demands that are made on the stuntman. Reuben Martin of the London Tough Guys Agency considers that a competent stuntman should be able to handle his body generally and have had some experience in boxing, acrobatics, wrestling, judo, karate and unarmed combat. He should be able to drive anything, crash a car and handle a sabre. He should have had some archery experience. He should be able to swim under water, climb a rope and dive. He should be able to do a long jump of no less than fifteen feet, fall fifty feet on dry land and seventy feet into water.[215] We might also add that he should be able to ride a horse.

There are perhaps fewer than forty stuntmen in the world with this all-round competence, and in fact most of them tend to specialise. Some, like Cliff Lyons, are best known for their work

H

with horses, others—Alf Joint is an obvious example—have made a particular reputation as high divers.*

Staying a stuntman

It is, of course, one thing to become a stuntman and another thing to remain in the profession. Training of one sort or another is a continuous process. General keep-fit work in a gymnasium is popular with many stuntmen, and constant weight control is essential. Regular walks and runs are used as methods of helping to control weight and also to keep a high level of general muscle tone. In the case of some specialisations, these will be specifically practised. A stuntman who specialises in horse work will naturally do a good deal more riding than will a stuntman with some other specialisation.

In some cases another occupation coincides with the stunt specialisation so that one activity helps the other. Rémy Julienne, for example, the French car stuntman, is also a champion motor-cross driver. A specialist in sword play will need to keep in constant practice in that specialism, as well as keeping up a general training programme. By contrast, the high-fall specialist cannot reasonably be expected to practice that specialism. But he will perhaps keep to a regular programme of diving practice which will not only keep him fit but help to preserve his judgement of heights.

The dangers of stunting

The conditions under which the modern stuntman works are very

---

*It is interesting to note that according to Cabat and Lévy (*Les Cascadeurs*), Gleb Rodjestvenski organised a group of professional stuntmen in Moscow in 1937. The entrance test for membership of the group was particularly stringent. It required a candidate to demonstrate a very high degree of skill in horsemanship, an ability to jump from at least a height of 16 feet, and skill in fencing, boxing and acrobatics. In the first year of the group's existence, of 500 applicants for membership only 40 were accepted. It was from this group that Eisenstein selected a dozen stuntmen to work with him on *Alexander Nevsky* (1938). The Russian view of the stuntman as essentially a specialist *actor*, is one that naturally commends itself to many Western stuntmen.

different from those that existed during the early days of the cinema. Stuntmen are no longer the 'crazy kids' who did anything to get into films, nor would such 'kids' last a moment in the profession as it exists today.

The stuntman is still entirely responsible for his own safety. He is, as we have seen, dependent on the skill of property men, special effects men, action directors and other stuntmen, but if he is injured in a stunt the responsibility is his. He can, of course, always refuse a particular stunt, or refuse to do it under the conditions that have been provided. The modern stuntman, in fact, does not allow himself to be engaged for a stunt that he believes contains an element of danger that he does not feel able to control. Stunting is dangerous, let us not be in any doubt about it, but what separates the modern professional stuntman from the rest of us is that he has a skill and judgement that allow him to come through that danger safely.

Reuben Martin considers the modern stuntman to be a responsible person who does as much as he can to eliminate the dangers of his trade. Les White says simply, 'Stuntmen don't get hurt.'[216] Few stuntmen would agree with the statement as it stands. Alf Joint has mentioned the injuries he has got through stunting. So has Jack Cooper. And Carpozi, talking of Gary Cooper's early experiences as a 'fall-down boy',[217] says: 'He realised, for one thing, that he couldn't go on indefinitely in such physically punishing work.'

And yet there is a strong element of truth in White's statement. It depends on how one interprets that word 'hurt'. If fractured bones, damaged spines and torn muscles are really too minor to be regarded as 'hurts', then White's statement is substantially true. Stuntmen very rarely get more seriously hurt than this, although Grace would no doubt question even that statement. They very rarely, in fact, lose their lives in stunting. Even John Van Orme, in one of the most turgidly dramatic articles on the terrors of stunting,[218] mentions only the death of Al Johnson during the making of *Hell's Angels* (1930) and the broken neck sustained by Grace during the making of the same picture, as examples of the dangers of stunting. The fact that Grace himself says that it was in the Fokker D7 crash for *Wings* that he broke his neck, a statement that is supported by William Wellman who directed the picture, does not in any case allow one to attach a great deal of importance to Orme's statements.

By contrast, May,[219] writing in 1939, says that there has been no mortality amongst stuntmen since 1928 when one of them was drowned canoeing in Alaska, and that Lloyds of London considered stuntmen a better insurance risk than policemen or firemen. In fact, Peters could write in 1956[220] that 'each stuntman in the Jock Easton agency is insured with Lloyds against injury for £5 per annum', a figure which certainly suggests that the risks were less than is popularly imagined, though Peters is careful to point out a little disconcertingly, 'there is no insurance against death'. In fact the statement, if it was true in 1956, is no longer true. One of the present writers, for example, has a death policy which would leave his dependants some £15,000. An insurance against injury for a professional stuntman today would cost something in the region of £20 per annum. By contrast, an insurance premium for a French stuntman in 1967 cost about 300,000 old francs (£250) a year.[221]

The rewards of stunting

The stuntman is in the position of any other self-employed person. He must make his own pension arrangements. He must invest whatever money he makes when times are good, according to his own business judgement. And like any other self-employed person he is allowed to offset against tax such legitimate expenses as those incurred in keeping himself fit and in providing such essential tools of his trade as protective padding.

One wonders, in fact, what the satisfactions of such a profession are when the disadvantages are so obviously considerable. There is of course the payment. 'The stuntmen's image is changing,' says Carvell.[222] 'Their salaries are now in the executive bracket.' In Britain, the earnings range of a top professional stuntman is between £3,000 and perhaps as much as £10,000 a year. Clearly this offers considerable compensation for the difficulties and dangers of the work. As long ago as 1939, May[223] gave the average earnings of the top American stuntmen—men like Harvey Parry, Cliff Lyons, Duke Green and Yakima Canutt—as $7,500 a year, with one or two of them earning $18,000 to $20,000.

A reply to a letter in the London *Daily Mirror* in 1956[224] asking for information about the pay that stuntmen receive, gives the following scales: £30 for falling off a horse, £160 for being dragged by a horse, £300 for a ninety-foot fall from a cliff. For the date, these figures do seem surprisingly high. This is understandable, because like any other responsible businessman the stuntman is reluctant to disclose the exact money he was paid for a particular stunt, and in consequence most figures that we see published in connection with the earnings of stuntmen are at best generalisations. The *Mirror* reply, however, is quite precise about one stunt payment: 'The highest fee for one scene was paid to stuntman Paul Mantz for crash-landing a Flying Fortress single handed in the film *Twelve O'Clock High*. This near-suicidal feat earned him £2,000.' By contrast with this, the basic stunt pay for film work in Britain is still only £15 a day, a figure which does not show any vast improvement over the $5 a day paid in the very early days of the cinema.

Payment to French stuntmen, according to Cabat and Levy,[225] varies from 300 NF (£23) for a 'usual' stunt to 5,000 NF (£375) for a 'particularly dangerous' stunt. They give a scale of payments which is of interest. For a fall from a horse for the cinema—20,000 AF (£15): for a similar fall for television—15,000 AF (£12). Falls down stairs are paid between 25 and 30,000 AF (£19–£23). For rolling a car over—100,000 to 200,000 AF (£75–£150); for falling into water at the wheel of a car—about 200,000 AF (£150). For being involved in an explosion—50–60,000 AF (£38–£46), and for falling from a motor cycle—about 250,000 AF (£190). For a fire stunt—'if the stuntman is burning like a torch'—a fee of between 30 and 50,000 AF (£23–£38) is paid, and the fee for being dragged by a horse varies from 50,000 AF (£38) to 80,000 AF (£62).

Attitudes to the stuntman

There is not a great deal beyond the cash payment that the stunt-man can look forward to in terms of recompense for his work. Nowdays, there is a reasonable chance that he will be given a credit somewhere in the titles for his work on a particular film or tele-vision programme. But he cannot hope to have that wide pro-fessional recognition that comes, for example, from a nomination for an Oscar, or for some other award carrying with it a certain international kudos. There are simply no awards that exist for stuntmen. Eason, despite his lifetime's work as an action director, never received the kind of formal recognition from his profession that even the meanest of public awards might have conferred.

Yet there is perhaps a certain kudos from the changing public attitude to the stuntman, for it is at last changing, even though 'so far as they have any public image it is entirely fanciful', according to Reuben Martin.[226] Maybe, but at least it is no longer true to say as Grace did in 1930: 'The stars think that a stunt man is just a little above an extra. The producers think he is a little below a moron. The public has never heard of him. They think that all thrills are faked or double printed.'[227] Nor would one any longer expect the casual cynicism of Bogart's remark: 'When I was making *Action in the North Atlantic* (1943), Raymond Massey and I had big mock arguments as to whose double was the bravest.'[228] Indeed, Charlton Heston put the more modern star's attitude in a television interview[229] when he said he regarded Joe Canutt, who was his double on *Ben-Hur* (1959), as 'perhaps the greatest stuntman of our time'.

The new image

The 'thick and stupid bruisers' image is cracking, and if the image that is replacing it—the more glamorous one of 'reckless James Bonds dicing with death'[230]—is still somewhat fanciful, it is none the less a little nearer the truth. The Bond image does argue a certain intelligence, which the stuntman must have. It argues a conscious courage different from the blind blundering of the 'bruisers', and that kind of courage the modern stuntman must have. Above all, it does argue a 'glamour', a certain magic which at one time was the exclusive possession of the stars. And this quality is being increasingly transferred from the star to the stuntman.

The star system in fact has militated against the star by diminishing that indefinable quality of 'magic' which gave him his superhuman appeal. By creating stars whose slightest indisposition could ruin the finances of a picture, it has cast doubts on the infallibility of the star—at least the star of action pictures—and such a quality of infallibility was part of his stock-in-trade. We cannot imagine a Valentino ever faltering—let alone failing—in his handling of a horse or a sword, any more than we can imagine Fairbanks missing a leap to a balcony, however great the distance. The star of the action picture did not fail, because infallibility in action was an essential ingredient of star quality. Pathé were well aware of this in the days of *The Perils of Pauline*, when even after the death of Stevenson, they still insisted that Pearl White did all her own stunts.[231] It was, in other words, deliberate studio policy to keep the stuntman out of the public eye because his very existence challenged the infallibility of the action star.

This anonymity is no longer possible. The stuntman has forced the attention of the public on himself by his increasingly spectacular feats and now challenges the very quality which has given the action star his appeal. It is significant, for example, that according to an official of the British Film Institute, more requests are received from young people for information on how to become stuntmen than on any other single aspect of cinema. This new and more glamorous image of the stuntman is reminiscent of the image projected by his Roman gladiatorial counterpart of whom Grant[232] says: 'graffiti at Pompeii reveal that members of the profession were loved with the passionate infatuation which teenage females reserve for the pop singer today.'

The satisfaction of stunting

The reasons that stuntmen give for being stuntmen are singularly unrevealing. They are, in fact, reminiscent of the reasons that the action stars of the twenties and thirties gave for being what they were. Les White says that 'stuntmen have to act more and more',[233] and no doubt this is an increasing attraction of cinema stunting. The stuntman has of course always been an actor, but this open recognition of the fact does encourage him to extend his range. Peterson[234] unconsciously echoes the surprise that many people still feel when faced with this fact: 'For a stuntman, Alf Joint looks and talks remarkably like an actor.' Bob Simmons in fact entered stunting from acting: 'I never made much money as an actor. But I did see a lot of tin-eared idiots trying to be stuntmen and I realised there was an opening for someone who could plan film stunts and bring some showmanship to them.'[235] Stressing the relationship between action and acting, Kirk Douglas said: 'I never lose myself in the part. An actor who loses himself in a fight scene will kill someone.'[236]

This real physical danger certainly does seem to have attracted some stuntmen into the profession. In Omar Locklear it seems to have amounted almost to a compulsive death wish, and there is undoubtedly a touch of the same quality in Grace, though he is reported to have said that he went into stunting initially for the money. Only later did he decide to stay in the profession 'for the thrills'.[237] Dave Crowley, too, admits to liking stunting and being in it 'for the thrills'.[238] The phrase is something of a blanket expression covering a range of sensations from the compulsive 'dicing with death' of Locklear and Grace to the 'It's beautiful' of Jack Cooper.[239] Kavanagh,[240] by contrast, says he entered stunting because he was too lazy to earn his living any other way, whilst John Van Orme[241] gives what is probably one of the most accurate reasons—force of circumstances. He was an out of work acrobat during the American depression and began doubling in the cinema.

We should not perhaps attach too much importance to the reasons stuntmen have given for being in their particular profession. Most of us might answer the question, 'Why are you in your present occupation?' with a straightforward 'I don't know'. Few of us deliberately choose a particular profession at an early age and then direct all our energies to entering it. With most of us, as with John Van Orme, circumstances play a very large part.

There is undoubtedly an attraction about pitting one's wits against such natural forces as gravity and demonstrating to a mass audience one's physical prowess. This kind of demonstration is what seems to have motivated men like Joe Bonomo and Frank Merrill. And there is a greater satisfaction in demonstrating this ability before the camera that in any other situation, for the camera can preserve ones prowess for later generations to marvel at. The ageing aerialist of the circus can only say, 'Ah, you should have seen me in my heyday!' The ageing stuntman of the cinema can say, 'Wait till I set up the projector. Wait till I get the can of film. I'll *show* you my heyday!' His greatest achievements are recorded forever. His youth, his total command of his body, his split-second judgement are still there to bring a gasp to the throat of a new generation.

The mythology of stunting

There is, too, the satisfaction of being part of a growing mythology, for as we have seen, the early days of cinema stunting have already slipped into the realms of myth. We can no longer be sure of the facts with any real accuracy, and as time passes and new accounts of them appear, we shall be a good deal less sure. It is difficult even to be certain of the spelling of some of the most evocative names. Locklear, for example, appears in one book[242] as 'Looklear', 'Look Lear' and 'Lock Lear', and is given the rank of Sergeant. His Christian name in various articles varies from Ormer, through Omar and Amer, to Omer. Again, it has been suggested that the use of boxes as the basis for high-fall rigs is attributable to a single incident. During a fire at a New York box factory the employees escaped by jumping from considerable heights on to piles of boxes, and this discovery came to be used by the stuntmen.[243] It does seem a surprising theory, considering the amount of thought and research that high-fallers have always given to their rigs, but it is another brick in the mythological structure already growing out of early cinema stunting.

Mythology, of course, has its roots in mystery, in a lack of well-established fact. Fernett[244] gives an example of this when he says of Tom Mix that he was 'born in Driftwood, Pennsylvania' and then adds the footnote: 'Or in Mix Run, Pennsylvania, or El Paso, Texas—depending upon whether you prefer to believe *Encyclopaedia Brittanica* [*sic*], *Motion Picture Almanac,* or Richard Shickel's book *The Stars.*' Much of stunting is surrounded by this kind of factual confusion. Partly it is that very few stuntmen have set down the facts in print. Grace is an almost unique example. And some of those who have—either by putting pen to paper themselves or through an intermediary—have left confused and sometimes fanciful records which it is difficult to take at their face value. To some extent this is understandable. As Khan says, 'it is easy to see why as a group they should be both scornful and suspicious of the outside world. Their professionalism is rarely recognised.'[245] There is very naturally a reticence on the part of a top stuntman to reveal specialist techniques that have cost him years of thought, experience and perhaps injury, when there is still a very good chance that his work will be critically dismissed as unworthy of serious attention.* None the less it does make it now virtually impossible to discover the truth. Even Pearl White's image is not secure. A recent book, claiming to be 'the first factual account of Pearl's colourful and dramatic life',[246] quotes her as

---

*In the 1072 pages of Leslie Halliwell's *The Filmgoer's Companion* (MacGibbon and Kee, London, 3rd ed., 1970) Yakima Canutt—without whom the Western as we have known it for the past thirty-odd years would not exist—has a three-line entry. In Rotha's *The Film Till Now* (Spring Books, London, 1967), which runs to more than 830 pages and has the apparently all-embracing sub-title of *A Survey of World Cinema,* there is no index entry for Canutt or Grace. There are many references to the films of Fairbanks Senior, yet none to Richard Talmadge without whom they just might not have been made. To Flynn, whose work cannot surely be ignored in any 'survey of world cinema', there is one dismissive reference.

saying: 'I never did those dangerous stunts like swinging down ropes and jumping off bridges. I had several men who doubled for me.' Her public, she claimed, had created the dare-devil image of her and 'somehow I had to live up to it'.

Attitudes to action

But there is something more to a mythology than a simple absence of facts. We spin mythologies around truths whose significance we sense, but with which we cannot come to grips in terms of conscious intellectual activity. For a mythology to grow, the phenomenon out of which it springs must have a sense of continuing relevance for us. It must gnaw at us so that we cannot leave it alone. Yet the more we consider it, the more possibilities do we see in it. So when we ask what it is that attracts us to action in entertainment, and particularly to that kind of violent action with which the cinema has always been concerned, we are asking a fairly fundamental question. We are asking a question about the nature of a phenomenon that has held a continuous fascination for humanity from the earliest recorded times.

It is also a phenomenon that has aroused more ire in critics and social scientists and representatives of law and order than any other single factor in entertainment. On January 1st, 1921, for example, Fred Bater, Mayor of Superior, Wisconsin, banned the showing of film serials on the grounds that the scenes of spectacular action they contained were responsible for the 'sudden wave of petty banditry and crime among juveniles in the city'.[247] This argument of the relationship between violence in entertainment and violence in real life is, of course, still with us, although the relationship itself is still very far from being established.

Another attack on spectacle and action is on the ground that it is intellectually 'shallow' and escapist: '. . . the cinema frankly makes use of all those elements of popular appeal which had served the melodrama in the past,' says Allardyce Nicoll.[248] 'Spectacularism is used there freely; appeal is made to that desire of throwing off the meanly sordid and monotonous surroundings of actual life in order to enter, if but for an hour, into a world of romance; as in the melodrama, the film exploits the world of crime and sensation.'

Even those closely associated with the cinema have contributed to the general denigration of spectacular action. Gilbert M. (Broncho Billy) Anderson who became 'the original movie cowboy and the daddy of all horse-opera heroes' said of Westerns: 'They cater to the low mentality that wants nothing but excitement and doesn't care why the stagecoach goes over the cliff as long as it goes over.'[249] 'The theme of most of these spectacles is superman,' says Chaplin.[250] 'The hero can outjump, outclimb, outshoot, out-fight, and outlove anyone in the picture. In fact every human problem is solved by these methods—except thinking.' These are recurrent themes—the unquestioned superiority of intellectual activity to physical activity and the essential 'escapist' quality of spectacle.

There is another theme that appears in adverse comment on action in entertainment, the theme of reality. The stuntman is clear enough, of course, about the difference between fictional reality and the reality of everyday life. 'A stunt, if it's properly planned, shouldn't be dangerous,' says Alf Joint.[251] 'The idea, of course, is to make it *look* dangerous. . . .' And Houdini, making the same distinction, says: 'The secret of showmanship consists not of what you really do, but what the mystery-loving public thinks you do.'[252] The distinction seems less clear to many critics. They appear not to grasp the essential fact that what happens within the entertainment context, although real enough within its own terms of reference is nevertheless different from what happens in 'real life'.

Dr Gerald Looney of the University of Arizona, talking recently in Chicago to the annual meeting of the American Academy of Paediatrics, is reported[253] as having said that by the time a child was fourteen he 'could expect to have seen 18,000 people killed on television', as if death on television—newsreels apart—was indistinguishable from death in 'real life'. There is a further confusion here: Dr Looney's statement—as reported—implies that for a child to witness fictional death on television is in some way traumatic.

If we accept the implication, then it is reasonable for us to assume that it is fictional death that is traumatic and not the medium on which it has appeared. If fictional death is damaging for a child to witness on television, then it is damaging for it to witness in the cinema and in the theatre. Yet many of the educationists who condemn fictional death on television or in the cinema are happy to organise school parties to visit theatre productions of *Macbeth*, *Hamlet*, *Romeo and Juliet* and *King Lear*. In *Macbeth* the children witness various forms of death and are shown the bleeding head of the decapitated Macbeth, and in *Hamlet* they see the stabbing of an old man and the violent deaths of four other people; *Romeo and Juliet* brings deaths by the sword, together with a poisoning and a suicide by dagger, and *King Lear*, one of the most savage of stage pieces, allows us to witness the blinding of Gloucester: 'Upon these eyes of thine, I'll set my foot.'

If the witnessing of fictional violence is traumatic, one cannot help wondering how much more damage has been caused to young minds by the plays of Shakespeare than by all the *Stagecoaches*, *Alamos* and *Bonnie and Clydes*. For we must not forget that in the cinema and on television we are merely seeing pictures of fictional death, whereas in the theatre it is happening in our presence. In the theatre, if we were sitting close enough, we could put out a hand and touch the weapon that is to destroy Hamlet, Laertes and the King.

Pictorial pleasure is certainly one of the satisfactions we get from action sequences in the cinema. There is an aesthetic satisfaction in seeing the unfolding of a choreographed movement pattern in sword play, for example, akin to the satisfaction derived from ballet. There is a similar pictorial satisfaction in seeing the visual patterns woven by the participants in a bar room brawl or a battle scene, the changing shapes, the shifting colours, the sheer spectacle.

But pictorial pleasure is not the thing that touches us most deeply. When we witness the final scene of *Bonnie and Clyde*, for example, it is not the pictorial effect of seeing the sagging bodies of the two principals criss-crossed by bullets that holds us. Pictorially, in fact, the scene is if anything revolting. What grips us is something central to tragedy. Bonnie and Clyde have flouted almost every law of society and God throughout the entire film. They have thumbed their noses at authority and respectability and social order. They have been guilty of *hubris* and they cannot, according to the tenets of tragedy, survive. Their end is inevitably bloody, as the ends of Hippolytus and Antigone are. Again, the pity and terror which in Aristotle's view are evoked in true tragedy are certainly feelings that we associate with many action scenes—the final battle sequence, for example, in *All Quiet On The Western Front*, the trapped paratroopers in the Ste-Mère-Église sequence from *The Longest Day*. Action, too, has a universality that transcends the barriers of language, and universality is a feature of tragedy.

Yet there is a sense in which the work of the stuntman, the action-specialist, transcends tragedy. 'The theme of most of these spectacles is superman,' says Chaplin, and indeed he is right. There is a quality of aspiration about the work of the stuntman that is immensely satisfying to an audience. The stuntman challenges all those restricting forces—gravity, death, age—that hem humanity in. Not only does he challenge them, he overcomes them. He is man as god. 'Movies represented an ideal of life,' said Olivia de Havilland in a television interview,[254] 'they represented gods and goddesses.' The stuntman challenges a view of life which defines man in narrow and restricting terms. Age weighs upon us, gravity holds us down, death awaits us. 'Not necessarily,' the stuntman appears to say, and his successful challenging of what seem to us unalterable facts of life is his greatest attraction. 'Study the spectacles devised, whether with full intent or not, to capture the public's loyalty, the public's obedience or the public's purse,' says Willson Disher of the fairground showman,[255] 'and you will see that the showman of today is as significant a figure as priest or emperor, for he belongs to the same trade.' He might well have been speaking of the stuntman in the cinema.

Notes

CHAPTER I

1 *Fairs, Circuses and Music Halls* by M. Willson Disher, Collins, London, 1942.
2 *Schools and Masters of Fence* by Egerton Castle, Bell, London, 1885.
3 *Gladiators* by Michael Grant, Weidenfeld and Nicolson, London, 1967.
4 *Development of the Theatre* by Allardyce Nicoll, Harrap, London, 3rd ed., 1948.
5 *Fairs, Circuses and Music Halls.*
6 *The Parade's Gone By* by Kevin Brownlow, Secker and Warburg, London, 1968.
7 *My Wonderful World of Slapstick* by Buster Keaton, with Charles Samuels, Allen and Unwin, London, 1967.
8 *British Drama* by Allardyce Nicoll, Harrap, London, 4th ed., 1947.
9 *Continued Next Week* by Kalton C. Lahue, University of Oklahoma Press, 1964.
10 *Continued Next Week.*
11 *The Parade's Gone By.*
12 *Les Cascadeurs* by Odilon Cabat and Jacques Levy, Société Le Gadenet, Paris, 1967.
13 *My Wonderful World of Slapstick.*
14 *The Parade's Gone By.*
15 *Houdini: The Man Who Walked Through Walls* by William Lindsay Gresham, Gollancz, London, 1960.
16 *My Wonderful World of Slapstick.*
17 *Houdini.*

18 *My Autobiography* by Charles Chaplin, The Bodley Head, London, 1964.

CHAPTER II

19 *My Autobiography.*
20 *My Wonderful World of Slapstick.*
21 *Comedy Films 1894–1954* by John Montgomery, Allen and Unwin, London, 2nd ed. 1968.
22 *The Parade's Gone By.*
23 *My Wicked, Wicked Ways* by Errol Flynn, Heinemann, London, 1960.
24 *The Big Man* by Mike Tomkies, Arthur Barker, London, 1971.
25 *Continued Next Week.*
26 *The Parade's Gone By.*
27 *The Parade's Gone By.*
28 *Continued Next Week.*
29 *The Parade's Gone By.*
30 *Continued Next Week.*
31 *My Wonderful World of Slapstick.*
32 *My Wonderful World of Slapstick.*
33 *Squadron of Death* by Dick Grace, Constable, London, 1930.
34 *Continued Next Week.*
35 *Continued Next Week.*
36 *The Parade's Gone By.*
37 *The Parade's Gone By.*

CHAPTER III

38 *The English Circus* by Ruth Manning-Sanders, Werner Laurie, London, 1952.
39 *The English Circus.*
40 'In Very Early Days' by Helen Gibson, in *Films in Review*, January 1968, pp. 28–34.

41 *The Gary Cooper Story* by George Carpozi Jr, Arlington House, New York, 1970.

42 'Underwriting Hollywood', news story in *Daily Telegraph*, October 22nd, 1959.

43 *The English Circus and Fair Ground* by Sir Garrard Tyrwhitt-Drake, Methuen, London, 1946.

44 'Stunt Men of the Movies' by George May, in *Life and Letters*, July, 1939.

45 'The Stuntmen' by Theodore Taylor, in *People Who Make Movies*, Doubleday, New York, 1967, pp. 101–109.

46 'What Hollywood Pays For Death' by John Van Orme, in *Picturegoer*, February 6th, 1932, p. 7.

47 *The Big Man.*

48 *Squadron of Death.*

49 *Next Time Drive Off The Cliff* by Gene Fernett, Cine-memories Publishing Co., Florida, USA, 1968.

50 In a correspondence with the authors dated January 6th, 1972.

51 *Next Time Drive Off The Cliff.*

52 *Les Cascadeurs.*

53 *The Fifty-Year Decline and Fall of Hollywood* by Ezra Goodman, Simon and Schuster, New York, 1961.

54 *The Parade's Gone By.*

55 *My Wicked, Wicked Ways.*

56 *Movie Horses: Their Treatment and Training* by Anthony Amaral, Dent, London, 1969.

57 *Is It Cruel? A Study of the Condition of Captive and Performing Animals* by Thomas Haining Gillespie, Herbert Jenkins, London, 1934.

58 'The Stuntmen'.

59 *Popular Entertainments Through the Ages* by Samuel McKechnie, Sampson Low, Marston, London, no date.

60 *The English Circus.*

61 *Menageries, Circuses and Theatres* by E. H. Bostock, Chapman and Hall, London, 1927.

62 *Continued Next Week.*

63 *The Fifty-Year Decline and Fall of Hollywood.*
64 *The Parade's Gone By.*
65 *Continued Next Week.*
66 *The Parade's Gone By.*

CHAPTER IV

67 Review by Felix Barker in the *Evening News*, London, August 18th, 1949.
68 *Railways in the Cinema* by John Huntley, Ian Allan, London, 1969.
69 *Railways in the Cinema.*
70 'In Very Early Days'.
71 'Stunt Men' by William K. Everson, in *Films in Review*, October 1955, pp. 394–402.
72 *Harold Lloyd's World of Comedy* by William Cahn, Allen and Unwin, London, 1966.
73 *Comedy Films.*
74 'No Way To Treat A Lady' by Alan McDowell, in the *Daily Telegraph Colour Supplement*, September 10th, 1970.
75 *Squadron of Death.*
76 *The Parade's Gone By.*
77 *The Fifty-Year Decline and Fall of Hollywood.*
78 'The Making of *Butch Cassidy and the Sundance Kid*', narrated by George Roy Hill, BBC TV, April 9th, 1971.
79 *The Kinematograph and Lantern Weekly*, London, January 22nd, 1914.
80 *The Kinematograph and Lantern Weekly*, London, January 29th, 1914.
81 Tom Milne in *The Financial Times*, London, October 30th, 1964.
82 *The Fifty-Year Decline and Fall of Hollywood.*
83 *Squadron of Death.*
84 'Crashing Cars for Films' by Reg Kavanagh, in *The Listener*, London, January 26th, 1939.

85 'Action Sequences by Bob Simmons', a Ken Gooding feature in *Photoplay*, June 1966, pp. 48–49, 55.

86 *Les Cascadeurs*.

87 Report in *The Times*, London, August 8th, 1970.

88 *The English Circus and Fair Ground*.

89 'A Prince of Dare-Devils' by L.V., in *Picturegoer*, December 1921, pp. 24–25.

90 December 1922, p. 30.

91 *The Parade's Gone By*.

92 *Squadron of Death*.

93 'Playing Safe With Danger' by Andrew Peters, in *Films and Filming*, June 1956, pp. 6–7.

94 *Gladiators*.

95 'The Stuntmen'.

96 *My Wonderful World of Slapstick*.

97 *The Parade's Gone By*.

98 *Harold Lloyd's World of Comedy*.

CHAPTER V

99 *The Parade's Gone By*.

100 *The English Circus*.

101 'When Tragedy Stalks The Studios' by Randolph Carroll Burke, in *Picturegoer*, February 13th, 1932.

102 *Comedy Films*.

103 'Man of Danger' by Derek Peterson, in *Photoplay*, May 1971, pp. 28–29, 61.

104 'Fall Guys For Hire' by Naseem Khan, in the *Guardian*, London, April 1st, 1971, p. 9.

105 'Fall Guys For Hire'.

106 *Falling For Stars*.

107 *The Guinness Book of Records* edited and compiled by Norris and Ross McWhirter, 1960 edition, Guinness Superlatives Limited, London.

108 'Action Sequences by Bob Simmons'.

109 *Squadron of Death.*
110 'The Hazards of Filming *Where Eagles Dare*' by Tony Toon, in *Photoplay*, London, February 1969, pp. 34–37.
111 'No Way To Treat A Lady'.
112 'Action Sequences by Bob Simmons'.
113 *Holinshed's Chronicles* edited by Allardyce and Josephine Nicoll, Dent, London, 1959.
114 *The English Circus.*
115 'Stunt Men of the Movies'.
116 'Stunt Girl' by Eric Random, in *Photoplay*, London, July 1965, pp. 18 and 66.
117 *The Big Man.*
118 *Buster Keaton* by J.-P. Lebel, Studio Vista, London, 1967.
119 *The Fifty-Year Decline and Fall of Hollywood.*

CHAPTER VI

120 *Circus Life and Circus Celebrities* by Thomas Frost, London, 1875.
121 'King of the Suicide Squad' by M. D. Phillips, in *Picture-goer*, April 30th, 1932, pp. 8–9.
122 *Fit For The Chase* by Raymond Lee, A. S. Barnes, New Jersey, 1969.
123 'The Stuntmen'.
124 *Continued Next Week.*
125 In *Speed Age*, November 1951, p. 13.
126 *Squadron of Death.*
127 'King of the Suicide Squad'.
128 *The Parade's Gone By.*
129 *The Parade's Gone By.*
130 Reply to letter in *Daily Mirror*, London, August 21st, 1956.
131 'King of the Suicide Squad'.

Notes

CHAPTER VII

132   In the Official Souvenir Programme of a jousting tournament held on the Knavesmire, York, England, on June 16th, 1971.

133   *Cynthia's Revels* (Act V, Scene iii).

134   *The English Master of Arms* by J. D. Aylward, Routledge and Kegan Paul, London, 1956.

135   'A Fight Can Be A Very Beautiful Thing' by Gordon Burn, in *Radio Times*, London, August 22nd–28th, 1970, p. 13.

136   'Medieval Road Show' by John Blunt, in *Yorkshire Evening Press*, York, England, November 30th, 1970.

137   *My Wicked, Wicked Ways*.

138   *My Wicked, Wicked Ways*.

139   'A Fight Can Be A Very Beautiful Thing'.

140   'Swordplay on the Screen' by Rudy Behlmer in *Films in Review*, June–July 1965, vol. XVI, no. 6, New York, pp. 362–375.

141   'Armaments of the Stage' by G. F. Laking in *The Connoisseur*, London, June 1911, vol. XXX, no. 118, pp. 105–108.

142   'Swordplay on the Screen'.

143   'Swordplay on the Screen'.

144   *My Wicked, Wicked Ways*.

145   'Swordplay on the Screen'.

146   'Swordplay on the Screen'.

147   In *Radio Times*, London, July 3rd–9th, 1971, p. 9.

148   *The Big Man*.

CHAPTER VIII

149   'Stunt Men of the Movies'.

150   *Gladiators*.

151   *The Parade's Gone By*.

152   'Royal Rumble' by Michael McNay, in the *Guardian*, London, June 28th, 1971, p. 8.

153 'Royal Rumble'.

154 *The Parade's Gone By.*

155 *My Autobiography.*

156 'No Way To Treat A Lady'.

157 'The Stuntmen'.

158 *The Parade's Gone By.*

159 'Playing Safe With Danger'.

160 'Royal Rumble'.

161 'Action Sequences by Bob Simmons'.

162 *Movie Horses.*

163 *The Fifty-Year Decline and Fall of Hollywood.*

164 *The Fifty-Year Decline and Fall of Hollywood.*

165 In an interview with one of the authors, Slough, England, June 3rd, 1971.

166 'Without Using Doubles' by Dorothy H. Cartwright, in *Picturegoer*, London, November 1929, pp. 30–31.

167 *Crashing Cars for Films.*

168 *Squadron of Death.*

169 *Movie Horses: Their Treatment and Training.*

170 'The Making of *Butch Cassidy and the Sundance Kid*'.

171 *Comedy Films.*

172 *The Parade's Gone By.*

173 *Railways in the Cinema.*

174 *The Film Till Now* by Paul Rotha, with an additional section by Richard Griffith, Spring Books, London, 1967.

175 'Stunt Men of the Movies'.

176 *Houdini.*

177 'King of the Suicide Squad'.

178 *Squadron of Death.*

179 'The Making of *Butch Cassidy and the Sundance Kid*'.

180 *The Fifty-Year Decline and Fall of Hollywood.*

181 In an interview on British Independent Television, May 16th, 1971.

182 'To Create a World' by Simon Butler, in *TV Times*, London, 1970, p. 10.

183 *The Parade's Gone By.*

184 *My Wonderful World of Slapstick.*
185 Reported in 'Talkies Come to Britain', BBC2 TV, May 26th, 1971.
186 'Man of Danger'.
187 *Continued Next Week.*
188 *The Parade's Gone By.*
189 *My Wicked, Wicked Ways.*
190 'Watch It! You Nearly Touched Me' by Gay Search, in *Daily Mirror Colour Magazine*, 1st issue 1969, London, pp. 44–45.
191 'When Carnage Comes to Order' by Ian Crichton, in *Daily Telegraph Magazine*, No. 324, London, January 8th, 1971, pp. 6–8.
192 *My Wicked, Wicked Ways.*
193 *Coryate's Crudities hastily gobbled up in Five Months' Travels in France, Italy, etc.* by Thomas Coryate, Glasgow, 1905 (1st ed. 1611).
194 *Popular Entertainments Through The Ages.*
195 *Houdini.*
196 In the *Daily Telegraph*, London, January 14th, 1971, p. 19.
197 *Continued Next Week.*
198 'Playing Safe With Danger'.
199 *The Stuntmen.*
200 *The Parade's Gone By.*
201 'His Targets Are Screen Stars', by Grant Jackson, in *Picturegoer*, London, February 13th, 1932.
202 *The Fifty-Year Decline and Fall of Hollywood.*
203 'Man of Danger'.
204 *The Parade's Gone By.*
205 *The Parade's Gone By.*
206 In an interview on BBC1 TV, October 3rd, 1971.
207 Dr Martin Cole in a Cambridge Union debate; 'Aquarius', London Weekend Television, November 7th, 1971.

CHAPTER IX

208 'Medieval Road Show'.
209 *The Big Man.*
210 'Fall Guys For Hire'.
211 'Falling For You' by Peter Carvell, in *Daily Telegraph Magazine*, London, November 7th, 1969.
212 'Stunt Girl'.
213 'Fall Guys For Hire'.
214 'Falling For You'.
215 'Falling For You'.
216 'Falling For You'.
217 *The Gary Cooper Story.*
218 'What Hollywood Pays For Death'.
219 'Stunt Men of the Movies'.
220 'Playing Safe With Danger'.
221 *Les Cascadeurs.*
222 'Falling For You'.
223 'Stunt Men of the Movies'.
224 *Daily Mirror*, London, August 21st, 1956.
225 *Les Cascadeurs.*
226 'Fall Guys For Hire'.
227 *Squadron of Death.*
228 *The Fifty-Year Decline and Fall of Hollywood.*
229 With Michael Parkinson, BBC1 TV, December 12th, 1971.
230 'Fall Guys For Hire'.
231 *Continued Next Week.*
232 *Gladiators.*
233 'Falling For You'.
234 'Man of Danger'.
235 'Action Sequences by Bob Simmons'.
236 Interview on BBC2 TV, May 8th, 1971.
237 'King of the Suicide Squad'.
238 'My Nine Lives As A Stunt Man' by Dave Crowley, in *The People*, London, April 20th, 1958.
239 'Fall Guys For Hire'.

240 'Crashing Cars For Films'.
241 'What Hollywood Pays For Death'.
242 *Les Cascadeurs.*
243 *Les Cascadeurs.*
244 *Next Time Drive Off The Cliff*
245 'Fall Guys For Hire'.
246 *Pearl White, The Peerless Fearless Girl* by Manuel Weltman and Raymond Lee, A. S. Barnes and Company, New York, 1969.
247 *Continued Next Week.*
248 *British Drama.*
249 *The Fifty-Year Decline and Fall of Hollywood.*
250 *My Autobiography.*
251 'Man of Danger'.
252 *Houdini.*
253 In *The Times*, London, October 19th, 1971, p. 1.
254 'The Movie Crazy Years', BBC1 TV, May 31st, 1971.
255 *Fairs, Circuses and Music Halls.*

Bibliography

AARONSON, CHARLES S., *International Motion Picture Almanac*, Quigley Publications, New York, 1962.

AMARAL, ANTHONY, *Movie Horses: Their Treatment and Training*, Dent, London, 1969.

ANON, 'Stunt Merchants', in *Picturegoer*, London, May 1921.

AYLWARD, J. D., *The English Master of Arms*, Routledge and Kegan Paul, London, 1956.

BARBOUR, ALAN G., 'The Stunt Men', in *Days of Thrills and Adventure*, Collier-Macmillan, London, 1970.

BARKER, DENNIS, 'Nosher's Knights Joust By Thames', in the *Guardian*, London, April 12th, 1971.

BARKER, FELIX, film review in the *Evening News*, London, August 18th, 1949.

BEHLMER, RUDY, 'Swordplay on the Screen', in *Films in Review*, June–July 1965, vol. XVI, no. 6, New York, pp. 362–375.

BEUNAT, MARIO, 'Tout Savoir Sur Les Cascadeurs', in *Le Nouveau Cinémonde*, no. 1847, December 1970, Paris, pp. 14–16.

BLUM, DANIEL, *A Pictorial History of the Talkies*, Spring Books, London, revised edition 1968.

BLUNT, JOHN, 'Medieval Road Show', in *Yorkshire Evening Press*, York, England, November 30th, 1970.

BONOMO, JOE, *The Strongman*, Bonomo Studios, New York, 1968.

BOSTOCK, E. H., *Menageries, Circuses and Theatres*, Chapman and Hall, London, 1927.

BROWNLOW, KEVIN, *The Parade's Gone By*, Secker and Warburg, London, 1968.

BURKE, RANDOLPH CARROLL, 'When Tragedy Stalks The Studios', in *Picturegoer*, London, February 13th, 1932.

Bibliography

BURN, GORDON, 'A Fight Can Be A Very Beautiful Thing', in *Radio Times*, London, August 22nd–28th, 1970, p. 13.

BURN, GORDON, 'Defying Death . . . to celebrate 50 years as a high-wire walker', in *Radio Times*, London, November 14th–20th, 1970.

BUTLER, SIMON, 'To Create A World', in *TV Times*, London, 1970.

CABAT, ODILON and LÉVY, JACQUES, *Les Cascadeurs*, Société Le Gadenet, Paris, 1967.

CAHN, WILLIAM, *Harold Lloyd's World of Comedy*, Allen and Unwin, London, 1966.

CAMERON, I. and E., *The Heavies*, Studio Vista, London, 1967.

CAMERON, I. and E., *Broads*, Studio Vista, London, 1969.

CARPOZI JR, GEORGE, *The Gary Cooper Story*, Arlington House, New York, 1970.

CARTWRIGHT, DOROTHY H., 'Without Using Doubles', in *Picturegoer*, London, November 1929, pp. 30–31.

CARVELL, PETER, 'Falling For You', in *Daily Telegraph Magazine*, London, November 7th, 1969.

CASTLE, EGERTON, *Schools and Masters of Fence*, Bell, London, 1885.

'Celluloid Casualties', in *Sunday Times Magazine*, London, November 2nd, 1969.

CHAPLIN, CHARLES, *My Autobiography*, The Bodley Head, London, 1964.

CORYATE, THOMAS, *Coryate's Crudities hastily gobbled up in Five Months' Travels in France, Italy, etc.*, Glasgow, 1905 (1st edition 1611).

CRAIG, JOHN D., *Danger is My Business*, Arthur Barker, London, 1938.

CRICHTON, IAN, 'When Carnage Comes To Order', in *Daily Telegraph Magazine*, no. 324, London, January 8th, 1971, pp. 6–8.

CROWLEY, DAVE, 'My Nine Lives As A Stunt Man', in *The People*, London, April 20th, 1958.

Daily Mirror, London, August 21st, 1956.

Daily Telegraph, Underwriting Hollywood, London, October 22nd, 1959.

Daily Telegraph, news story, London, January 14th, 1971, p. 19.

DEXTER, T. F. G., *The Pagan Origin of Fairs*, New Knowledge Press, Perranporth, England, no date.

DISHER, M. WILLSON, *Fairs, Circuses and Music Halls*, Collins, London, 1942.

DOMINIK-MILHAKIEV, KOSTIA, 'Les Cascadeurs Ne Sont Pas Des Kamikazes!', in *Revue du Cinema*, no. 7, Paris, October–November 1969, pp. 36–37.

DWIGGINS, DON, *Hollywood Pilot: The Biography of Paul Mantz*, Doubleday, New York, 1967.

EDWARDS, COURTENAY, 'Air Bags: Will They Work?', in *Daily Telegraph Magazine*, no. 325, London, January 15th, 1971, pp. 36–38.

EVERSON, WILLIAM K., 'Stunt Men', in *Films in Review*, New York, October 1955, pp. 394–402.

EVERSON, WILLIAM K., *The Art of W. C. Fields*, Allen and Unwin, London, 1968.

The Factual Film, Oxford University Press, London, 1947.

FERNETT, GENE, *Next Time Drive Off The Cliff*, Cinememories Publishing Company, Cocoa, Florida, 1968.

FLYNN, ERROL, *My Wicked, Wicked Ways*, Heinemann, London, 1960.

FROBOESS, HARRY, *The Reminiscing Champ*, Pageant Press, New York, 1953.

Froissart's Chronicles, edited and translated by John Jolliffe, Harvill Press, London, 1967.

FROST, THOMAS, *Circus Life and Circus Celebrities*, London, 1875.

GIBSON, HELEN, 'In Very Early Days', in *Films in Review*, New York, January 1968, pp. 28–34.

GIFFORD, DENIS, *British Cinema*, Zwemmer, London, 1968.

GILLESPIE, THOMAS HAINING, *Is It Cruel? A study of the condition of captive and performing animals*, Herbert Jenkins, London, 1934.

GOODING, KEN, 'Action Sequences by Bob Simmons', in *Photoplay*, London, June 1966, pp. 48–49, 55.

GOODMAN, EZRA, *The Fifty-Year Decline and Fall of Hollywood*, Simon and Schuster, New York, 1961.

GRACE, DICK, '"Stunt Men", the Boys Who Risk Their Lives to Thrill', in *Photoplay*, New York, August 1925, pp. 32–35, 129.

GRACE, DICK, *Squadron of Death*, Constable, London, 1930.

GRACE, DICK, *I Am Still Alive*, Rand McNally, New York, 1931.

GRAHAM, PETER, *A Dictionary of the Cinema*, Zwemmer, London, revised edition 1968.

GRANT, MICHAEL, *Gladiators*, Weidenfeld and Nicolson, London, 1967.

GRANT, PAUL, 'Gone Swimming—In Leg-Irons And Handcuffs', in *Weekend*, London, December 4th–10th, 1968, p. 19.

GRESHAM, WILLIAM LINDSAY, *Houdini: The Man Who Walked Through Walls*, Gollancz, London, 1960.

HAGNER, JOHN G., *Falling For Stars*, El' Jon Publications, Los Angeles, 1964.

HAGNER, JOHN G., *The Greatest Stunts Ever*, El' Jon Publications, Los Angeles, 1967.

HALLIWELL, LESLIE, *The Filmgoer's Companion*, MacGibbon and Kee, London, 3rd edition 1970.

HILL, GEORGE ROY, (narrator), 'The Making of *Butch Cassidy and the Sundance Kid*', BBC1 TV, April 9th, 1971.

HOBBS, WILLIAM, *Techniques of the Stage Fight*, Studio Vista, London, 1967.

HUNT, JOHN, *The Ascent of Everest*, Hodder and Stoughton, London, 1953.

HUNTLEY, JOHN, *Railways in the Cinema*, Ian Allan, London, 1969.

JACKSON, GRANT, 'His Targets Are Screen Stars', in *Picturegoer*, London, February 13th, 1932.

JENKINSON, PHILIP, notes in *Radio Times*, London, July 3rd–9th, 1971, p. 9.

KAVANAGH, REG, 'Crashing Cars for Films', in *The Listener*, London, January 26th, 1939.

KEATON, BUSTER, with Charles Samuels, *My Wonderful World of Slapstick*, Allen and Unwin, London, 1967.

KHAN, NASEEM, 'Fall Guys For Hire', in the *Guardian*, London, April 1st, 1971, p. 9.

LAHUE, KALTON C., *Continued Next Week*, University of Oklahoma Press, 1964.

LAKING, G. F., 'Armaments of the Stage', in *The Connoisseur*, London, June 1911, vol. XXX, no. 118, pp. 105–108.

LEBEL, J.-P., *Buster Keaton*, Zwemmer, London, 1967.

LECKY, WILLIAM EDWARD HARTPOLE, *History of European Morals from Augustus to Charlemagne*, Longmans Green, London, 1911.

LEE, RAYMOND, *Fit For The Chase*, A. S. Barnes, New Jersey, 1969.

LLOYD, JAMES, *My Circus Life*, Noel Douglas, London, 1925.

LOW, RACHEL, *The History of the British Film 1906–1914*, Allen and Unwin, London, 1949.

LOW, RACHEL, *The History of the British Film 1914–1918*, Allen and Unwin, London, 1950.

MCDOWELL, ALAN, 'No Way To Treat A Lady', in *Daily Telegraph Magazine*, September 10th, 1970.

MCKECHNIE, SAMUEL, *Popular Entertainments Through the Ages*, Sampson Low, Marston, London, no date.

MCNAY, MICHAEL, 'Royal Rumble', in the *Guardian*, London, June 28th, 1971, p. 8.

MCWHIRTER, NORRIS and ROSS, (eds.), *Guinness Book of Records*, Guinness Superlatives Limited, London, editions of 1960, 1965 and 1971.

MANNING-SANDERS, RUTH, *The English Circus*, Werner Laurie, London, 1952.

MANTZIUS, KARL, *A History of Theatrical Art in ancient and modern times*, translated by Louise von Cossel and C. Archer, Duckworth, London, 1903–21.

MAY, GEORGE, 'Stunt Men of the Movies', in *Life and Letters*, London, July 1939.

MILNE, TOM, review in *The Financial Times*, London, October 30th, 1964.

MONTGOMERY, JOHN, *Comedy Films 1894–1954*, Allen and Unwin, London, 2nd edition 1968.

National Film Archive Catalogue, British Film Institute, London, part 3, 1966.

Bibliography

NICOLL, ALLARDYCE, *British Drama*, Harrap, London, 4th edition 1947.

NICOLL, ALLARDYCE, *Development of the Theatre*, Harrap, London, 3rd edition 1948.

NICOLL, ALLARDYCE and JOSEPHINE, (eds.), *Holinshed's Chronicles*, Dent, London, 1959.

NOBLE, PETER, *The British Film Yearbook*, British Yearbooks, London, no date.

Official Souvenir Programme of a jousting tournament held on the Knavesmire, York, England, on June 16th, 1971.

ORME, JOHN VAN, 'What Hollywood Pays For Death', in *Picturegoer*, London, February 6th, 1932, p. 7.

PETERS, ANDREW, 'Playing Safe With Danger', in *Films and Filming*, London, June 1956, pp. 6–7.

PETERSON, DEREK, 'Man of Danger', in *Photoplay*, London, May 1971, pp. 28–29, 61.

PHILLIPS, M. D., 'King of the Suicide Squad', in *Picturegoer*, London, April 30th, 1932, pp. 8–9.

RANDOM, ERIC, 'Stunt Girl', in *Photoplay*, London, July 1965, pp. 18, 66.

RICHARDSON, ANTHONY, *Crash Kavanagh*, Max Parrish, London, 1953.

ROBINSON, DAVID, *Hollywood In The Twenties*, Zwemmer, London, 1968.

ROTHA, PAUL, *The Film Till Now*, Spring Books, London, 1967.

RUSSELL, SINCLAIR, 'Topical Thrills In The Making', in *Picturegoer*, London, April 1921, pp. 8–9.

SANDWELL, ROGER, 'Stand-In For Danger', in *The Film Fan's Bedside Book No. 2*, Co-ordination (Press and Publicity) Ltd., London, 1949, pp. 76–80.

SCOTT, AUDREY, *I Was A Hollywood Stunt Girl*, Dorrance, Philadelphia, 1969.

SEARCH, GAY, 'Watch It! You Nearly Touched Me', in *Daily Mirror Colour Magazine*, London, 1st issue 1969, pp. 44–45.

SHIPMAN, DAVID, *The Great Movie Stars: The Golden Years*, Hamlyn, London, 1970.

Bibliography

SHULMAN, IRVING, *Valentino*, Leslie Frewin, London, 1968.

SPEARS, JACK, '2nd-Unit Director', in *Films in Review*, New York, March 1955, pp. 108–112.

STERNBERG, JOSEF VON, *Fun In A Chinese Laundry*, Secker and Warburg, London, 1966.

STUART, RAY, *Immortals of the Screen*, Spring Books, London, 1967.

'The Stunt Men', in *Photoplay*, London, February 1966, pp. 22–23.

TAYLOR, JOHN RUSSELL, *The Penguin Dictionary of the Theatre*, Penguin, London, 1966.

TAYLOR, THEODORE, 'The Stuntmen', in *People Who Make Movies*, Doubleday, New York, 1967, pp. 101–109.

'They're Dying—For A Bit Of Fun', in *Weekend*, London, September 29th–October 5th, 1971, pp. 3–5.

The Times, London, August 8th, 1970.

The Times, London, October 19th, 1971.

TOMKIES, MIKE, *The Big Man*, Arthur Barker, London, 1971.

TOON, TONY, 'The Hazards of Filming *Where Eagles Dare*', in *Photoplay*, London, February 1969, pp. 34–37.

TYRWHITT-DRAKE, SIR GARRARD, *The English Circus and Fair Ground*, Methuen, London, 1946.

V. L., 'A Prince of Dare-Devils', in *Picturegoer*, December 1921, pp. 24–25.

WARRINGTON, JOHN, (ed.), *The Diary of Samuel Pepys*, Dent, London, revised edition 1953.

WELTMAN, MANUEL and LEE, RAYMOND, *Pearl White, The Peerless Fearless Girl*, A. S. Barnes, New Jersey, 1969.

WISE, ARTHUR, *Weapons in the Theatre*, Longmans, London, 1968.

WOOD, ROBIN, *Arthur Penn*, Studio Vista, London, 1967.

Index

Index

Index

Index

Index